Pictorial History of Morals

Pictorial History of
MORALS

Edited by H. E. Wedeck, Ph.D.

PETER OWEN · LONDON

PETER OWEN LIMITED
50 Old Brompton Road London SW7

★

First published in the British Commonwealth 1964
© 1963 Philosophical Library, New York
Printed in the USA
Bound in Great Britain

Contents

"ACCABUSSADE" OF A PROSTITUTE
"Dunking" as a corrective measure was widely practiced in 17th Century Europe.

Love and the French
Cassell & Co., Ltd., London

[1]

ZEUS AND IO

Correggio (1494-1534)

INTRODUCTION

This book is in the nature of a survey, with illustrative aids, of man's social and amatory life through the centuries. It ranges from Biblical and classical antiquity to the present day, and extends in scope from European mores to the Orient. In the course of its investigations into the normal and aberrational phases of such erotic incidence, this study embraces the sexual and emotional relationships of men and women in a variety of manifestations: aberrant and strange cults that have been associated with the genesiac impulses; marriage rites and phallic symbolism; sacred and secular prostitution; incest and adultery. In addition, it also takes under consideration factors that have contributed to amatory compulsiveness: notably, the emphasis on the nude in art presentations; the function of the bed in its historical and social evolution; the emergence of the bath as an ancillary enticement in promoting erotic excitations; and the sadistic and orgiastic impulses aroused by great social and national upheavals, particularly the onset of aggressive wars.

H. E. W.

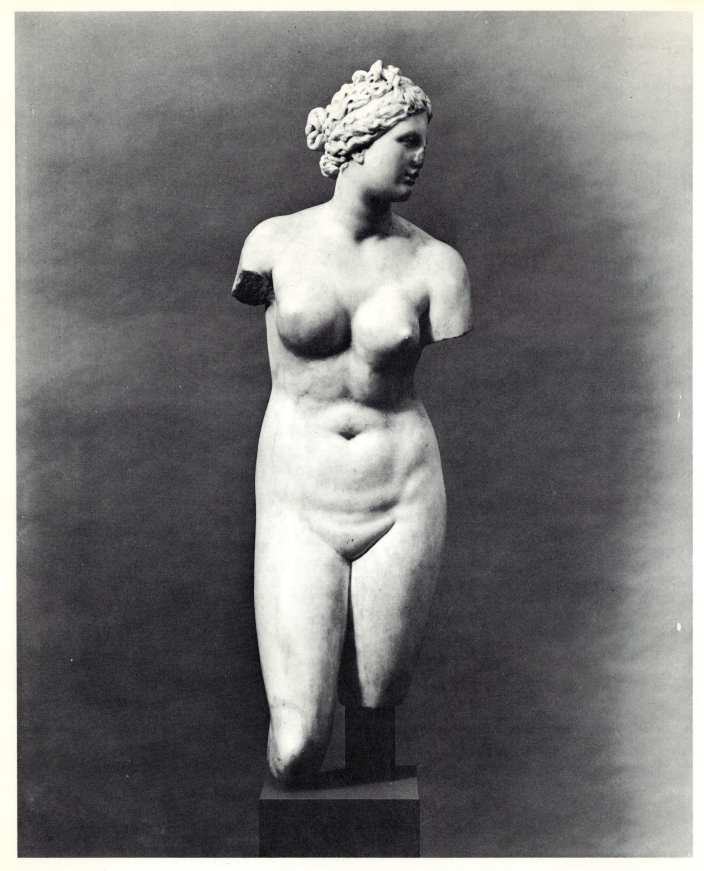

APHRODITE

c. 300 B.C.
Metropolitan Museum of Art. N.Y.

Love In Antiquity

Love In Antiquity

Erotic practices pervaded all ancient life. But these practices were basically associated with religious beliefs, with cosmic creativeness, and with the sense of human continuity. Not until highly sophisticated times were they considered obscene or licentious in themselves in contrast with an idealistic, metaphysical, or social concept of innocence or purity.

Virility was exultant and free from stigma, though not from indirect comment. In the fifth century B.C. the apogee of Greek cultural achievement, Alcibiades, the famous political leader, was noted for his physiological vigor. His amorous inclinations were so urgent that on his coat of arms there was the design of Eros, god of love, hurling lightning. Diogenes Laërtius, the historian who flourished in the third century A.D. says that Alcibiades, when a young man, separated wives from their husbands.

The Romans, although basically a more earthy people, had their spokesmen of love too, particularly Propertius, Tibullus, Catullus, and Ovid. On osculation as an aphroditic technique, Ovid says in his Amores:

> I saw their frenzied kisses, linking
> tongue with tongue.

Other provocative means are mentioned, not so ancient, not at all unknown in these days. They include speaking with expressive eyebrows, gesturing, making conversation with the eyes, expressing affection with the lips.

The goddess Aphrodite, goddess of love through whom, as the poet Lucretius sings, all things are conceived, was known by a variety of names according to her special functions in the amatory arts. As Ambologera, she was the postponer of old age. She was the animating agent. Prayers were addressed to this deity by those interested in retaining vigor or in acquiring rejuvenescence.

The same kind of supplication is mentioned centuries later by the Roman epigrammatist Martial:

> Suppliantly he begs, both for himself
> and for two miserable persons: make
> this one young, O Cytherean goddess,
> and this one make virile.

In the goddess' honor a popular Greek festival was held, known as the Aphrodisia. On this occasion prostitutes and hetairae, a euphemistic name for amatory companions, participated.

At the busy harbor of Corinth, constantly thronged with sailors and traders, the festival was celebrated with the utmost sexual license, the women causing provocation by dress, speech, and gesture.

This festival and similar ceremonials and rites prevalent in ancient times amply demonstrate the universality of the erotic theme and its forthright acceptance as a basic force not only in human life but in the cosmic procreative design as well.

The Greek hetairae, to increase their enticing charms, used every available opportunity to enhance their amatory attractiveness. Hair was dyed black. Grease-paint, false hair and colored ribbons were used as additional adornments. The hetairae were also familiar with eye-paint, seaweed paint, white lead, hair nets and girdles, combs and necklaces, earrings and Coan silk robes, buckles on arms, and rings and jewels. In addition, the hetairae were taught by professional beldames how to conduct themselves, how to inspire jealousy, how to dress provokingly, how to increase their income, and how to extract the utmost profit from their fleeting beauty.

Ancient Greek comedy frequently comments on the

swaying and writhing of the female body as an erotic excitation. This feminine practice was known as periproctian.

As patroness of love, Aphrodite presided over every sexual manifestation. As Aphrodite Hetaira she was the goddess of the female amatory companions of the Greeks. Under the name of Aphrodite Porne she was the divine protectress of prostitutes and of a variety of sexual activities.

In Sparta she was also known as Aphrodite Peribaso, Aphrodite the Streetwalker. As Aphrodite Trymalitis, she symbolized the ultimate sexual consummation.

In poetry and in sculpture she was represented as endowed with such alluring charms and such sexual enticements as to infatuate even the wise men, as Homer suggests. Throughout Greece, in temples dedicated to the divinity, her callipygian beauty was stressed as a factor in her worship.

On the testimony of the Greek poet Hesiod, in his *Theogony*, which describes the origins of the divinities, Aphrodite sprang from the severed membrum of Uranus, the sky god. Hence Aphrodite was considered under two forms. As Aphrodite Urania, she was the goddess of pure, wedded love. As Aphrodite Pandemos, she was the goddess of free love that was open to purchase.

WALL PAINTING

Pompeii

In Greece, the five-day festival of the Thesmophoria was celebrated, by women only, in honor of the two divinities Persephone and Demeter. This was symbolically a propagation rite and involved women, married life, and procreation. In the course of time the festival spread through all the colonies of Greece, to Sicily, to the shores of the Black Sea, to Asia Minor.

In Attica, the women participants were required to observe sexual abstinence for nine days before the festival. The ostensible reason, said the priests, was an act of piety, but actually the abstinence merely goaded toward unrestrained sexual orgies.

At Paphos in Cyprus, a festival was held annually in honor of Aphrodite. Men and women participated in the ceremonies, which were marked by orgiastic sexual rites. Centuries later, the Roman Fathers of the Church, among them Clement of Alexandria and Arnobius, fulminated against these practices. The initiated member gave a gift of a coin for the goddess, for which he received in turn a phallus and some salt.

Sexual indulgence, in short, was in Greece virtually a religious duty, consistent with the worship of Aphrodite. Hence it is easy to appreciate the religious status of the hierodouloi, the sacred temple prostitutes.

Such temple slaves were known to many cults in various countries, to the Egyptians and to the peoples of Asia Minor.

The temple of Aphrodite at Byblos in Phoenicia was especially noted for its hierodouloi. So too with the cult of Mylitta in Babylonia.

In Cyprus, at Amathos and Paphos, the hierodouloi of the temples were dedicated to Aphrodite Astarte. Among the Romans, in the temple of Venus Erycina on Mount Eryx in Sicily, the hierodouloi had a widespread reputation.

At Cnidus and Olympia and elsewhere, there were pandokeia, inns, that ostensibly constituted shelters for visitors and travelers but in practice were haunts for sexual enjoyments. Greek inns, in general, were frequently managed by women, who often used their premises as brothels. Theophrastus, a Greek philosopher of the third century B.C., considered inns and brothels synonymous.

Among a number of Greek romances that have come down to us are the story of Chaereas and Kallirrhoe, by Chariton, who lived in the second century A.D., and the love story of Abrocomes and Antheia, by Xenophon of Ephesus. Heliodorus of Emesa produced the tale of Theagenes and Chariclea. Longus of Lesbos is the author of the romance of Daphnis and Chloe.

All the varieties of erotic practices and aberrations were known to the ancients. Cuckoldry appears in Homer, who traditionally belongs in the ninth century B.C. In Book 8 of

But pimps —male and female— are accused, and, if they are convicted, are punished with death, since while those who are greedy for lust are shy of coming together, they in addition practice their own shamelessness for recompense and finally make the attempt and come to an agreement.

Lysistrata, a comedy by Aristophanes (c. 450 — c. 385 B.C.), has a theme that has made the play of timeless interest. The subject is the power of sex in the life of a community. In spite of the frank expression of sexual phenomena the play has been frequently presented on the stage, for the forcefulness of the arguments and situations is beyond cavil. The play was produced in 411 B.C., at a time when Athens was fighting for survival in a war against Sparta. The conflict might have been concluded years before, in 425 B.C., but now the final and almost disastrous climax was upon the Athenians. Peace must be secured at all costs. And women find a way. Lysistrata, the protagonist, proposes that the women of Greece should compel their husbands to sue for peace. Otherwise, the women will refuse all amorous associations. The plan seems ideal and would be rapidly effective. But the participants concerned

SATYR AND HERMAPHRODITE
The satyr in ancient mythology was a half-human, half bestial creature, the essence of lust, while the hermaphrodite combined the male and female principles.

Marble Group
Antiquarium, Berlin

the Odyssey, Hephaestus, husband of the goddess Aphrodite, becomes the victim when Aphrodite joins forces with Ares, the war god. The episode is told at a banquet in honor of Odysseus, at the court of King Alcinous, ruler of Phaeacia.

Aeschines, the Greek orator who belongs in the fourth century B.C., describes the punishment meted out to a woman taken in adultery:

The woman may put on no ornament and may not visit the public temples, lest she should corrupt women who were beyond reproach: but if she does so or adorns herself, then the first man who meets her may tear her clothes from her body, take her ornaments from her and beat her; but he may not kill her or make her a cripple, if only he makes her a dishonored woman and deprives her of all pleasure in life.

SATYR AND NYMPH
Museo Comunale, Rome

in the plan are women, and hesitant to deprive themselves of their own erotic privileges.

The concept of love itself is described by the philosopher Plato (c. 429 - 347 B.C.) in the Symposium, one of his philosophical dialogues:

> Each of us when separated is always looking for his other half; such a nature is prone to love and ready to return love. And when he finds his other half, the pair are lost in an amazement of love and friendship and intimacy, and one will not be out of the other's sight, as I may say, even for a moment; these are they who pass their lives with one another. For the entire yearning which each of them has toward the other does not appear to be the desire of intercourse, but of something else which the soul desires and cannot tell, and of which she has only a dark and doubtful presentiment.

Among the Romans, one of the most popular pleasure resorts was Baiae. It was the focal point of all kinds of erotic experiment, unbridled debauchery, amorous intrigues and excitations, sexual encounters and aberrations.

The philosopher and tutor to the Emperor Nero, the Stoic Seneca, inveighs against the abandoned and lascivious atmosphere of the resort. It is, he declares in one of his Letters, characterized by all-night revelry, drunkenness on the beach, banquets in boats, and uninhibited festivities and orgies. All this, apart from the hot sulphur springs that were the ostensible object of visitors who sought curative treatments, tended to extreme aphroditic diversions.

The Circus Maximus, the scene of public racing contests, was, among the Romans, a kind of hotbed of incitements, by the very nature of the sadistic features of the performances, to sexual expression. Hence, as a vast and turbulent outlet, the proximity of numberless prostitutes who were lodged in this area of the city.

The Church Fathers, particularly Tertullian and Augustine, inveigh against these practices, in which both betting on the results of the chariot races and wild promiscuities were involved.

Luxorius, a poet of the fifth century A.D., has left a large number of poems descriptive of these activities. He ranges over all types of perversions. Among his subjects are: Hermaphrodites and prostitutes, cuckolds, an effeminate charioteer who never won a race, lechers and adulterers. The totality of the pieces suggests a degenerate, unrestrained, and perturbed society, in which eunuchs, pederasts, and deviates of all kinds are not uncommon figures.

The ancient Romans, in the early centuries, frowned upon dancing, especially by women, as they considered it an erotic, licentious inducement. One Roman historian, Sallust, comments that a certain Sempronia danced more gracefully than a respectable woman should.

The Roman poet Ovid, on the other hand, recommends dancing to all girls who are in love.

At banquets and public performances of various kinds professional dancing-girls appeared. Generally, they were imported from Spain or Syria. Skilled in erotic movements and manipulations, they readily provoked the spectators. The Roman satirist Juvenal describes them as writhing and wriggling frantically to the musical accompaniment of their own castanets, to excite sluggish lovers. Other Roman poets, among them Propertius, Horace, and the epigrammatist Martial say similar things about the amatory provocations of such dancers.

Lascivious Ionic dances, too, although condemned by grave elders, were popular among Roman girls.

Tertullian, one of the Roman Church Fathers, belonging in the third century A.D., attacks pagan rites, Roman public festivals and entertainments as virtual sexual orgiastic stimulants. To Tertullian, public shows are a 'gathering of the wicked.' The Roman theatre, he continues, is the shrine of Venus, licentious and unbridled. Venus and Bacchus, in conjunction, are demons of lust. The Roman theatre is packed with filth, in the gestures of the actors, in the words of the farces, in the motions of the buffoon who plays the part of a woman. All sense of sexual shame is banished. The very prostitutes, victims of the public lust, are brought on the stage . . . they are paraded before the faces of every rank and age . . . announcement is made of their dwelling, the fee they charge, their sexual reputation. Both tragedies and comedies teach outrage and lust; they are virtually and actually erotic excitements.

In his treatise on Women's Toilette, Tertullian makes a comprehensive attack on Roman women's enticing use of pomades, perfumes, oils, rouge, paste, ornamentation of hair, all deliberately directed toward the stimulation of men's sexual appetites.

In the matter of women's fondness for certain fashions in dressing, the Stoic Seneca makes sharp comments on Roman practices:

> I see silken clothes, if they can be called clothes, with which the body or only the private parts could be covered. Dressed in them, a women can hardly swear with a clear conscience that she is not naked.

H. E. W.

DANAË
The legend of Danaë represents basically the allurement of gold as the price of chastity.

Rembrandt (1606-1669)
Hermitage, Leningrad

[11]

Priapus

THE ADULATION OF VENUS

Priapus

In ancient mythology, Priapus is the divinity whose symbol is the phallus. He is the son of Dionysus and Aphrodite, and represents the crude physical principle of Eros.

There is extant a body of Latin poems, entitled Priapeia, that deal with the erotic activities, the phallus as a motif, and Priapus as the guardian and patron.

ON THE WORSHIP OF PRIAPUS

Men, considered collectively, are at all times the same animals, employing the same organs, and endowed with the same faculties: their passions, prejudices, and conceptions, will of course be formed upon the same internal principles, although directed to various ends, and modified in various ways, by the variety of external circumstances operating upon them. Education and science may correct, restrain, and extend; but neither can annihilate or create: they turn and embellish the currents; but can neither stop nor enlarge the springs, which, continuing to flow with a perpetual and equal tide, return to their ancient channels, when the causes that perverted them are withdrawn.

The first principles of the human mind will be more

ORGIES AT THE END OF THE WORLD

directly brought into action, in proportion to the earnestness and affection with which it contemplates its object; and passion and prejudice will acquire dominion over it, in proportion as its first principles are more directly brought into action. On all common subjects, this dominion of passion and prejudice is restrained by the evidence of sense and perception; but, when the mind is led to the contemplation of things beyond its comprehension, all such restraints vanish: reason has then nothing to oppose to the phantoms of imagination, which acquire terrors from their obscurity, and dictate uncontrolled, because

unknown. Such is the case in all religious subjects, which, being beyond the reach of sense or reason, are always embraced or rejected with violence and heat. Men think they know, because they are sure they feel; and are firmly convinced, because strongly agitated. Hence proceed that haste and violence with which devout persons of all religions condemn the rites and doctrines of others, and the furious zeal and bigotry with which they maintain their own; while perhaps, if both were equally well understood, both would be found to have the same meaning, and only to differ in the modes of conveying it.

OFFERING TO PRIAPUS

Priapus, the phallic deity, was anciently the object of worship and supplication on the part of both men and women.

J. Raoux: 1735

Of all the profane rites which belonged to the ancient polytheism, none were more furiously inveighed against by the zealous propagators of the Christian faith, than the obscene ceremonies performed in the worship of Priapus; which appeared not only contrary to the gravity and sanctity of religion, but subversive of the first principles of decency and good order in society. Even the form itself, under which the god was represented, appeared to them a mockery of all piety and devotion, and more fit to be placed in a brothel than a temple. But the forms and ceremonials of a religion are not always to be understood in their direct and obvious sense; but are to be considered as symbolical representations of some hidden meaning, which may be extremely wise and just, though the symbols themselves, to those who know not their true signification, may appear in the highest degree absurd and extravagant. It has often happened, that avarice and superstition have continued their symbolical representations for ages after

their original meaning has been lost and forgotten; when they must of course appear nonsensical and ridiculous, if not impious and extravagant.

Such is the case with the rite now under consideration, than which nothing can be more monstrous and indecent, if considered in its plain and obvious meaning, or as a part of the Christian worship; but which will be found to be a very natural symbol of a very natural and philosophical system of religion, if considered according to its original use and intention.

What this is, I shall endeavor in the following sheets to explain as concisely and clearly as possible. Those who wish to know how generally the symbol, and the religion which it represented, once prevailed, will consult the great and elaborate work of Mr. D'Hancarville, who, with infinite learning and ingenuity, has traced its progress over the whole earth. My endeavor will be merely to show, from what original principles in the human mind it was

POPPAEA

Poppaea was one of the most infamous figures in Roman history. She was first the mistress, then the wife, of the Emperor Nero. Beautiful, wealthy, ruthless, licentious, the historian Tacitus says of her that she had every asset but goodness. Her amorous promiscuities became a public byword.

Capitol Museum, Rome

first adopted, and how it was connected with the ancient theology: matters of very curious inquiry, which will serve, better perhaps than any others, to illustrate that truth, which ought to be present in every man's mind when he judges of the actions of others, that in morals, as well as physics, there is no effect without an adequate cause. If in doing this, I frequently find it necessary to differ in opinion with the learned author above-mentioned, it will be always with the utmost deference and respect; as it is to him that we are indebted for the only reasonable method of explaining the emblematical works of the ancient artists.

Whatever the Greeks and Egyptians meant by the symbol in question, it was certainly nothing ludicrous or licentious; of which we need no other proof, than its having been carried in solemn procession at the celebration of those mysteries in which the first principles of their religion, the knowledge of the God of Nature, the First, the Supreme, the Intellectual, were preserved free from the vulgar superstitions, and communicated, under the

[17]

LEDA AND THE SWAN

After Leonardo da Vinci
Collection: Spiridon, Rome

strictest oaths of secrecy, to the initiated; who were obliged to purify themselves, prior to their initiation, by abstaining from venery, and all impure food. We may therefore be assured, that no impure meaning could be conveyed by this symbol; but that it represented some fundamental principle of their faith. What this was, it is difficult to obtain any direct information, on account of the secrecy under which this part of their religion was guarded. Plutarch tells us, that the Egyptians represented Osiris with the organ of generation erect, to show his generative and prolific power: he also tells us, that Osiris was the same Deity as the Bacchus of the Greek Mythology; who was also the same as the first begotten Love of Orpheus and Hesiod. This deity is celebrated by the ancient poets as the creator of all things, the father of gods and men; and it appears, by the passage above referred to, that the organ of generation was the symbol of his great characteristic attribute. This is perfectly consistent with the general practice of the Greek artists, who (as will be made appear hereafter) uniformly represented the attributes of the deity by the corresponding properties observed in the objects of sight. They thus personified the epithets and titles applied to him in the hymns and litanies, and conveyed their ideas of him by forms, only intelligible to

[18]

LEDA

The theme of Leda and her seducer, Zeus, in the assumed body of a swan, frequently presented in art, is basically the erotic theme in its most unbridled form, divorced from all moral concepts.

Michelangelo   (1475-1564)
Musée Correr, Venice

FAUN AND NYMPH

Wall Painting in Pompeii
National Museum, Naples

the initiated, instead of sounds, which were intelligible to all. The organ of generation represented the generative or creative attribute, and in the language of painting and sculpture, signified the same as the epithet *pangenetos* in the Orphic litanies.

This interpretation will perhaps surprise those who have not been accustomed to divest their minds of the prejudices of education and fashion; but I doubt not, but it will appear just and reasonable to those who consider manners and customs as relative to the natural causes which produced them, rather than to the artificial opinions and prejudices of any particular age or country. There is naturally no impurity or licentiousness in the moderate and regular gratification of any natural appetite; the turpitude consisting wholly in the excess or perversion. Neither are organs of one species of enjoyment naturally to be considered as subjects of shame and concealment more than those of another; every refinement of modern manners on this head being derived from acquired habit, not from nature: habit, indeed, long established; for it seems to have been as general in Homer's days as at present; but which certainly did not exist when the mystic symbols of the ancient worship were first adopted. As these symbols were intended to express abstract ideas by objects of sight, the contrivers of them naturally selected those objects whose characteristic properties seemed to have the greatest analogy with the Divine attributes which they wished to represent. In an age, therefore, when no prejudices of artificial decency existed, what more just and natural image could they find, by which to express their idea of the beneficent power of the great Creator, than that organ which endowed them with the power of procreation, and made them partakers, not only of the felicity of the Deity, but of his great characteristic attribute, that of multiplying his own image, communicating his blessings, and extending them to generations yet unborn?

In the ancient theology of Greece, preserved in the Orphic Fragments, this Deity, the *Eros protogenos*, or first-begotten Love, is said to have been produced, together with Aether, by Time, or Eternity (Kronos), and Necessity (Ananke), operating upon inert matter (Chaos). He is described as eternally begetting; the Father of Night, called in later times the lucid or splendid, because he first appeared in splendor; of a double nature, as possessing the general power of creation and generation, both active and passive, both male and female. Light is his necessary and primary attribute, co-eternal with himself, and with him brought forth from inert matter by necessity. Hence the purity and the sanctity always attributed to light by the Greeks. He is called the Father of Night, because by attracting the light to himself, and becoming the fountain which distributed it to the world, he produced night, which is called eternally-begotten, because it had eternally existed, although mixed and lost in the general mass. He is said to pervade the world with the motion of his wings, bringing pure light; and thence to be called the splendid, the ruling Priapus, and self-illuminated. It is to be observed that the word *Priapus*, afterwards the name of a subordinate deity, is here used as a title relating to one of his attributes; the reasons for which I shall endeavor to explain hereafter. Wings are figuratively attributed to him as being the emblems of swiftness and incubation; by the first of which he pervaded matter, and by the second fructified the egg of Chaos. The egg was carried in procession at the celebration of the mysteries, because, as Plutarch says, it was the material of generation containing the seeds and germs of life and motion, without being actually possessed of either. For this reason, it was a very proper symbol of Chaos, containing the seeds and materials of all things, which, however, were barren and useless, until the Creator fructified them by the incubation of his vital spirit, and released them from the restraints of inert matter, by the efforts of his divine strength. The incubation of the vital spirit is represented on the colonial medals of Tyre, by a serpent wreathed around an egg; for the serpent, having the power of casting his skin, and apparently renewing his youth, became the symbol of life and vigor, and as such is always made an attendant on the mythological deities presiding over health. It is also observed, that animals of the serpent kind retain life more pertinaciously than any others except the Polypus, which is sometimes represented upon the Greek Medals, probably in its stead. I have myself seen the heart of an adder continue its vital motions for many minutes after it has been taken from the body, and even renew them, after it has been cold, upon being moistened with warm water, and touched with a stimulus.

The Creator, delivering the fructified seeds of things from the restraints of inert matter by his divine strength, is represented on innumerable Greek medals by the Urus, or wild Bull, in the act of butting against the Egg of Chaos, and breaking it with his horns. It is true, that the egg is not represented with the bull on any of those which I have seen; but Mr. D'Hancarville has brought examples from other countries, where the same system prevailed, which, as well as the general analogy of the Greek theology, prove that the egg must have been understood, and that the attitude of the bull could have no other meaning. I shall also have occasion hereafter to show by other examples, that it was no uncommon practice, in these mystic monuments, to make a part of a group represent the whole. It was from this horned symbol of the power of the Deity that horns were placed in the portraits of kings to show that their power was derived from

LOVING COUPLE

Wall Painting in Pompeii
National Museum, Naples

A scene in a bridal chamber: Aphrodite dresses the bride: Hymenaeus, associated with marriage, sits at the threshold: on the far side, musicians. The Roman poet Catullus has an epithalamium in which this ancient marriage rite is described.

4th century B.C.
Vatican, Rome

Heaven, and acknowledged no earthly superior. The moderns have indeed changed the meaning of this symbol, and given it a sense of which, perhaps, it would be difficult to find the origin, though I have often wondered that it has never exercised the sagacity of those learned gentlemen who make British antiquities the subjects of their laborious inquiries. At present, it certainly does not bear any character of dignity or power; nor does it ever imply that those to whom it is attributed have been particularly favored by the generative or creative powers. But this is a subject much too important to be discussed in a digression; I shall therefore leave it to those learned antiquarians who have done themselves so much honor, and the public so much service, by their successful inquiries into customs of the same kind. To their indefatigable industry and exquisite ingenuity I earnestly recommend it, only observing that this modern acceptation of the symbol is of considerable antiquity, for it is mentioned as proverbial in the Oneirocritics of Artemidorus; and that it is not now confined to Great Britain, but prevails in most parts of Christendom, as the ancient acceptation of it did formerly in most parts of the world, even among that people from whose religion Christianity is derived; for it is a common mode of expression in the Old Testament, to say that the horns of any shall be exalted, in order to signify that he shall be raised into power or pre-eminence; and when Moses descended from the Mount with the spirit of God still upon him, his head appeared horned.

To the head of the bull was sometimes joined the organ of generation, which represented not only the strength of the Creator, but the peculiar direction of it to the most beneficial purpose, the propagation of sensitive beings.

Sometimes this generative attribute is represented by the symbol of the goat, supposed to be the most salacious of animals, and therefore adopted upon the same principles as the Bull and the serpent. The choral odes, sung in honor of the generator Bacchus, were hence called tragodiai, or songs of the goat; a title which is now applied to the dramatic dialogues anciently inserted in these odes, to break their uniformity. On a medal, struck in honor of Augustus, the goat terminates in the tail of a fish, to show the generative power incorporated with water. Under his feet is the globe of the earth, supposed to be fertilized by this union; and upon his back, the cornucopia, representing the result of this fertility.

Mr. D'Hancarville attributed the origin of all these symbols to the ambiguity of words; the same term being employed in the primitive language to signify God and a Bull, the Universe and a Goat, Life and a Serpent. But words are only the types and symbols of ideas, and therefore must be posterior to them, in the same manner as ideas are to their objects. The words of a primitive language, being imitative of the ideas from which they sprung, and of the objects they meant to express, as far as the imperfections of the organs of speech will admit, there must necessarily be the same kind of analogy between them as between the ideas and objects themselves. It is impossible, therefore, that in such a language any ambiguity of this sort could exist, as it does in secondary languages; the words of which, being collected from various sources, and blended together without having any natural connection, become arbitrary signs of convention, instead of imitative representations of ideas. In this case it often happens, that words, similar in form, but different in meaning, have been adopted from different sources, which, being blended together, lose their little difference of form, and retain their entire difference of meaning. Hence ambiguities arise, such as those above mentioned, which could not possibly exist in an original tongue.

The Greek poets and artists frequently give the per-

DIONYSIAC FESTIVAL

The Maenads, Thyiades, and Bacchae, as they were variously termed, were women inspired by Dionysiac frenzy, the spirit of Dionysus, god of wine and fertility. Roaming the woods, they led the life of animals. They were associated with nocturnal dances, wild revelries, amorous excesses. Their ways are vividly described in the Greek dramatist Euripides' Bacchae.

Attic School: 500 B.C.
State Museum, Berlin

sonification of a particular attribute for the Deity himself; hence he is called *Taurozoas, Tauropos, Tauromorphos,* etc., and hence the initials and monograms of the Orphic epithets applied to the Creator, are found with the bull, and other symbols, on the Greek medals. It must not be imagined from hence, that the ancients supposed the Deity to exist under the form of a bull, a goat, or a serpent: on the contrary, he is always described in the Orphic theology as a general pervading spirit, without form, or distinct locality of any kind; and appears, by a curious fragment preserved by Proclus, to have been no other than *attraction* personified. The self-created mind of the Eternal Father is said to have spread the heavy bond of love through all things, in order that they might endure for ever. This Eternal Father is Kronos, time or eternity, personified; and so taken for the unknown Being that fills eternity and infinity. The ancient theologists knew that we could form no positive idea of infinity, whether of power, space, or time; it being fleeting and fugitive, and eluding the understanding by a continued and boundless progression. The only notion we have of it is from the addition or division of finite things, which suggest the idea of infinite, only from a power we feel in ourselves of still multiplying and dividing without end. The Schoolmen

indeed were bolder, and, by a summary mode of reasoning, in which they were very expert, proved that they had as clear and adequate an idea of infinity, as of any finite substance whatever. Infinity, said they, is that which has no bounds. This negation, being a positive assertion, must be founded on a positive idea. We have therefore a positive idea of infinity.

The Eclectic Jews, and their followers, the Ammonian and Christian Platonics, who endeavored to make their own philosophy and religion conform to the ancient theology, held infinity of space to be only the immensity of the divine presence. God is Everywhere was their dogma, which, is now inserted into the Confessional of the Greek Church. This infinity was distinguished by them from common space, as time was from eternity. Whatever is eternal or infinite, said they, must be absolutely indivisible; because division is in itself inconsistent with infinite continuity and duration: therefore space and time are distinct from infinity and eternity, which are void of all parts and gradations whatever. Time is measured by years, days, hours, etc., and distinguished by past, present, and future; but these, being divisions, are excluded from eternity, as locality is from infinity, and as both are from the Being who fills both; who can therefore feel no succession of events, nor know any gradation of distance; but must comprehend infinite duration as if it were one moment, and infinite extent as if it were but a single point. Hence the Ammonian Platonics speak of him as concentered in his own unity, and extended through all things, but participated of by none. Being of a nature more refined and elevated than intelligence itself, he could not be known by sense, perception, or reason; and being the cause of all, he must be anterior to all, even to eternity itself, if considered as eternity of time, and not as the intellectual unity, which is the Deity himself, by whose emanations all things exist, and to whose proximity or distances they owe their degrees of excellence or baseness. *Being* itself, in its most abstract sense, is derived from him; for that which is the cause and beginning of all *Being,* cannot be a part of that *All* which sprung from himself: therefore he is not *Being,* nor is *Being* his Attribute; for that which has no attribute cannot have the abstract simplicity of pure unity. All *Being* is in its nature finite; for, if it was otherwise, it must be without bounds every way; and therefore could have no gradation of proximity to the first cause, or consequent pre-eminence of one part over another: for, as all distinctions of time are excluded from infinite duration, and all divisions of locality from infinite extent, so are all degrees of priority from infinite progression. The mind *is* and *acts* in itself; but the abstract unity of the first cause is neither in itself, nor in another; — not in itself, because that would imply modification, from which abstract simplicity is necessarily exempt; nor in another, because then there would be an hypostatical duality, instead of absolute unity. In both cases there would be a locality of hypostasis, inconsistent with intellectual infinity. As all physical attributes were excluded from this metaphysical abstraction, which they called their first cause, he must of course be destitute of all moral ones, which are only generalized modes of action of the former. Even simple abstract truth was denied him; for truth, as Proclus says, is merely the relative to falsehood; and no relative can exist without a positive or correlative. The Deity therefore who has no falsehood, can have no truth, in our sense of the word.

As metaphysical theology is a study very generally, and very deservedly, neglected at present, I thought this little specimen of it might be entertaining, from its novelty, to most readers; especially as it is intimately connected with the ancient system, which I have here undertaken to examine. Those, who wish to know more of it, may consult Proclus on the Theology of Plato, where they will find the most exquisite ingenuity most wantonly wasted. No persons ever showed greater acuteness or strength of reasoning than the Platonics and Scholastics; but having quitted common sense, and attempted to mount into the intellectual world, they expended it all in abortive efforts which may amuse the imagination, but cannot satisfy the understanding.

The ancient Theologists showed more discretion; for, finding that they could conceive no idea of infinity, they were content to revere the Infinite Being in the most general and efficient exertion of his power, attraction; whose agency is perceptible through all matter, and to which all motion may, perhaps, be ultimately traced. This power, being personified, became the secondary Deity, to whom all adoration and worship were directed, and who is therefore frequently considered as the sole and supreme cause of all things. His agency being supposed to extend through the whole material world, and to produce all the various revolutions by which its system is sustained, his attributes were of course extremely numerous and varied. These were expressed by various titles and epithets in the mystic hymns and litanies, which the artists endeavored to represent by various forms and characters of men and animals. The great characteristic attribute was represented by the organ of generation in that state of tension and rigidity which is necessary to the due performance of its functions. Many small images of this kind have been found among the ruins of Herculaneum and Pompeii, attached to the bracelets which the chaste and pious matrons of antiquity wore round their necks and arms. In these, the organ of generation appears alone, or only accompanied with the wings of incubation, in order to show that the devout wearer devoted herself wholly and solely to procreation, the great end for which she was ordained. So expressive a symbol, being constantly in her view, must keep her attention fixed on its natural object, and continually remind her of the gratitude she owed the Creator, for having taken her into his service, made her a partaker of his most valuable blessings, and employed her as the passive instrument in the exertion of his most beneficial power.

The female organs of generation were revered as symbols of the generative powers of nature or matter, as the male were of the generative powers of God. They are usually represented emblematically, by the Shell, or *Concha Veneris,* which was therefore worn by devout persons of antiquity, as it still continues to be by pilgrims, and many of the common women of Italy. The union of both was

THE ORIGIN OF THE MILKY WAY

Tintoretto (1518-1594)
National Gallery, London

ARIADNE AND DIONYSUS

Falling in love with Theseus, Ariadne helped him to kill the Minotaur. Then he fled with her, but abandoned her on Naxos. Dionysus, the fertility god, found her there and married her.

Wall Painting in Pompeii
National Museum, Naples

expressed by the hand mentioned in Sir William Hamilton's letter; which being a less explicit symbol, has escaped the attention of the reformers, and is still worn, as well as the shell, by the women of Italy, though without being understood. It represented the act of generation, which was considered as a solemn sacrament, in honor of the Creator, as will be more fully shown hereafter.

The male organs of generation are sometimes found represented by signs of the same sort, which might properly be called the symbols of symbols. One of the most remarkable of these is a cross, in the form of the letter T, which thus served as the emblem of creation and generation, before the church adopted it as the sign of salvation; a lucky coincidence of ideas, which, without doubt, facilitated the reception of it among the faithful. To the representative of the male organs was sometimes added a human head, which gives it the exact appearance of a crucifix. On an ancient medal, found in Cyprus, which,

from the style of workmanship, is certainly anterior to the Macedonian conquest, it appears with the chaplet or rosary, such as is now used in the Romish churches; the beads of which were used, anciently, to reckon time. Their being placed in a circle, marked its progressive continuity; while their separation from each other marked the divisions, by which it is made to return on itself, and thus produce years, months, and days. The symbol of the creative power is placed upon them, because these divisions were particularly under his influence and protection; the sun being his visible image, and the centre of his power, from which his emanations extended through the universe. Hence the Egyptians, in their sacred hymns, called upon Osiris, as the being who dwelt concealed in the embraces of the sun; and hence the great luminary itself is called *Kosmocratoz* in the Orphic Hymns.

This general emanation of the pervading Spirit of God, by which all things are generated and maintained, is

SATYR CARRYING OFF NYMPH
Wall Painting in Pompeii
National Museum, Naples

beautifully described by Virgil, in the following lines:

> For God pervades all lands, and the expanse of Ocean, and the vault of heaven. Hence come cattle and herds, men and the entire race of beasts: everything that is born acquiring for itself the slenderness of life. All things, too, in dissolution, return in due course and are restored to the same source. Nor is there any place for death, but living things soar into the stars and reach the deep heavens.

The Ethereal Spirit is here described as expanding itself through the universe, and giving life and motion to the inhabitants of earth, water, and air, by a participation of its own essence, each particle of which returned to its native source, at the dissolution of the body which is animated. Hence, not only men, but all animals, and even vegetables, were supposed to be impregnated with some particles of the Divine Nature infused into them, from which their

various qualities and dispositions, as well as their powers of propagation, were supposed to be derived. These appeared to be so many emanations of the Divine attributes, operating in different modes and degrees, according to the nature of the beings to which they belonged. Hence the characteristic properties of animals and plants were not only regarded as representations, but as actual emanations of the Divine Power, consubstantial with his own essence. For this reason, the symbols were treated with greater respect and veneration than if they had been merely signs and characters of convention. Plutarch says, that most of the Egyptian priests held the bull Apis, who was worshipped with so much ceremony, to be only an image of the Spirit of Osiris. This I take to have been the real meaning of all the animal worship of the Egyptians, about which so much has been written, and so little discovered. Those animals or plants, in which any particular attribute of the Deity seemed to predominate, became the symbols of that

[27]

MINERVA TRIUMPHANT OVER IGNORANCE
*Mythologically, the worship of Minerva, goddess of wis-
dom, spread at the expense of the war god Mars himself.
The ancients were familiar with female warriors: such as
the Amazons, who participated in the Trojan War.*
Kunsthistorisches Museum, Vienna

attribute, and were accordingly worshipped as the images of Divine Providence, acting in that particular direction. Like many other customs, both of ancient and modern worship, the practice, probably, continued long after the reasons upon which it was founded were either wholly lost, or only partially preserved, in vague traditions. This was the case in Egypt; for, though many of the priests knew or conjectured the origin of the worship of the bull, they could give no rational account why the crocodile, the ichneumon, and the ibis received similar honors. The symbolical characters, called hieroglyphics, continued to be esteemed by them as more holy and venerable than the conventional representations of sounds, notwithstanding their manifest inferiority; yet it does not appear, from any accounts extant, that they were able to assign any reason for this preference. On the contrary, Strabo tells us that the

Egyptians of his time were wholly ignorant of their ancient learning and religion, though impostors continually pretended to explain it. Their ignorance in these points is not to be wondered at, considering that the most ancient Egyptians, of whom we have any authentic accounts, lived after the subversion of their monarchy and destruction of their temples by the Persians, who used every endeavor to annihilate their religion; first, by command of Cambyses, and then of Ochus. What they were before this calamity, we have no direct information; for Herodotus is the earliest traveler, and he visited this country when in ruins.

It is observable in all modern religions, that men are superstitious in proportion as they are ignorant, and that those who know least of the principles of religion are the most earnest and fervent in the practice of its exterior rites and ceremonies. We may suppose from analogy, that this was the case with the Egyptians. The learned and rational merely respected and revered the sacred animals, whilst the vulgar worshipped and adored them. The greatest part of the former being, as is natural to suppose, destroyed by the persecution of the Persians, this worship and adoration became general; different cities adopting different animals as their tutelar deities, in the same manner as the Catholics now put themselves under the protection of different saints and martyrs. Like them, too, in the fervency of their devotion for the imaginary agent they forgot the original cause.

The custom of keeping animals as images of the Divine attributes, seems once to have prevailed in Greece as well as Egypt; for the God of Health was represented by a living serpent at Epidaurus, even in the last stage of their religion. In general, however, they preferred wrought images, not from their superiority in art, which they did not acquire until after the time of Homer, when their theology was entirely corrupted; but because they had thus the means of expressing their ideas more fully, by combining several forms together, and showing, not only the Divine attribute, but the mode and purpose of its operation. For instance; the celebrated bronze in the Vatican has the male organs of generation placed upon the head of a cock, the emblem of the sun, supported by the neck and shoulders of a man. In this composition, they represented the generative power of the Eros, the Osiris, Mithras, or Bacchus, whose centre is the sun, incarnate with man. By the inscription on the pedestal, the attribute this personified, is styled The Savior of the World; a title always venerable, under whatever image it be represented.

The Egyptians showed this incarnation of the Deity by a less permanent, though equally expressive symbol. At Mendes a living goat was kept as the image of the generative power, to whom the women presented themselves naked, and had the honor of being publicly enjoyed by him. Herodotus saw the act openly performed and calls it a prodigy. But the Egyptians had no such horror of it; for it was to them a representation of the Deity, and the communication of his creative spirit to man. It was one of the sacraments of that ancient church, and was, without doubt, beheld with that pious awe and reverence with which devout persons always contemplate the mysteries of their faith, whatever they happen to be; for, as the learned and orthodox Bishop Warburton, whose authority it is not for me to dispute, says, *from the nature of any action morality cannot arise, nor from its effects;* therefore, for aught we can tell, this ceremony, however shocking it may appear to modern manners and opinions, might have been in-

THE THIRTEENTH LABOR OF HERCULES
Hercules, the ancient exemplar of strength, performed twelve amazing tasks. To these twelve legendary labors the artist imaginatively adds a thirteenth labor.
Dominique Vivant Denon (1747-1826)

[29]

trinsically meritorious at the time of its celebration, and afford a truly edifying spectacle to the saints of ancient Egypt. Indeed, the Greeks do not seem to have felt much horror or disgust at the imitative representation of it, whatever the historian might have thought proper to express at the real celebration. Several specimens of their sculpture in this way have escaped the fury of the reformers, and remained for the instruction of later times. One of these, found among the ruins of Herculaneum, and kept concealed in the Royal Museum of Portici, is well known. Another exists in the collection of Mr. Townley, which I have thought proper to have engraved for the benefit of the learned. It may be remarked, that in these monuments the goat is passive instead of active; and that the human symbol is represented as incarnate with the divine, instead of the divine with the human; but this is in fact no difference; for the Creator, being of both sexes, is represented indifferently of either. In the other symbol of the bull, the sex is equally varied; the Greek medals having sometimes a bull, and sometimes a cow, which, Strabo tells us, was employed as the symbol of Venus, the passive generative power, at Momemphis, in Egypt. Both the bull and the cow are also worshipped at present by the Hindoos, as symbols of the male and female, or generative and nutritive, powers of the Deity. The cow is in almost all their pagodas; but the bull is revered with superior solemnity and devotion. At Tanjour is a monument of their piety to him, which even the inflexible perseverance, and habitual industry of the natives of that country, could scarcely have erected without greater knowledge in practical mechanics than they now possess. It is a statue of a bull lying down, hewn, with great accuracy, out of a single piece of hard granite, which has been conveyed by land from the distance of one hundred miles, although its weight, in its present reduced state, must be at least one hundred tons. The Greeks sometimes made their Taurine Bacchus, or bull, with a human face, to express both sexes, which they signified by the initial of the epithet *Liphnes* placed under him. Over him they frequently put the radiated asterisk, which represents the sun, to show the Deity, whose attribute he was intended to express. Hence we may perceive the reason why the Germans, who, according to Caesar, worshipped the sun, carried a brazen bull, as the image of their God, when they invaded the Roman dominions in the time of Marius; and even the chosen people of Providence, when they made unto themselves an image of the God who was to conduct them through the desert, and cast out the ungodly, from before them, made it in the shape of a young bull, or calf.

The Greeks, as they advanced in the cultivation of the imitative arts, gradually changed the animal for the human form, preserving still the original character. The human head was at first added to the body of the bull; but afterwards the whole figure was made human, with some of the features, and general character of the animal, blended with it. Oftentimes, however, these mixed figures had a peculiar and proper meaning, like that of the Vatican Bronze: and were not intended as mere refinements of art. Such are the fawns and satyrs, who represent the emanations of the Creator, incarnate with man, acting as his angels and ministers in the work of universal generation. In copulation with the goat, they represent the reciprocal incarnation of man with the deity, when incorporated with universal matter: for the Deity, being both male and female, was both active and passive in procreation; first animating man by an emanation from his own essence, and then employing that emanation to reproduce, in conjunction with the common productive powers of nature, which are no other than his own prolific spirit transfused through matter.

A Discourse on the Worship of Priapus
Richard Payne Knight. *1786.*

DIANA ASLEEP

St. Quentin, 1765

Love in the Orient

ORIENTAL BATH

Ingres (1780-1867)
Louvre, Paris

[34]

Love in the Orient

The Orient has always been wise in the ways of men: and particularly in the ways of men and women. Arabic, Hindu, Chinese treatises expound amatory techniques and mores, on the metaphysical plane as evidence of the cosmic scheme of continuity and creativeness, and on the physiological and realistic level that involves the erotic functional performances.

In the fourteenth century Hasan ibn Mohammed, surnamed Sherif ed-Din and known as Rami, produced his Anis El-'Oushshak, a study of feminine form, with citations from the Persian poets. It is a literary glorification of woman, an exultant paean of man to his cosmic partner. And although it probes into anatomical directions, it is, in essence, free from occidental prurience.

In China, Taoist manuals and erotic tales have contributed to amatory knowledge. Concubinage was prevalent in Chinese culture. Courtesans had special, segregated quarters. Lesbianism was not infrequent. There were actually secret associations of women who took an oath never to marry. Assassination by the other female members followed the breaking of the pledge.

In India, the Ananga-Ranga holds a major position in the corpus of erotology. It is a Sanskrit manual by a certain Kalyanamalla, who belongs in the sixteenth century. It deals with thirty-three different erotic themes and offers some one hundred and thirty prescriptions relative to the subject. Virtually, it is an Oriental Ars Amatoria. In addition to translations into the Indian languages, there is an English rendering by Sir Richard Burton. The Kama Sutra belongs in the same category: there are, too, a number of other versified guides that emphasize certain erotic themes that the other treatises have touched on.

Arabs have their own standards of feminine pulchritude. The Arab ideal includes a body white as ivory, teeth like rice in whiteness and glow, the gait and step of a young, spirited mare or a doe. This ideal woman's hair is black, and hangs in thick tresses. Her lashes are curved, her breasts firm, her hips wide.

In figure she should stand upright, like a palm tree that grows skyward in the oasis. With her narrow waist, and perfumed with myrrh, and adorned with tinkling jewelry, she can allure any man by her seductive presence without the aid of any other contrived aphrodisiacs.

Of all peoples, the Arabs have made almost a science of erotic literature. Their writings abound in studies and manuals that discuss the physiology of love, amorous skills, aphrodisiacs and anaphrodisiacs, and in a wider sense the entire range of sexual relationships, both acceptable and abnormal.

The Perfumed Garden, by the Sheikh Nefzawi, is one

CIRCASSIAN SLAVE MARKET

John H. Ramberg

of the major erotic handbooks originally intended for Moslem use. It is full of anecdotes illustrating some particular phase of amatory activity—pervaded in most cases, by expressions of devoutness, sanctity, poetic imagery, and glorifying verse. In this respect, the work is highly reminiscent of the content of the Arabian Nights. In some degree, it is the forerunner of Boccaccio and Rabelais.

Underlying the widespread indulgence in sexual activity in Moslem countries lies a religious motif, an explicit injunction governing erotic mores as a sacred function and a devout duty. Sexual desires, according to Arab concepts,

SLAVE MARKET

C. Delort

should therefore not be discouraged, but rather actively stimulated. Hence, in line with such positive prescriptions, the continuous search for foods, drugs, and other aphrodisiac devices and aids in the prolongation and promotion of sexual capacity.

The author of The Perfumed Garden, Sheikh Nefzawi,

on occasion exalts woman, breaking out into rapturous eulogy:

Then the Almighty has plunged women into a sea of splendors, of voluptuousness, and of delights, and covered her with

HASHISH

Willens Schellenks
Musée Guimet, Paris

precious vestments with brilliant girdles
and provoking smiles.
He has also gifted her with eyes that
inspire love, and with eyelashes like polished
blades.

According to the testimony of a Dutch physician, Dr.
L. A. Schlegel, the Chinese are the most passionate people.
In a book published in 1880 he discusses their amatory
mores. Erotic books and engravings, he asserts, are largely
employed as sexual excitants. Immense quantities of
these are to be met with everywhere. Nearly all of them,

The harem was the Oriental laboratory of eroticism, where women were trained for the whims and fantasies of the male.

Guérard, 1853
Bibliotheque Nationale, Paris

EVIDENCE OF VIRTUE
*This type of post-connubial ritual, imposed on the bride,
was practiced for centuries, and is still in vogue in Moslem
countries.*

Chinese painting on silk

light pieces, novels, anecdotes are full of expressions of so cynical a nature that it is almost impossible to choose among them.

In the Tschoen Koeng Ise — Erotic Poems — history is brought forward for the sole purpose of describing the most scandalous affairs in the vilest language.

The governing authorities, adds the author, allow these works to circulate without restriction. . . In certain regions of China, little articulated and movable puppets are manufactured, in porcelain or ivory, extremely obscene, and known under the name of Tschoen Koeng Siang.

In the literary field, the Chin P'ing Mei in an outstand-

ing picaresque erotic novel. It is a long adventurous tale, written during the sixteenth century, pervaded, in the vein of Apuleius' Metamorphoses, by amorous encounters, scenes in bordellos, feasts of lanterns, astrological lore, spells and aphrodisiac matter, bawdry and cuckoldry, erotic techniques and sexual stimuli. Among the large number of characters that move through the episodes are Golden Lotus herself, Porphyry, and Hsi-Mên Ch'ing, young boys and old beldames familiar with every lubricity, every love charm, incantation, and philtre.

In some respects, Hindu ideals of feminine perfection coincide with those of Arab countries. The face should

[40]

AN AINU SUCKLES BEAR CUBS

Oriental viewpoint. The tales are packed with erotic episodes, with sages and traders, slaves, charlatans, eunuchs, wives and concubines. Love and brutality, sexual perversions, piety and lasciviousness, romance and indecency, roguery and fantasy mingle merrily and unresentfully in this panoramic conspectus of Oriental amatory life. One of the best English translations is that of Sir Richard Burton, published by the Burton Club in seventeen volumes and containing elaborate commentaries.

Among notable erotic treatises are the Bah-Numeh, the Book of Pleasure. This is of Turkish origin, the author being Abdul Hagg Effendi. The Book of the Bridal and the Brides is an Arabic manual by Al-Jahiz. El Ktab deals with the Secrets of Love, in the vein of Omar Haleby. It was published in Paris in 1893, with a commentary by P. de Regla. Ibn Sina was a medieval Hispano-Arab who wrote a Treatise on Love that has been translated into English. The Kitab Nawazir Al-Ayk Fi Al-Nayk — The Green Splendors of the Copse in Copulation — is also in the same genre. It is ascribed to a certain Jala Al-Din Al-Siyuti.

be as pleasing as the new moon. The body should be soft as the mustard flower. A fine fair, tender skin is a requisite. Eyes bright as those of a fawn. Bosom full and firm. The nose straight. A swan-like gliding gait. The voice low and musical, while the garments should be white, flowing, adorned with jewels.

In the Hindu love manuals, special chapters are devoted to charms and drugs intended to attract and retain love, as well as recipes whose purpose was to achieve complete mastery over the person loved.

Arabic literature contains a vast corpus of erotology. The Arabian Nights, possibly, may represent the essential

SUTTEE

It was a custom for a Hindu widow to immolate herself on the pyre of her dying husband. This rite of suttee was not confined to India: the self-immolation of Dido in Vergil's Aeneid belongs in the same category.

HINDU SCULPTURE

The Black Pagoda, India

[42]

Erotic sculpture on a temple façade at Konarak, Orissa. The cosmic principle of creation, in Hindu mythology, was a metaphysical concept, akin to Lucretius' alma Venus genetrix.

Archaeological Survey
Government of India

The lingam ritual prevalent among the Hindu adherents of Vishnu was expounded and interpreted, from a historical-mythological viewpoint, by Pierre Sonnerat (1745-1814), a French traveler who produced a Voyage aux Indes Orientales et à la Chine, published in two volumes, in Paris, in 1782.

In Egypt there were dancing girls known as awalim. They alternated with prostitutional activities. From the earliest times, in fact, dancing has been associated with amatory and sexual manifestations. The association is manifest in ancient temple worship, in Greece, in the Middle East, and in India.

The famous Egyptologist, Sir William Flinders Petrie, presents, in his translation of The Doulaq Papyrus, dating in the second millennium B.C., the ancient religious associations with prostitution. The hierodouloi, the female temple practitioners, were dedicated to Aphrodite or her epichorial counterpart.

H. E. W.

[43]

Sculptures on façade of Mahamandapa Kandarya Mahadeo Temple. Like the frescoes of Pompeii, Hindu temples are known for their extreme representations of erotic practices.

Department of Archaeology
Government of India

Slave trading post in not too distant days of Arabia.

SLAVE DEALER

[46]

Polyandry

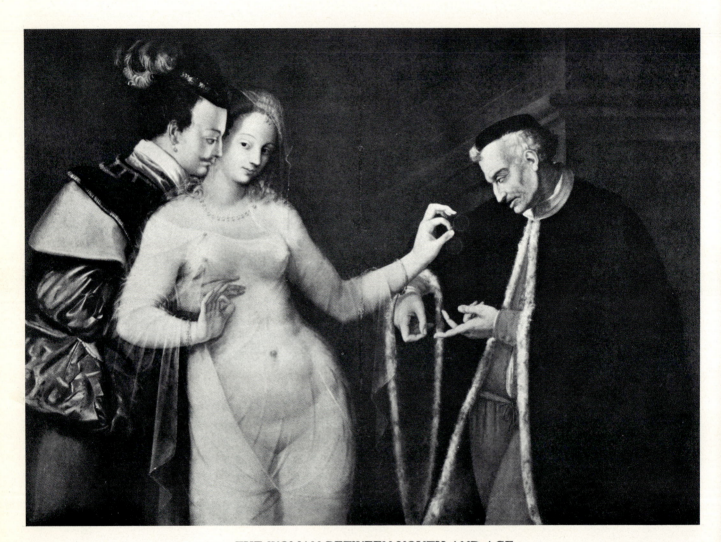

THE WOMAN BETWEEN YOUTH AND AGE

French School, c. 1575
Museum of Rennes

Polyandry

Polyandry is the marriage of one woman to several men. This is a relatively rare form of marriage. The best known people practicing polyandry were the Todas of India prior to the period of British influence. The Todas also practiced female infanticide.

The Polynesians of the Marquesas Islands also had a system of polyandry. Young girls, approximately twelve years of age, were considered nubile, and from that age a girl had two or more husbands.

In Tibet, too, among the Ladakhs, polyandry is an established custom. The practice, in a more restricted degree, also appears among the Tibetan Bhotias. Here the custom is confined to the brothers of one family.

H. E. W.

POLYANDRY IN TIBET

In Tibet, where polyandry has long been in vogue, the polyandrous wife wears this head-dress, made of wool and cane, and adorned with turquoise and coral. The husbands are usually brothers. The marriage of cousins is not permitted.

[49]

THE FEAST OF ACHELOUS

Rubens (1577-1640)
Metropolitan Museum of Art

FEAST OF THE GODS

The lusts of mortals are reflected in the orgies of ancient mythology, the anthropomorphic deities merely imitating man's immoralities.

Abraham Bloemaert (1564-1651)
Alte Pinakothek, Munich

| 51 |

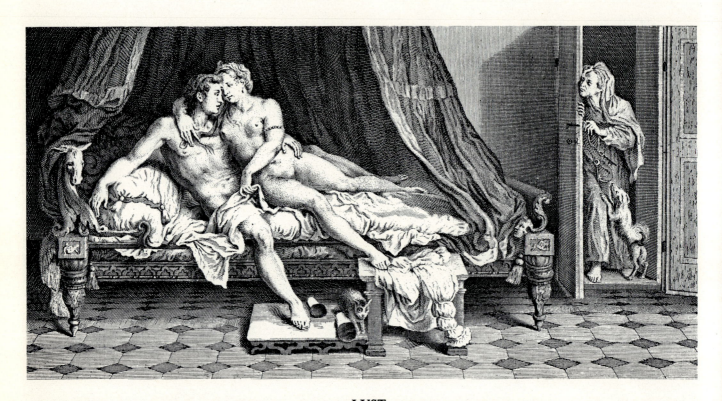

LUST

Giulio Romano (1499-1546)

Great Lovers

VENUS LISTENING TO MUSIC

Titian (1477-1576)
Museo del Prado, Madrid

Great Lovers

DON JUAN

Don Juan belongs in the legendary and literary roster of the great amatory adventurers. The original Don Juan is believed to have been a certain Spanish Don Miguel Mañara Vicentelo de Leca.

In literature, the name appears somewhere about 1620, with the performance of a play by the monk Gabriel Tellez, called Tirso de Molina (1571-1648). The piece was El Burlador de Sevilla y Convidado de Piedra. The theme of seducer and libertine belonged to popular Spanish mythology. But there existed other instances of a Don Juan Tenorio. The most famous was a favorite of Peter I, the Cruel, king of Castile. According to Gregorio Marañon, however, the actual prototype of Tirso de Molina was a certain Duke of Villamediana, a notorious roué of his time. Some twenty years after the appearance of El Burlador, a young man of Seville was so impressed by the character of the dramatic protagonist that he iden-

tified himself with this Don Juan. His name is Miguel de Leca y Colona y Mañara y Vicentelo.It is difficult to assert that Molière knew of this Don Juan when he produced his own Don Juan ou Le Festin de Pierre, c. 1665: but one of the episodes in Molina appears again in Molière.

Don Juan became the seducer incarnate, but the anti-Tristan, the passionless seducer, in love not with a woman, but with Woman.

In this traditional sense, Don Juan is the man of pleasure, devoid of romantic despair, amorous for the moment. He is fundamentally an enemy of the divinity. He is in quest, not of pleasure so much as of conquest. His joy and his vocation are synthesized in seduction. Unlike Tristan, Don Juan, finding his ultimate delight in subjugation, postulates an eternal infidelity.

Don Juan has been the subject of many literary and metaphysical studies: notably by Otto Rank, Stefan Zweig, Alfred Fabre, Denis de Rougemont, Claude Elser, and Gregorio Marañon.

CASANOVA

Casanova de Seingalt, depicted in one of his amorous adventures.

Giacomo Girolamo (1725-1798)

CASANOVA

Giacomo Casanova de Seingalt (1725-1798) was the professional libertine, the dedicated exemplar of erotic mores. In his extreme old age, like some exhausted satyr, he composed his personal reminiscences. Produced originally in French, these Memoirs were delivered by his grandson Carlo Angiolini, in 1820, to a German publisher, and were issued in Germany in twelve volumes, in 1823.

In his early youth, Casanova had already begun to reveal certain erotic tendencies. At table, he expounded a lewd couplet in Latin with an equally salacious grammatical comment.

The contents of the Memoirs cover Casanova's life from boyhood to late maturity, and touch on most countries, and the major cities, of Europe. For his life was constant movement, from boudoir to banquet, from gambling den to house of assignation, from social gatherings to fairs, always in quest: for wealth, women, comforts and ease.

Many translations and private editions, in the interest of bibliophiles, have appeared in the last century. The most recent re-publication is Memoirs of Casanova. 4 volumes. Translated by Arthur Machen. New York: Dover, 1961.

A mere survey of the chapter headings alone indicates the trend and interests of Casanova. He takes minor orders. He has an adventure with Lucie. He is expelled from the seminary, where he finds homosexuality practiced among the students. He goes to Rome, and to Bologna, to Venice and to Parma, to Geneva and Vienna, to Madrid and Ferrara, to Dresden and to Paris. He makes contacts with lawyers and diplomats, with scoundrels and priests,

A woman entertainer of 18th Century European aristocracy.

with innkeepers and cardinals. There are French ladies and the nobility, young girls and married matrons, actresses and nondescripts. Casanova participates in social circles, attends the opera, dines in elegance. He drops his clerical garb and becomes a military adventurer, a kind of free lance mercenary: which does not last long. He finds amorous opportunities at any moment, in any spot: in carriages and boudoirs, in inns and at intimate suppers. The names of his equally willing conquests follow in rapid sequence: Angela and Christine, Cécile and Thérèse, Marchetti and Henriette.

On occasion he becomes meditative, almost scholarly, and makes a sober allusion to Cicero's Tusculan Disputations. He quotes a couplet in Italian, or a phrase from Horace. Or goes off into philosophical speculation.

He had wanton eyes and groping hands, a lust for flesh no less than for flesh-pots, an impassioned and boundless desire. Casanova depicts his total character, his secret ways and views, stating the most intimate details without subterfuge, with a rare apology. For, on his amatory coat of arms, was emblazoned his supreme concept, stemming from his personal experience, but in a literary sense deriving from Rabelais: Nature has needs that must be satisfied.

A frivolous, inconsequential life was his: interspersed with arrests and flight, sexual encounters, meetings with ambassadors and royalty and celebrities: followed by darker times, imprisonment and agonies. Yet everywhere he discovers Priapus, Aphrodite, and Eros in wait for him, ready to aid him in his libidinous enterprises, that are the condition and explanation of his being. Yet there is also a certain ingenuousness in the narration of such encounters.

In a literary sense, Casanova has the gift of presenting

[57]

A PICNIC LUNCH

E. Manet (1832-1883)
Louvre, Paris

a living picture by the accumulation of circumstantial details, as in the affair of the ravishing C.C.

At times, Casanova stops recounting his amatory victories, not from exhaustion, but merely to analyze the nature and purpose of love. What is love? he asks himself:

I have read numberless ancient writings on this theme. I have also read most of what the moderns say. But neither all that is said about it, nor all that I myself have said about it either when I was young or now that I am no longer young, nothing, absolutely nothing will make me admit that love is a trifle or a vanity. It is a kind of madness, agreed, but one over which philosophy has no power. It is a sickness to which man is subject at every age and it is incurable if it extends into old age. Love, being, sentiment that cannot be defined! Lord of Nature! Sweet bitterness. Cruel bitterness! Love! Alluring monster that is beyond definition. In the midst of a thousand tortures that you inflict upon life, you implant so much pleasure in human existence that but for you being and non-being would be united and conjoined!

Catherine II of Russia (1729-1796): Catherine the Great. Called the Semiramis of the North. Her life was notorious for her amatory adventures, her succession of lovers, her flaunting disdain of all conventions, of every lewd scandal. She deposed Peter III with the aid of her lover Grigor Orlov. Childless with her husband, the grandson of Peter the Great, she was advised by her Chancellor that the Empire urgently required an heir to maintain the stability of her position.

Imperialistic and at the same time completely realistic, Catherine ordered her chef to prepare caviar and sturgeon for a dinner at which Saltikoff, an officer of the guard, was invited. As a consequence of her gastronomic perception not devoid of its amatory associations, she safeguarded her Empire with an heir.

H. E. W.

The Toilette

THE BATH

Gius Barbaglia

The Toilette

To heighten their physical and emotional attractiveness, women at all times, in all levels of society, primitive as well as highly sophisticated, ancient and contemporary, have used an amazing battery of beautifying aids and adjuncts: unguents and cosmetics, hair-arrangements and dyes, Coan silk diaphanous robes, jewelry and perfumes, paint and powder. The Orient, in particular, has produced in the Kama Sutra, the Ananga-Ranga, and The Perfumed Garden specific guidance in this area of erotic seductiveness.

In the Occident, the Roman poet Ovid, arch-priest of eroticism, left a brief, unfinished, but enlightening versified guide to facial treatment:

> Learn, girls, the care that embellishes the face and the means of protecting your beauty. Cultivation has forced the unfertile earth to produce the gifts of Ceres: the stinging bramble-bushes have gone. Cultivation too remedies the bitter juices in fruits, and the split tree receives adoptive resources. What is adorned gives pleasure: lofty roofs are covered with gold ornaments. The black earth is hidden by the marble edifices erected thereon. Fleece undergoes frequent dye tinctures in the Tyrian bronze cauldrons: India offers for our delight ivory minutely carved.

Perhaps, under king Tatius, the Sabine women of antiquity would have preferred to cultivate the fields of their fathers rather than their own beauty. Then the ruddy-hued matron, sitting on her high bench, would weave her hard task continuously with her thumb; and she herself enclosed in the fold the lambs that her daughter had taken out to graze. She herself then tended the fire, throwing twigs and cut wood upon it. But your mothers produced delicate daughters. You want your bodies draped in gold-embroidered robes: you want to perfume your hair and vary your coiffure. You want your hands glittering with jeweled-rings. You adorn your neck with precious stones culled from the East, so heavy that two stones drooping from one ear are a burden.

But one must not resent this. You should care to please, since in our own time men are well turned out. Your husbands adopt feminine tastes and the wife scarcely has anything to add to their luxurious ways. Women live hidden in the country and arrange their hair-do. Though lofty Mt. Athos conceals them, lofty Athos will find them well adorned. To please even oneself is a certain pleasure. Maidens are concerned and take delight in their beauty. The bird of Juno unfolds its swift wings when they are praised by men and silently the bird swells with pride in its beauty.

In this way love will blossom, rather than by potent herbs that the witch's hand cut with horrendous skill. Nor put any trust in simples, nor juices compounded in philtres, nor try the noxious venom of the rutting mare. Snakes are not split in two by the incantations of Marsians, nor does the water return to its own source by their aid. And,

SUSANNA AT THE BATH

Tintoretto (1518-1594)
Art Gallery, Vienna

although a person were to beat repeatedly on brazen Temesaean drums, never would the moon be thrown from her horse-drawn chariot.

Let your first care, girls, be to safeguard your character. A face pleases, when there are, in addition, spiritual qualities. Love, based on character, endures; age will ravage beauty, and your charming face will be furrowed with wrinkles. A time will come, when you will regret having looked into your mirror and this grief will be another cause for wrinkles. Virtue is sufficient, and endures through life, however long, and throughout all the years love will survive thereby.

Come now, when sleep relaxes your delicate limbs, by what means can your white skin acquire a glow? Take barley that the farmers of Libya have sent by boat; take off the straw and the coverings. Let an equal measure of ers be soaked in ten eggs but let the hulled barley weigh two full pounds. When this mixture is dried in the windy air have it pounded slowly by an ass, under a worn millstone. Pulverize also the first sprouting horn of a living

THE TOILETTE

School of Fontainebleau
Louvre, Paris

stag: add a sixth of a full as of this. And now when the flour is crushed and pulverized, forthwith pass the whole mixture through an infinitely fine-meshed sieve. Add twelve bulbs of narcissus without the skins, and crush them in a clean marble mortar with vigorous hands. Then two ounces of gum with Tuscan flour of wheat, and to this add nine times as much honey. Any woman that smears her face with this cosmetic will glow, smoother than her own mirror. Do not hesitate either to crush pale lupins and at the same time cook beans, large-sized. Let

there be six pounds of each equally; crush both items under black mill-stones. Do not fail to add cerussa nor the spume of red nitre and iris that comes from Illyrian soil. Work all this with young and vigorous arms; and let the crushed ingredients weigh exactly an ounce.

Ingredients taken from the nest of plaintive birds cause blotches on the face to disappear: this application is called aleyoneum. If you ask what is the proper dose for these ingredients, the amount is the weight of an ounce divided into two parts. To make the mixture adhere and cover the

[65]

BATHING

Kornelius Holsteyn
Art Gallery, Kassel

whole body, add Attic honey from golden honey-combs.

Though incense appeases the gods and the angered divinities, it must not all be offered on the burning altars. When you have mixed incense with nitre that smooths the body, and let there be of each the same weight, a third of a pound, add, less than a fourth part, gum taken from the bark of a tree and a quantity of rich myrrh. After pulverizing all this, sift it through a fine strainer, and crush the powder, mixing it with honey.

It is beneficial too to add fennel to sweet-smelling myrrh — five scruples of fennel and nine of myrrh — and a bunch of dry roses, and male incense with ammoniac salt. Sprinkle thereon cream of barley, and let the incense with the salt equal the weight of the roses. If a delicate face is smeared with this application, for however short a time, all the redness will disappear. I have seen a woman soak poppies in cold water, crush them, and smear her tender cheeks with them.

De Medicamine Faciei Femineae. Ovid.
Transl. by *H. E. W.*

[66]

Marriage: The Status of Women

Marriage:
The Status of Women

Marriage, one of the basic human institutions that date back to proto-historic times, has, through the ages, become encrusted with strange rituals and taboos, with moral restrictions and religious injunctions and inhibitions. Marriage has, through the centuries and in every region, been used as a kind of corpus vile of fantastic experiments and ceremonials. And as men became more knowledgeable and society became more material and earthy and luxury-loving, marriage itself became an object of humor and ribaldry, of hilarious farce and contemptuous disdain. Sometimes it assumed the aspect of slavery, in a domestic sense, not disjoined from torture: on occasion, too, becoming a remote ideal, that remained, in the chivalric ages, a romantic concept of supreme love.

Marriage, being a human institution, acquired associations of infidelities and aberrations, adultery and incest and cuckoldry. It is to be observed that in ancient Greece, in a general sense, no stigma was attached to a husband who sought change and stimulus with a hetaira. Yet Aristotle proposed loss of civil rights for the errant husband or wife. Catullus, the Roman erotic poet, composed a sensuous glorification of the marriage state: while the Restoration dramatists of England stressed in their plays that marriage à la mode had become merely another diversionary and temporary amatory motif.

THE POSITION OF WOMEN

In the long series of moral revolutions that have been described in the foregoing chapters, I have more than once had occasion to refer to the position that was assigned to woman in the community, and to the virtues and vices that spring directly from the relations of the sexes. I have not, however, as yet discussed these questions with a fulness at all corresponding to their historical importance, and I propose, in consequence, before concluding this volume, to devote a few pages to their examination. Of all the many questions that are treated in this work, there is none which I approach with so much hesitation, for there is probably none which it is so difficult to treat with clearness and impartiality, and at the same time without exciting any scandal of offence. The complexity of the problem, arising from the very large place which exceptional institutions or circumstances, and especially the influence of climate and race, have had on the chastity of nations, I have already noticed, and the extreme delicacy of the matters with which this branch of ethics is connected must be palpable to all. The first duty of an historian, however, is to truth; and it is absolutely impossible to present a true picture of the moral condition of different ages, and to form a true estimate of the moral effects of different re-

[69]

ligions, without adverting to the department of morals, which has exhibited most change, and has probably exercised most influence.

It is natural that, in the period when men are still perfect barbarians, when their habits of life are still nomadic, and when, war and the chase, being their sole pursuits, the qualities that are required in these form their chief measure of excellence, the inferiority of women to men should be regarded as undoubted, and their position should be extremely degraded. In all those qualities which are then most prized, women are indisputably inferior. The social qualities in which they are especially fitted to excel have no sphere for their display. The ascendancy of beauty is very faint, and, even if it were otherwise, few traces of female beauty could survive the hardships of the savage life. Woman is looked upon merely as the slave of man, and as the minister to his passions. In the first capacity, her life is one of continual, abject, and unrequited toil. In the second capacity, she is exposed to all the violent revulsions of feeling that follow, among rude men, the gratification of the animal passions.

Even in this early stage, however, we may trace some rudiments of those moral sentiments which are destined at a later period to expand. The institution of marriage exists. The value of chastity is commonly in some degree felt, and appears in the indignation which is displayed against the adulterer. The duty of restraining the passions is largely recognised in the female, though the males are only restricted by the prohibition of adultery.

The first two steps which are taken towards the elevation of woman are probably the abandonment of the custom of purchasing wives, and the construction of the family on the basis of monogamy. In the earliest periods of civilization, the marriage contract was arranged between the bridegroom and the father of the bride, on the condition of a sum of money being paid by the former to the latter. This sum, which is known in the laws of the barbarians as the 'mundium,' was in fact a payment to the father for the cession of his daughter, who thus became the bought slave of her husband. It is one of the most remarkable features of the ancient laws of India, that they forbade this gift, on the ground that the parent should not sell his child; but there can be little doubt that this sale was at one time the ordinary type of marriage. In the Jewish writings we find Jacob purchasing Leah and Rachel by certain services to their father; and this custom, which seems to have been at one time general in Judea, appears in the age of Homer to have been general in Greece. At an early period, however, of Greek history, the purchase-money was replaced by the dowry, or sum of money paid by the father of the bride for the use of his daughter; and this, although it passed into the hands of the husband,

contributed to elevate the wife, in the first place, by the dignity it gave her, and, in the next place, by special laws, which both in Greece and Rome secured it to her in most cases of separation. The wife thus possessed a guarantee against ill-usage by her husband. She ceased to be his slave, and became in some degree a contracting party. Among the early Germans, a different and very remarkable custom existed. The bride did not bring any dowry to her husband, nor did the bridegroom give anything to the father of the bride; but he gave his gift to the bride herself, on the morning after the first night of marriage, and this, which was called the 'Morgengab,' or morning gift, was the origin of the jointure.

Still more important than the foregoing was the institution of monogamy, by which, from its earliest days, the Greek civilization proclaimed its superiority to the Asiatic civilizations that had preceded it. We may regard monogamy either in the light of our intuitive moral sentiment on the subject of purity, or in the light of the interests of society. In its Oriental or polygamous stage, marriage is regarded almost exclusively, in its lowest aspect, as a gratification of the passions; while in European marriages the mutual attachment and respect of the contracting parties, the formation of a household, and the long train of domestic feelings and duties that accompany it, have all their distinguished place among the motives of the contract, and the lower element has comparatively little prominence. In this way it may be intelligibly said, without any reference to utilitarian considerations, that monogamy is a higher state than polygamy. The utilitarian arguments in its defence are also extremely powerful, and may be summed up in three sentences. Nature, by making the number of males and females nearly equal, indicates it as natural. In no other form of marriage can the government of the family, which is one of the chief ends of marriage, be so happily sustained, and in no other does woman assume the position of the equal of man.

Monogamy was the general system in Greece, though there are said to have been slight and temporary deviations into the earlier system, after some great disasters, when an increase of population was ardently desired. A broad line must, however, be drawn between the legendary or poetical period, as reflected in Homer and perpetuated in the tragedians, and the later historical period. It is one of the most remarkable, and to some writers one of the most perplexing, facts in the moral history of Greece, that in the former and ruder period women had undoubtedly the highest place, and their type exhibited the highest perfection. Moral ideas, in a thousand forms, have been sublimated, enlarged, and changed, by advancing civilization; but it may be fearlessly asserted that the types of female excellence which are contained in the Greek poems, while

VENUS AND MARS CAUGHT IN VULCAN'S NET

Adultery was the ultimate social immorality, even in the Homeric epics. Divine reprobation is manifest in the assembled deities, in spite of laughter.

Martin van Heemskerck (1498-1574)
Kunsthistorisches Museum, Vienna

they are among the earliest, are also among the most perfect in the literature of mankind. The conjugal tenderness of Hector and Andromache; the unwearied fidelity of Penelope, awaiting through the long revolving years the return of her storm-tossed husband, who looked forward to her as to the crown of all his labours; the heroic love of Alcestis, voluntarily dying that her husband might live; the filial piety of Antigone; the majestic grandeur of the death of Polyxena; the more subdued and saintly resignation of Iphigenia, excusing with her last breath the father who had condemned her; the joyous, modest, and loving Nausicaa, whose figure shines like a perfect idyll among the tragedies of the Odyssey — all these are pictures of perennial beauty, which Rome and Christendom, chivalry and modern civilization, have neither eclipsed nor transcended. Virgin modesty and conjugal fidelity, the graces as well as the virtues of the most perfect womanhood, have never been more exquisitely portrayed. The female figures stand out in the canvas almost as prominently as the male ones, and are surrounded by an almost equal reverence. The whole history of the Siege of Troy is a history of the catastrophes that followed a violation of the nuptial tie. Yet, at the same time, the position of women was in some respects a degraded one. The custom of purchase-money given to the father of the bride was general. The husbands appear to have indulged largely, and with little or no censure, in concubines. Female captives of the highest rank were treated with great harshness. The inferiority of women to men was strongly asserted, and it was illustrated and defended by a very curious physiological notion, that the generative power belonged exclusively to men, women having only a very subordinate part in the production of their children. The woman Pandora was said to have been the author of all human ills.

In the historical age of Greece, the legal position of women had in some respects slightly improved, but their moral condition had undergone a marked deterioration. Virtuous women lived a life of perfect seclusion. The foremost and most dazzling type of Ionic womanhood was the courtesan, while, among the men, the latitude accorded by public opinion was almost unrestricted.

The facts in moral history, which it is at once most important and most difficult to appreciate, are what may be called the facts of feeling. It is much easier to show what men did or taught than to realize the state of mind that rendered possible such actions or teaching; and in the case before us we have to deal with a condition of feeling so extremely remote from that of our own day, that the difficulty is preeminently great. Very sensual, and at the same time very brilliant societies, have indeed repeatedly existed, and the histories of both France and

Italy afford many examples of an artistic and intellectual enthusiasm encircling those who were morally most frail; but the peculiarity of Greek sensuality is, that it grew up, for the most part, uncensured, and indeed even encouraged, under the eyes of some of the most illustrious of moralists. If we can imagine Ninon de l'Enclos at a time when the rank and splendour of Parisian society thronged her drawing-rooms, reckoning a Bossuet or a Fénelon among her followers—if we can imagine these prelates publicly advising her about the duties of her profession, and the means of attaching the affections of her lovers—we shall have conceived a relation scarcely more strange than that which existed between Socrates and the courtesan Theodota.

In order to reconstruct, as far as possible, the modes of feeling of the Greek moralists, it will be necessary in the first place to say a few words concerning one of the most delicate, but at the same time most important, problems with which the legislator and the moralist have to deal.

It was a favourite doctrine of the Christian Fathers, that concupiscence, or the sensual passion, was 'the original sin' of human nature; and it must be owned that the progress of knowledge, which is usually extremely opposed to the ascetic theory of life, concurs with the theological view, in showing the natural force of this appetite to be far greater than the well-being of man requires. The writings of Malthus have proved, what the Greek moralists appear in a considerable degree to have seen, that its normal and temperate exercise in the form of marriage, would produce, if universal, the utmost calamities to the world, and that, while nature seems in the most unequivocal manner to urge the human race to early marriages, the first condition of an advancing civilization in populous countries is to restrain or diminish them. In no highly civilized society is marriage general on the first development of the passions, and the continual tendency of increasing knowledge is to render such marriages more rare. It is also an undoubted truth that, however much moralists may enforce the obligation of extra-matrimonial purity, this obligation has never been even approximately regarded; and in all nations, ages, and religions a vast mass of irregular indulgence has appeared, which has probably contributed more than any other single cause to the misery and the degradation of man.

There are two ends which a moralist, in dealing with this question, will especially regard—the natural duty of every man doing something for the support of the child he has called into existence, and the preservation of the domestic circle unassailed and unpolluted. The family is the centre and the archetype of the State and the happiness and goodness of society are always in a very great degree dependent upon the purity of domestic life. The essentially exclusive nature of marital affection, and the

HENRY VIII AND ANNE BOLEYN
Henry VIII, King of England, had six wives in succession:
two of whom, Anne Boleyn and Catherine Howard, were
beheaded on the charge of adultery.

J. L. G. Ferris: 1895

natural desire of every man to be certain of the paternity of the child he supports, render the incursions of irregular passions within the domestic circle a cause of extreme suffering. Yet it would appear as if the excessive force of these passions would render such incursions both frequent and inevitable.

Under these circumstances, there has arisen in society a figure which is certainly the most mournful, and in some respects the most awful, upon which the eye of the moralist can dwell. That unhappy being whose very name is a shame to speak; who counterfeits with a cold heart the transports of affection, and submits herself as the passive instrument of lust; who is scorned and insulted as the vilest of her sex, and doomed, for the most part, to disease and abject wretchedness and an early death, appears in every age as the perpetual symbol of the degradation and the sinfulness of man. Herself the supreme type of vice, she is ultimately the most efficient guardian of virtue. But for her, the unchallenged purity of countless happy homes would be polluted, and not a few who, in the pride of their untempted chastity, think of her with an indignant shudder, would have known the agony of remorse and of despair. On that one degraded and ignoble form are concentrated the passions that might have filled the world with shame. She remains, while creeds and civilizations rise and fall, the eternal priestess of humanity, blasted for the sins of the people.

In dealing with this unhappy being, and with all of her

[73]

REDEMPTION WITH A GIFT
An illustration of the Ius Primae Noctis, when the lord of the manor made a bride within his domain the object of his prior privilege, unless her family redeemed her.
Woodcut: 15th century

sex who have violated the law of chastity, the public opinion of most Christian countries pronounces a sentence of extreme severity. In the Anglo-Saxon nations especially, a single fault of this kind is sufficient, at least in the upper and middle classes, to affix an indelible brand which no time, no virtues, no penitence can wholly efface. This sentence is probably, in the first instance, simply the expression of the religious feeling on the subject, but it is also sometimes defended by powerful arguments drawn from the interests of society. It is said that the preservation of domestic purity is a matter of such transcendent importance that it is right that the most crushing penalties should be attached to an act which the imagination can easily transfigure which legal enactments can never efficiently control, and to which the most violent passions may prompt. It is said, too, that an anathema which drives into obscurity all evidences of sensual passions is pecu-

liarly fitted to restrict their operation; for, more than any other passions, they are dependent on the imagination, which is readily fired by the sight of evil. It is added, that the emphasis with which the vice is stigmatised produces a corresponding admiration for the opposite virtue, and that a feeling of the most delicate and scrupulous honour is thus formed among the female population, which not only preserves from gross sin, but also dignifies and ennobles the whole character.

In opposition to these views, several considerations of much weight have been urged. It is argued that, however persistently society may ignore this form of vice, it exists nevertheless, and on the most gigantic scale, and that evil rarely assumes such inveterate and perverting forms as when it is shrouded in obscurity and veiled by an hypocritical appearance of unconsciousness. The existence in England of certainly not less than fifty thousand unhappy women, sunk in the very lowest depths of vice and misery, shows sufficiently what an appalling amount of moral evil is festering uncontrolled, undiscussed, and unalleviated, under the fair surface of a decorous society. In the eyes of every physician, and indeed in the eyes of most continental writers who have adverted to the subject, no other feature of English life appears so infamous as the fact that an epidemic, which is one of the most dreadful now existing among mankind, which communicates itself from the guilty husband to the innocent wife, and even transmits its taint to her offspring, and which the experience of other nations conclusively proves may be vastly diminished, should be suffered to rage unchecked because the Legislature refuses to take official cognisance of its existence, or proper sanitary measures for its repression. If the terrible censure which English public opinion passes upon every instance of female frailty in some degree diminishes the number, it does not prevent such instances from being extremely numerous, and it immeasurably aggravates the suffering they produce. Acts which in other European countries would excite only a slight and transient emotion spread in England, over a wide circle, all the bitterness of unmitigated anguish. Acts which naturally neither imply nor produce a total subversion of the moral feelings, and which, in other countries, are often followed by happy, virtuous, and affectionate lives, in England almost invariably lead to absolute ruin. Infanticide is greatly multiplied, and a vast proportion of those whose reputations and lives have been blasted by one momentary sin, are hurled into the abyss of habitual prostitution — a condition which, owing to the sentence of public opinion and the neglect of legislators, is in no other European country so hopelessly vicious or so irrevocable.

It is added, too, that the immense multitude who are thus doomed to the extremity of life-long wretchedness are not always, perhaps not generally, of those whose dispositions seem naturally incapable of virtue. The victims of seduction are often led aside quite as much by the ardour of their affections, and by the vivacity of their intelligence, as by any vicious propensities. Even in the lowest grades, the most dispassionate observers have detected remains of higher feelings, which, in a different moral atmosphere, and under different moral husbandry, would have undoubtedly been developed. The statistics of prostitution show that a great proportion of those who have fallen into it have been impelled by the most extreme poverty, in many instances verging upon starvation.

These opposing considerations, which I have very briefly indicated, and which I do not propose to discuss or to estimate, will be sufficient to exhibit the magnitude of the problem. In the Greek civilization, legislators and moralists endeavoured to meet it by the cordial recognition of two distinct orders of womanhood — the wife, whose first duty was fidelity to her husband; the hetaera, or mistress, who subsisted by her fugitive attachments. The wives of the Greeks lived in almost absolute seclusion. They were usually married when very young. Their occupations were to weave, to spin, to embroider, to superintend the household, to care for their sick slaves. They lived in a special and retired part of the house. The more wealthy seldom went abroad, and never except when accompanied by a female slave; never attended the public spectacles; received no male visitors except in the presence of their husbands, and had not even a seat at their own tables when male guests were there. Their pre-eminent virtue was fidelity, and it is probable that this was very strictly and very generally observed. Their remarkable freedom from temptations, the public opinion which strongly discouraged any attempt to seduce them, and the ample sphere for illicit pleasures that was accorded to the other sex, all contributed to protect it. On the other hand, living, as they did, almost exclusively among their female slaves, being deprived of all the educating influence of male society, and having no place at those public spectacles which were the chief means of Athenian culture, their minds must necessarily have been exceedingly contracted. Thucydides doubtless expressed the prevailing sentiment of his countrymen when he said that the highest merit of woman is not to be spoken of either for good or for evil; and Phidias illustrated the same feeling when he represented the heavenly Aphrodite standing on a tortoise, typifying thereby the secluded life of a virtuous woman.

In their own restricted sphere their lives were probably not unhappy. Education and custom rendered the purely domestic life that was assigned to them a second nature, and it must in most instances have reconciled them to the extramatrimonial connections in which their husbands too frequently indulged. The prevailing manners were very gentle. Domestic oppression is scarcely ever spoken of; the husband lived chiefly in the public place; causes of jealousy and of dissension could seldom occur; and a feeling of warm affection, though not a feeling of equality, must doubtless have in most cases spontaneously arisen. In the writings of Xenophon we have a charming picture of a husband who had received into his arms his young wife of fifteen, absolutely ignorant of the world and of its ways. He speaks to her with extreme kindness, but in the language that would be used to a little child. Her task, he tells her, is to be like a queen bee, dwelling continually at home and superintending the work of her slaves. She must distribute to each their tasks, must economize the family income, and must take especial care that the house is strictly orderly — the shoes, the pots, and the clothes always in their places. It is also, he tells her, a part of her duty to tend her sick slaves; but here his wife interrupted him, exclaiming, 'Nay, but that will indeed be the most agreeable of my offices, if such as I treat with kindness are likely to be grateful, and to love me more than before.' With a very tender and delicate care to avoid everything resembling a reproach, the husband persuades his wife to give up the habits of wearing high-heeled boots, in order to appear tall, and of colouring her face with vermilion and white lead. He promises her that if she faithfully performs her duties he will himself be the first and most devoted of her slaves. He assured Socrates that when any domestic dispute arose he could extricate himself admirably, if he was in the right; but that, whenever he was in the wrong, he found it impossible to convince his wife that it was otherwise.

We have another picture of Greek married life in the writings of Plutarch, but it represents the condition of the Greek mind at a later period than that of Xenophon. In Plutarch the wife is represented not as the mere housekeeper, or as the chief slave of her husband, but as his equal and his companion. He enforces, in the strongest terms, reciprocity of obligations, and desires that the minds of women should be cultivated to the highest point. His precepts of marriage, indeed, fall little if at all below any that have appeared in modern days. His letter of consolation to his wife, on the death of their child, breathes a spirit of the tenderest affection. It is recorded of him that, having had some dispute with the relations of his wife, she feared that it might impair their domestic happiness, and she accordingly persuaded her husband to accompany her on a pilgrimage to Mount Helicon, where they offered up together a sacrifice to Love, and prayed that their affection for one another might never be diminished.

In general, however, the position of the virtuous Greek woman was a very low one. She was under a perpetual tutelage: first of all to her parents, who disposed of her hand, then to her husband, and in her days of widowhood to her sons. In cases of inheritance her male relations were preferred to her. The privilege of divorce, which, in Athens, at least, she possessed as well as her husband, appears to have been practically almost nugatory, on account of the shock which public declarations in the law court gave to the habits which education and public opinion had formed. She brought with her, however, a dowry, and the recognized necessity of endowing daughters was one of the causes of those frequent expositions which were perpetrated with so little blame. The Athenian law was also peculiarly careful and tender in dealing with the interests of female orphans. Plato had argued that women were equal to men; but the habits of the people were totally opposed to this theory. Marriage was regarded chiefly in a civic light, as the means of producing citizens, and in Sparta it was ordered that old or infirm husbands should cede their young wives to stronger men, who could produce vigorous soldiers for the State. The Lacedaemonian treatment of women, which differed in many respects from that which prevailed in the other Greek States, while it was utterly destructive of all delicacy of feeling or action, had undoubtedly the effect of producing a fierce and masculine patriotism; and many fine examples are recorded of Spartan mothers devoting their sons on the altar of their country, rejoicing over their deaths when nobly won, and infusing their own heroic spirit into the armies of the people. For the most part, however, the names of virtuous women seldom appear in Greek history. The simple modesty which was evinced by Phocion's wife, in the period when her husband occupied the foremost position in Athens, and a few instances of conjugal and filial affection, have been recorded; but in general the only women who attracted the notice of the people were the hetaerae, or courtesans.

In order to understand the position which these last assumed in Greek life, we must transport ourselves in thought into a moral latitude totally different from our own. The Greek conception of excellence was the full and perfect development of humanity in all its organs and functions, and without any tinge of asceticism. Some parts of human nature were recognized as higher than others; and to suffer any of the lower appetites to obscure the mind, restrain the will and engross the energies of life, was acknowledged to be disgraceful; but the systematic repression of a natural appetite was totally foreign to Greek modes of thought. Legislators, moralists, and the general voice of the people, appear to have applied these principles almost unreservedly to intercourse between the sexes, and the most virtuous men habitually and openly entered into relations which would now be almost universally censured.

The experience, however, of many societies has shown that a public opinion may accord, in this respect, almost unlimited licence to one sex, without showing any corresponding indulgence to the other. But, in Greece, a concurrence of causes had conspired to bring a certain section of courtesans into a position they have in no other society attained. The voluptuous worship of Aphrodite gave a kind of religious sanction to their profession. Courtesans were the priestesses in her temples, and those of Corinth were believed by their prayers to have averted calamities from their city. Prostitution is said to have entered into the religious rites of Babylon, Biblis, Cyprus, and Corinth, and these as well as Miletus, Tenedos, Lesbos, and Abydos became famous for their schools of vice, which grew up under the shadow of the temples.

In the next place, the intense aesthetic enthusiasm that

A woman's faithfulness is in question, but the interrogation is composed of men. Morality had one standard for men, another for women, and in a male-dominated society, as Euripides observed, the woman was invariably the defendant.

Lucas Cranach (1472-1553)
Schleissheim Gallery

[77]

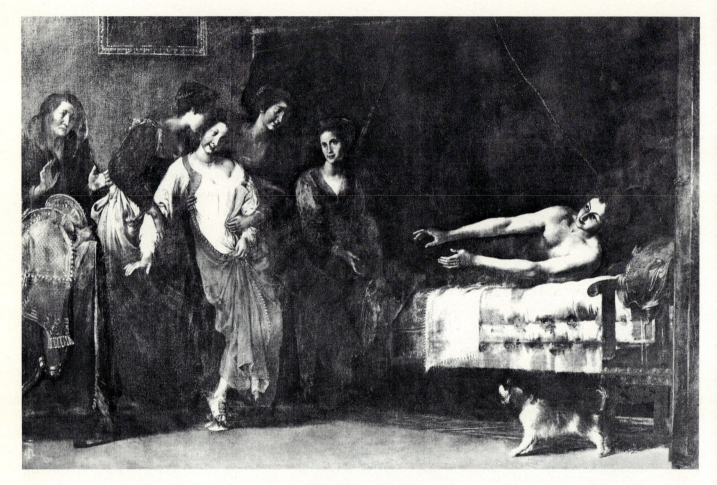

THE NEW BRIDE

Giovanni da San Giovanni
Uffizi Gallery, Florence

prevailed was eminently fitted to raise the most beautiful to honour. In a land and beneath a sky where natural beauty developed to the highest point, there arose a school of matchless artists both in painting and in sculpture, and public games and contests were celebrated, in which supreme physical perfection was crowned by an assembled people. In no other period of the world's history was the admiration of beauty in all its forms so passionate or so universal. It coloured the whole moral teaching of the time, and led the chief moralists to regard virtue simply as the highest kind of supersensual beauty. It appeared in all literature, where the beauty of form and style was

the first of studies. It supplied at once the inspiration and the rule of all Greek art. It led the Greek wife to pray, before all other prayers, for the beauty of her children. It surrounded the most beautiful with an aureole of admiring reverence. The courtesan was often the queen of beauty. She was the model of the statues of Aphrodite, that commanded the admiration of Greece. Praxiteles was accustomed to reproduce the form of Phryne, and her statue, carved in gold, stood in the temple of Apollo at Delphi; and when she was accused of corrupting the youth of Athens, her advocate, Hyperides, procured her acquittal by suddenly unveiling her charms before the dazzled

[78]

eyes of the assembled judges. Apelles was at once the painter and the lover of Laïs, and Alexander gave him, as the choicest gift, his own favourite concubine, of whom the painter had become enamoured while portraying her. The chief flower-painter of antiquity acquired his skill through his love of the flower-girl Glycera, whom he was accustomed to paint among her garlands. Pindar and Simonides sang the praises of courtesans, and grave philosophers made pilgrimages to visit them, and their names were known in every city.

It is not surprising that, in such a state of thought and feeling, many of the more ambitious and accomplished women should have betaken themselves to this career, nor yet that they should have attained the social position which the secluded existence and the enforced ignorance of the Greek wives had left vacant. The courtesan was the one free woman of Athens, and she often availed herself of her freedom to acquire a degree of knowledge which enabled her to add to her other charms an intense intellectual fascination. Gathering around her the most brilliant artists, poets, historians, and philosophers, she flung herself unreservedly into the intellectual and aesthetic enthusiasms of her time, and soon became the centre of a literary society of matchless splendour. Aspasia, who was as famous for her genius as for her beauty, won the passionate love of Pericles. She is said to have instructed him in eloquence, and to have composed some of his most famous orations; she was continually consulted on affairs of state; and Socrates, like other philosophers, attended her assemblies. Socrates himself has owned his deep obligations to the instructions of a courtesan named Diotima. The courtesan Leontium was among the most ardent disciples of Epicurus.

Another cause probably contributed indirectly to the elevation of this class, to which it is extremely difficult to allude in an English book, but which it is impossible altogether to omit, even in the most cursory survey of Greek morals. Irregular female connections were looked upon as ordinary and not disgraceful incidents in the life of a good man, for they were compared with that lower abyss of unnatural love, which was the deepest and strangest taint of Greek civilization. This vice, which never appears in the writings of Homer and Hesiod, doubtless arose under the influence of the public games, which, accustoming men to the contemplation of absolutely nude figures, awoke an unnatural passion, totally remote from all modern feelings, but which in Greece it was regarded as heroic to resist. The popular religion in this, as in other cases, was made to bend to the new vice. Hebe, the cupbearer of the gods, was replaced by Ganymede, and the worst vices of earth were transported to Olympus. Artists sought to reflect the passion in their statues of the Herma-

phrodite, of Bacchus, and the more effeminate Apollo; moralists were known to praise it as the bond of friendship, and it was spoken of as the inspiring enthusiasm of the heroic Theban legion of Epaminondas. In general, however, it was stigmatised as unquestionably a vice, but it was treated with a levity we can now hardly conceive. We can scarcely have a better illustration of the extent to which moral ideas and feelings have changed, than the fact that the first two Greeks who were considered worthy of statue by their fellow-countrymen are said to have been Harmodius and Aristogeiton, who were united by an impure love, and who were glorified for a political assassination.

It is probable that cause conspired with the others to dissociate the class of courtesan from the idea of supreme depravity with which they have usually been connected. The great majority, however, were sunk in this, as in all other ages, in abject degradation; comparatively few attained the condition of hetaerae, and even of these it is probable that the greater number exhibited the characteristics which in all ages have attached to their class. Faithlessness, extreme rapacity, and extravagant luxury, were common among them; but yet it is unquestionable that there were many exceptions. The excommunication of society did not press upon or degrade them; and though they were never regarded with the same honour as married women, it seems generally to have been believed that the wife and the courtesan had each her place and her function in the world, and her own peculiar type of excellence. The courtesan Leaena, who was a friend of Harmodius, died in torture rather than reveal the conspiracy of her friend, and the Athenians, in allusion to her name, caused the statue of a tongueless lioness to be erected to commemorate her constancy. The gentle manners and disinterested affection of a courtesan named Bacchis were especially recorded, and a very touching letter paints the character, and describes the regret that followed her to the tomb. In one of the most remarkable of his pictures of Greek life, Xenophon describes how Socrates, having heard of the beauty of the courtesan Theodota, went with his desciples to ascertain for himself whether the report was true; how with a quiet humour he questioned her about the sources of the luxury of her dwelling, and how he proceeded to sketch for her the qualities she should cultivate in order to attach her lovers. She ought, he tells her, to shut the door against the insolent, to watch her lovers in sickness, to rejoice greatly when they succeed in anything honourable, to love tenderly those who love her. Having carried on a cheerful and perfectly unembarrassed conversation with her, with no kind of reproach on his part, either expressed or implied, and with no trace either of the timidity or effrontery of conscious guilt upon hers, the best and wisest of the Greeks left his hostess with a graceful compliment to her beauty.

My task in describing this aspect of Greek life has been an eminently unpleasing one, and I should certainly not have entered upon even the baldest and most guarded disquisition on a subject so difficult, painful, and delicate, had it not been absolutely indispensable to a history of morals to give at least an outline of the progress that has been effected in this sphere. What I have written will sufficiently explain why Greece, which was fertile, beyond all other lands, in great men, was so remarkably barren of great women. It will show, too, that while the Greek moralists recognized, like ourselves, the distinction between the higher and the lower sides of our nature, they differed very widely from modern public opinion in the standard of morals they enforced. The Christian doctrine, that it is criminal to gratify a powerful and transient physical appetite, except under the condition of a lifelong contract, was altogether unknown. Strict duties were imposed upon Greek wives. Duties were imposed at a later period, though less strictly, upon the husband. Unnatural love was stigmatised, but with a levity of censure which to a modern mind appears inexpressibly revolting. Some slight legal disqualifications rested upon the whole class of hetaerae, and, though more admired, they were less respected than women who had adopted a domestic life; but a combination of circumstances had raised them, in actual work and in popular estimation, to an unexampled elevation, and an aversion to marriage became very general, and extra-matrimonial connections were formed with the most perfect frankness and publicity.

If we now turn to the Roman civilization, we shall find that some important advances had been made in the condition of women. The virtue of chastity has, as I have shown, been regarded in two different ways. The utilitarian view, which commonly prevails in countries where a political spirit is more powerful than a religious spirit, regards marriage as the ideal state, and to promote the happiness, sanctity, and security of this state is the main object of all its precepts. The mystical view which rests upon the natural feeling of shame, and which, as history proves, has prevailed especially where political sentiment is very low, and religious sentiment very strong, regards virginity as its supreme type, and marriage as simply the most pardonable declension from ideal purity. It is, I think, a very remarkable fact, that at the head of the religious system of Rome we find two sacerdotal bodies which appear respectively to typify these ideas. The Flamens of Jupiter and the Vestal Virgins were the two most sacred orders in Rome. The ministrations of each were believed to be vitally important to the State. Each could officiate only within the walls of Rome. Each was appointed with the most imposing ceremonies. Each was honoured with the most profound reverence. But in one important respect they differed. The Vestal was the type of virginity, and her purity was guarded by the most terrific penalties. The Flamen, on the other hand, was the representative of Roman marriage in its strictest and holiest form. He was necessarily married. His marriage was celebrated with the most solemn rites. It could only be dissolved by death. If his wife died, he was degraded from his office.

Of these two orders, there can be no question that the Flamen was the most faithful expression of the Roman sentiments. The Roman religion was essentially domestic, and it was a main object of the legislator to surround marriage with every circumstance of dignity and solemnity. Monogamy was, from the earliest times, strictly enjoined; and it was one of the great benefits that have resulted from the expansion of Roman power, that it made this type dominant in Europe. In the legends of early Rome we have ample evidence both of the high moral estimate of women, and of their prominence in Roman life. The tragedies of Lucretia and of Virginia display a delicacy of honour, a sense of the supreme excellence of unsullied purity, which no Christian nation could surpass. The legends of the Sabine women interceding between their parents and their husbands, and thus saving the infant republic, and of the mother of Coriolanus averting by her prayers the ruin impending over her country, entitled women to claim their share in the patriotic glories of Rome. A temple of Venus Calva was associated with the legend of Roman ladies, who, in an hour of danger, cut off their long tresses to make bowstrings for the soldiers. Another temple preserved to all posterity the memory of the filial piety of that Roman woman who, when her mother was condemned to be starved to death, obtained permission to visit her in her prison, and was discovered feeding her from her breast.

The legal position, however, of the Roman wife was for a long period extremely low. The Roman family was constituted on the principle of the uncontrolled authority of its head, both over his wife and over his children, and he could repudiate the former at will. Neither the custom of gifts to the father of the bride, nor the custom of dowries, appears to have existed in the earliest period of Roman history; but the father disposed absolutely of the hand of his daughter, and sometimes even possessed the power of breaking off marriages that had been actually contracted. In the forms of marriage, however, which were usual in the earlier periods of Rome, the absolute power passed into the hands of the husband, and he had the right, in some cases, of putting her to death. Law and public opinion combined in making matrimonial purity most

NIGHT

Aristide Maillol (1861-1944)
Albright Art Gallery, Buffalo, N.Y.

strict. For five hundred and twenty years, it was said, there was no such thing as a divorce in Rome. Manners were so severe, that a senator was censured for indecency because he had kissed his wife in the presence of their daughter. It was considered in a high degree disgraceful for a Roman mother to delegate to a nurse the duty of suckling her child. Sumptuary laws regulated with the most minute severity all the details of domestic economy. The courtesan class, though probably numerous and certainly uncontrolled, were regarded with much contempt. The disgrace of publicly professing themselves members of it was believed to be a sufficient punishment; and an old law, which was probably intended to teach in symbol the duties of married life, enjoined that no such person should touch the altar of Juno. It was related of a certain aedile, that he failed to obtain redress for an assault which had been made upon him, because it had occurred in a house of ill-fame, in which it was disgraceful for a Roman magistrate to be found. The sanctity of female purity was believed to be attested by all nature. The most savage animals became tame before a virgin. When a woman walked naked round a field, caterpillars and all loathsome insects fell dead before her. It was said that drowned men floated on their backs, and drowned women on their faces; and this, in the opinion of Roman naturalists, was due to the superior purity of the latter.

HISTORY OF EUROPEAN MORALS
W. E. H. Lecky

Candaules shows his wife to his favorite Gyges. An episode in voyeurism.
Narrated by Herodotus.

Jacob Jordaens (1593-1678)
National Museum, Stockholm.

Famous Mistresses

Famous Mistresses

MADAME POMPADOUR

Among the mistresses whose names have been recorded, Madame Pompadour, here depicted as Venus, was the adviser and paramour of Louis XV, King of France.

Francois Boucher (1703-1770)

The mistress or concubine appear in the earliest periods of human history, from Homer to King Solomon, from Sumer to Egypt. Names have vanished, but the status remains. Yet it is remarkable that the position of courtesan or mistress had merely a nugatory stigma attached to it, or virtually and for the most part none at all. In the course of social evolution and the progression in the complexities of living, the mistress acquired sometimes a dominant if at the same time a notorious status. Leaena, a Greek courtesan, was ready to suffer torture and even death rather than reveal the participation of her lover in a conspiracy.

Lerne was the mistress of the orator Stratocles: but her favors were conditioned by mercenary motives too. And she was known for her price as Didrachmos.

Phryne, one of the most beautiful, the most famous but also the most dangerous of the hetairae in Athens, was a model for the sculptor Praxiteles.

Lais was the mistress of Aristippus the philosopher. Thaïs was the mistress of Alexander the Great. Lamia is recorded in history and legend: so too with Gnathaena. These women were the mistresses of kings and artists, poets and orators: Apelles and Hippolochus belong to this category, while the statesman Pericles was associated with the concubine or hetaira Aspasia.

In some Greek contexts the concubine appears to have a status analogous to that of a member of the domestic household. For Demosthenes, the Greek orator, refers to a law in which mother, wife, sister, daughter, concubine are listed together.

Cyrus the younger had a mistress called Milto. Darius, the Persian monarch who was crushed by Alexander, had with him, even on his military campaigns, some 360 concubines.

Demosthenes had a mistress by whom he had children. The Greek poets and dramatists, the ancient historians and satirists have chronicled these relationships with virtual objectivity. Hyperides' mistress was Myrrhina. Agathocleia became the concubine of Ptolemy IV Philopator, Pharaoh of Egypt. Catullus had his Lesbia, whom he glorifies or rebukes in his lyric passions. Tibullus chanted his Lycoris. Propertius had his Cynthia. Ovid, married, glorifies his Corinna. Alciphron, Greek author of a number of revealing domestic and character sketches, provides intimate glimpses of these women, their ambitions and their wiles and sometimes their distorted affections. The ancient texts in general ring with the names of Nicylla and Leontis, Niko, Euphro and Boidion, Aristocleia and Glycera.

Belestiche was the mistress of the Pharaoh Ptolemy II of Philadelphia. According to the Greek biographer Plutarch, he built a temple dedicated to her, and named her Aphrodite Belestiche.

The philosopher Epicurus had a mistress, a certain Leontion, who was also his pupil in philosophy. The Empress Theodora had been the Emperor Justinian's mistress before she became his consort.

In the Mostellaria, a comedy by the Roman poet Plautus, the hero sets up his mistress by selling his patrimony. The Emperor Constantius had a mistress named Helena.

Augustine admits, in his Confessions, that while he was studying at Carthage, as a young man, he had a mistress: her name, however, he does not reveal.

In the Middle Ages the clergy, under the ban against marriage, resorted in many cases to the possession of a mistress. Many prominent churchmen — the Venerable Bede, Bishops, Popes — fulminated against this degeneration of asceticism and the disintegration of spiritual morality. Yet the Popes themselves, in many instances, especially during the Renaissance, had their mistresses.

THEODORA (c. 508-548): This Empress is the subject of forthright comment by Procopius, the Byzantine chronicler, in his Anecdota or Secret History: and also by Gibbon in his Decline and Fall of the Roman Empire. Gibbon describes her as follows:

The beauty of Theodora was the subject of more flattering praise, and the source of more exquisite delight. Her features were delicate and regular; her complexion, though somewhat pale, was tinged with a natural color; every sensation was instantly expressed by the vivacity of her eyes; her easy motions displayed the graces of a small but elegant figure; and even love or adulation might proclaim, that painting and poetry were incapable of delineating the matchless excellence of her form. But this form was degraded by the facility with which it was exposed to the public eye and prostituted to licentious desire. Her venal charms were abandoned to a promiscuous crowd of citizens and strangers, of every rank, and of every profession; the fortunate lover who had been promised a night of enjoyment was often driven from her bed by a stronger or more wealthy favorite; and, when she passed through the streets, her presence was avoided by all who wished to escape either the scandal or the temptation. The satirical historian has not blushed to describe the naked scenes which Theodora was not ashamed to exhibit in the theatre. After exhausting the arts of sensual pleasure, she most ungratefully murmured against the parsimony of Nature; but her murmurs, her pleasures, and her arts must be veiled in the obscurity of a learned language. After reigning for some time, the delight and contempt of the capital, she condescended to accompany Ecebolus, a native of Tyre, who had obtained the government of the African Pentapolis. But this union was frail and transient; Ecebolus soon rejected an expensive or faithless concubine; she was reduced at Alexandria to extreme distress;

MARIE LOUISE O'MURPHY
Mistress of Louis XV, King of France.

Francois Boucher (1703-1770)
Louvre, Paris

The Duchess of Alba, unclothed.

and, in her laborious return to Constantinople, every city of the East admired and enjoyed the fair Cyprian, whose merit appeard to justify her descent from the peculiar island of Venus. The vague commerce of Theodora, and the most detestable precautions, preserved her from the danger which she feared; yet once, and once only, she became a mother. The infant was saved and educated in Arabia, by his father, who imparted to him on his death-bed that he was the son of an empress. Filled with ambitious hopes, the unsuspecting youth immediately hastened to the palace of Constantinople, and was admitted to the presence of his mother. As he was never more seen, even after the decease of Theodora, she deserves the foul imputation of extinguishing with his life a secret so offensive to her Imperial virtue.

In the most abject state of her fortune and reputation, some vision, either of sleep or of fancy, had whispered to Theodora the pleasing assurance that she was destined to become the spouse of a potent monarch. Conscious of her approaching greatness, she returned from Paphlagonia to Constantinople; assumed, like a skilful actress, a more decent character; relieved her poverty by the laudable industry of spinning wool; and affected a life of chastity and solitude in a small house, which she afterwards changed into a magnificent temple. Her beauty, assisted by art or accident, soon attracted, captivated, and fixed the patrician Justinian, who already reigned with absolute sway under the name of his uncle. Perhaps she contrived to enhance the value of a gift which she had so often lavished on the meanest of mankind; perhaps she inflamed, at first by modest delays, and at last by sensual allurements, the desires of a lover, who from nature or devotion was addicted to long vigils and abstemious diet. When his first transports had subsided, she still maintained the same ascendant over his mind, by the more solid merit of temper and understanding. Justinian delighted to ennoble and enrich the object of his affection; the treasures of the East were poured at her feet; and the nephew of Justin was determined, perhaps by religious scruples, to bestow on his concubine the sacred and legal character of a wife. But the laws of Rome expressly prohibited the marriage of a senator with any female who had been dishonored by a servile origin or theatrical profession; the empress Lupicina, or Euphemia, a barbarian of rustic manners but of irreproachable virtue, refused to accept a prostitute for her niece; and even Vigilantia, the superstitious mother of Justinian, though she acknowledged the wit and beauty of Theodora, was seriously apprehensive lest the levity

The favorite model of Goya, the Duchess of Alba, "dressed".

Francisco José de Goya y Lucientes (1746-1828)
Museo del Prado

and arrogance of that artful paramour might corrupt the piety and happiness of her son. These obstacles were removed by the inflexible constancy of Justinian. He patiently expected the death of the empress; he despised the tears of his mother, who soon sunk under the weight of her affliction; and a law was promulgated in the name of the emperor Justin, which abolished the rigid jurisprudence of antiquity. A glorious repentance (the words of the edict) was left open for the unhappy females who had prostituted their persons on the theatre, and they were permitted to contract a legal union with the most illustrious of the Romans. This indulgence was speedily followed by the solemn nuptials of Justinian and Theodora; her dignity was gradually exalted with that of her lover; and, as soon as Justin had invested his nephew with the purple, the patriarch of Constantinople placed the diadem on the heads of the emperor and empress of the East. But the usual honors which the severity of Roman manners had allowed to the wives of princes could not justify either the ambition of Theodora or the fondness of Justinian. He seated her on the throne as an equal and independent colleague in the sovereignty of the empire, and an oath of allegiance was imposed on the governors of the provinces in the joint names of Justinian and Theodora.

The Eastern world fell prostrate before the genius and fortune of the daughter of Acacius. The prostitute who, in the presence of innumerable spectators, had polluted the theatre of Constantinople, was adored as a queen in the same city, by grave magistrates, orthodox bishops, victorious generals, and captive monarchs.

Those who believe that the female mind is totally depraved by the loss of chastity will eagerly listen to all the invectives of private envy or popular resentment, which have dissembled the virtues of Theodora, exaggerated her vices, and condemned with rigor the venal or voluntary sins of the youthful harlot. From a motive of shame or contempt, she often declined the servile homage of the multitude, escaped from the odious light of the capital, and passed the greatest part of the year in the palaces and gardens which were pleasantly seated on the sea-coast of the Propontis and the Bosphorus. Her private hours were devoted to the prudent as well as grateful care of her beauty, the luxury of the bath and table, and the long slumber of the evening and the morning. Her secret apartments were occupied by the favorite women and eunuchs, whose interests and passions she indulged at the expense of justice; the most illustrious personages of the state were crowded into a dark and sultry antechamber, and when at last, after

NELL GWYNN

*Nell Gwynn, one of the most notorious women of her time,
was the mistress of Charles II of England.*

Peter Lely (1618-1680)

tedious attendance, they were admitted to kiss the feet of Theodora, they experienced, as her humor might suggest, the silent arrogance of an empress or the capricious levity of a comedian. Her rapacious avarice to accumulate an immense treasure may be excused by the apprehension of her husband's death, which could leave no alternative between ruin and the throne; and fear as well as ambition might exasperate Theodora against two generals, who, during a malady of the emperor, had rashly declared that they were not disposed to acquiesce in the choice of the capital. But the reproach of cruelty, so repugnant even to her softer vices, has left an indelible stain on the memory of Theodora. Her numerous spies observed, and jealously reported every action, or word, or look, injurious to their royal mistress. Whomsoever they accused were cast into her peculiar prisons, inaccessible to the inquiries of justice; and it was rumored that the torture of the rack or scourge had been inflicted in the presence of a female tyrant, insensible to the voice of prayer or of pity.

Belonging to the Byzantine period, like Theodora, was Antonina. We learn of her ways through the Greek historian Procopius. Born in Caesarea, he was attached to the court of the Emperor Justinian I, in the sixth century

A.D. He was an imperial secretary, in which capacity he visited Africa, Asia, and Italy. His reputation rests on his history of contemporary events. Among other books, he produced the Anecdota, or Secret History, that exposed the scandals of notable figures of his time.

In particular, he reveals the private life of the general Belisarius and of his wife Antonina. Antonina's father was a charioteer: her mother, a public wench who hung around the theatrical area, while Antonina herself was a known harlot. Before her marriage she had already had a number of children. As the wife of Belisarius, she became the mistress of a Christianized young man named Theodosius. Her passion for him knew no restraints, even in the presence of her husband, of her attendants. When Theodosius, conscience-stricken, became a monk, Antonina went into domestic and public mourning. Later, however, Theodosius returned to Antonina. Procopius declares that he finally succumbed to dysentery: but the historian Gibbon suggests an amatory finality as the cause of his death.

LORME, MARION DE (c. 1612 - c. 1652): Mistress of the Marquis de Cinq-Mars, Saint-Evrémond, Condé, and the Duke of Buckingham. Traditionally, she is believed to

[92]

have fled to London, where she lived many years beyond the assumed date of her death. She appears in Alfred de Vigny's Cinq-Mars. Also in Victor Hugo's drama Marion Delorme.

LENCLOS, ANNE (1620-1705): Called Ninon de Lenclos. French mistress of a long succession of lovers. Her reputation induced appraisals by Voltaire and Saint-Simon. Her name is associated with La Rochefoucauld, Condé, and Saint-Evrémond, among many other admirers.

THEROIGNE DE MERICOURT (1762-1817): Heroic figure during the French Revolution. She led the assault on the Bastille. Called The Amazon of Liberty. She was the mistress of many personalities prominent in the Revolutionary period.

HAMILTON, EMMA (c. 1761-1815): Lady Hamilton was the mistress of Charles Greville: later, of Lord Nelson, by whom she had a daughter named Horatia. She has been the subject of several intimate studies.

LAMB, CAROLINE, LADY (1875-1828): Author of three novels. Mistress of Lord Byron. Became passionately enamoured of the poet, with whom she spent some nine months. Her end was tragic. Confronted by the funeral procession of her old lover, she became insane.

MERODE, CLEO DE: Mistress of King Leopold II of Belgium, with whom she was linked repeatedly in the satirical press of Europe.

MONTESPAN, MARQUISE DE (1641-1707): Françoise Athénaïs Rochechouart. Mistress of King Louis XIV. When she realized that the king's interest in her was waning, she resorted to occult and Satanic practices that were promoted by a witch and fortune-teller known as Cathérine La Voisin.

MAINTENON, MARQUISE DE (1635-1719): Françoise d'Aubigné. Mistress, then wife, of King Louis XIV. She exerted a beneficent influence over the king, especially in a religious direction, as well as in his domestic and foreign policies. Apart from her personal attractions, she had intellectual capacities, from the evidence of her extant correspondence.

DU BARRY, COMTESSE (1746-1793): Marie Jeanne Bécu. Mistress of King Louis XV, over whom and over whose court she exercised a marked influence. Her end was the guillotine, but her life was adventurous.

In more recent times, there is the name of Céleste Mogador (1824-1909). Dancer, equestrienne, and actress, she became the Comtesse Lionel de Moreton de Chabrillan. In addition, she acquired an extended notoriety by publishing her memoirs.

Among other mistresses, particularly such as had eminent royal or political associations, were:

Nell Gwynn, mistress of Charles II, king of England:

Mlle. de la Vallière, mistress of Louis XIV:

Mlle. Fontange, mistress of Louis XIV:

The Dancer Barberini, mistress of Frederick II:

The Countess Cosel, mistress of Augustus the Strong:

Sophie de Rüffet, mistress of Mirabeau:

The Dancer Agatha, mistress of Karl Eugene of Würtemberg:

The Countess Lichtenau, mistress of Frederick Wilhelm II of Prussia.

H. E. W.

MORNING

Francois Boucher (1703-1770)
Louvre, Paris

Incest

VENUS, CUPID AND VULCAN

Jacopo Palina
State Collection of Art, Kassel

Incest

BEATRICE CENCI

The Renaissance artist Guido Reni is here depicted paint-
ing Beatrice Cenci's portrait. Victim of her father's brutality,
she conspired with her family to secure his death. On her
father's death, the members of the Cenci family were all
executed. P. B. Shelley has made Beatrice the subject of a
tragedy.

Guido Reni (1575-1642)
Castel S. Angelo, Rome

From antiquity to current times, incest has been prevalent among both primitive and civilized peoples. It has been the subject of drama, as in Oedipus Rex and the Restoration plays, of fiction and ballads, art and sermons.

Euripides, the Greek dramatist, comments in his Andromache, on this custom among the Persians:

Such is all the race of the barbarians: father has intercourse with daughter, son with mother.

During the dominance of Pericles in Athens, a certain Cimon had intercourse with his sister Epinike and was as a consequence forced to go into exile.

A notable case of incest is that of Roland, Charlemagne's son, with his sister Gisèle.

Psychoanalytically, the love of a son for a mother is known as the Oedipus Complex, while the love of the daughter for her father is called the Electra Complex.

Apart from the Oedipus-Jocasta association, incest occurs, historically, in the case of the Roman Clodia and her brother Clodius Pulcher: and, centuries later, in that of Casanova.

H. E. W.

TRIUMPH OF CHASTITY
*In this allegorical picture, Renaissance society becomes aware of the conflict
between chastity and the frenzy of contemporary mores.*

Lorenzo Lotto (1480-1556)
Palazzo Pallavicini, Rome

Sex in the Bible

SUSANNA AND THE ELDERS
In the Apocryphal story of Susanna, the virtuous wife of Joachim is charged with adultery by accusers who had themselves tried to assail her chastity.

Tintoretto   (1518-1594)
Art Gallery, Vienna

Sex in the Bible

POTIPHAR'S WIFE

Rembrandt (1606-1669)
Bibliotheque Nationale, Paris

In addition to the normal sex relationships, Biblical literature illustrates a remarkable range of erotic deviations and aberrations. Life was lavish and complex in the framework of both nomadic custom and of stabilized urban society. Hence the communal fabric and individual and personal characterial composition reflect all instances of sexual associations. King and peasant, princelings and queens and, in a wider sense, a variety of ethnic communities stand revealed as branded by their passions, their furtive lusts, their readiness to abandon the barriers and shackles of prescribed codes. So that again and again there appear injunctions and prohibitions and threats designed to control those febrile urgencies and to direct them into more sedate, more acceptable channels. There are thus constant fulminations against onanism and sodomy, against seduction and prostitution, against acceptance of obscene deities and lascivious mores, harlotry and adultery, homosexuality and incest. The character of the twin cities of Sodom and Gomorrah alone presents startling testimony of the degree of degeneracy, profligacy, and sexual corruption that could, thousands of years ago, be reached without benefit of modernistic and highly developed adventitious aids and counsel. Sensuality was so pervasive that restrictions, both legalistic and religious, were completely abrogated and disdained: as in the case of the Golden Calf.

The incident involving Joseph and Potiphar's wife, which Thomas Mann has fictionally expanded into a monumental trilogy is briefly told in Genesis 39.7-14:

> And it came to pass after these things, that his master's wife cast her eyes upon Joseph; and she said, Lie with me.
>
> But he refused, and said unto his master's wife, Behold, my master wottest not what is with me in the house, and he hath committed all that he hath to my hand;

HAGAR

Hagar, handmaid of Abram's sterile wife, was given to Abram as his wife. An instance involving the preservation of the family line.

D. Bray

There is none greater in this house than I; neither hath he kept back anything from me but thee, because thou art his wife; how then can I do this great wickedness, and sin against God?

And it came to pass, as she spake to Joseph day by day, that he hearkened not unto her, to lie by her, or to be with her.

And it came to pass about this time, that Joseph went into the house to do his business; and there was none of the men of the house there within.

And she caught him by his garment, saying, lie with me: and he left his garment in her hand, and fled, and got him out.

And it came to pass, when she saw that he had left his garment in her hand, and was fled forth,

That she called unto the men of her house, and spake unto them, saying, See, he hath brought in an Hebrew unto us to mock us; he came in unto me to lie with me, and I cried with a loud voice:

And it came to pass, when he heard that I lifted up my voice and cried, that he left his garment with me, and fled, and got him out.

David's relationship with Bath-sheba is described in 2 Samuel 11. 2-5—

And it came to pass in an eveningtide, that David arose from off his bed, and walked upon the roof of the king's house: and from the roof he saw a woman washing herself; and the woman was very beautiful to look upon.

And David sent and enquired after the woman. And one said, Is not this Bath-sheba, the daughter of Eliam, the wife of Uriah the Hittite?

And David sent messengers, and took her; and she came in unto him, and he lay with her; for she was purified from her uncleanness: and she returned unto her house.

And the woman conceived, and sent and told David, and said, I am with child.

Later in years, David was advised to practice what became known as Shunammitism. The incident occurs in 1 Kings 1. 1-4:

Now King David was old and stricken in years; and they covered him with clothes, but he got no heat.

Wherefore his servants said unto him, Let there be sought for my lord the king a young virgin; and let her stand before the king, and let her cherish him, and let her be in thy bosom, that my lord the king may get heat.

So they sought for a fair damsel throughout all the coasts of Israel, and found Abinhag a Shunammite, and brought her to the king.

LOT AND HIS DAUGHTERS

And the damsel was very fair, and cherished the king, and ministered to him; but the king knew her not.

An instance of incest appears in Genesis 19. 31-36:

And the firstborn said unto the younger, Our father is old, and there is not a man in the earth to come in unto us after the manner of all the earth:

Come, let us make our father drink wine, and we will lie with him, that we may preserve seed of our father.

And they made their father drink wine that night: and the firstborn went in, and lay with her father; and he perceived not when she lay down, nor when she arose.

And it came to pass on the morrow, that the firstborn said unto the younger, Behold, I lay yesternight with my father; let us make him drink wine this night also; and go thou in, and lie with him, that we may preserve seed of our father.

And they made their father drink wine that night also; and the younger arose, and lay with him; and he perceived not when she lay with him; nor when she arose.

Thus were both the daughters of Lot with child by their father.

Adultery is expressly forbidden in Deuteronomy 22.22:

If a man be found lying with a woman married to an husband, then they shall both of them die, both the man that lay with the woman, and the woman: so shalt thou put away evil from Israel.

THE TEMPTATION OF ST. ANTHONY

THE URIAS LETTER

Franciabigio (1482-1525)
Deutsche Fotothek, Dresden

Rape occurs in Deuteronomy 22.25:

But if a man find a betrothed damsel in the field, and the man force her, and lie with her: then the man only that lay with her shall die.

Incest again appears in Deuteronomy 22.30:

A man shall not take his father's wife, nor discover his father's skirt.

Harlotry is described in Proverbs 7. 7-14:

I discerned among the youth, a young man void of understanding.

Passing through the street near her corner; and he went the way to her house,

In the twilight, in the evening, in the black and dark night;

And behold, there met him a woman with the attire of an harlot, and subtil of heart.

She is loud and stubborn; her feet abide not in her house:

Now she is without, now in the streets, and lieth in wait at every corner.

So she caught him, and kissed him, and with an impudent face said unto him,

I have peace offerings with me; this day have I paid my vows.

The episode of Judah and Tamar illustrates the status of incest and prostitution: Genesis 38. 6-26:

And Judah took a wife for Er his firstborn, whose name was Tamar.

And Er, Judah's firstborn, was wicked in the sight of the Lord, and the Lord slew him.

And Judah said unto Onan, Go in unto thy brother's wife, and marry her, and raise up seed to thy brother.

And Onan knew that the seed should not be his; and it came to pass, when he went in unto his brother's wife, that he spilled it on the ground, lest that he should give seed to his brother.

And the thing that he did displeased the Lord: wherefore he slew him also.

Then said Judah to Tamar his daughter in law, Remain a widow at thy father's house, till Shelah my son be grown: for he said, Lest peradventure he die also, as his brethren did. And Tamar went and dwelt in her father's house.

And in process of time the daughter of Shuah Judah's wife died; and Judah was comforted and went up unto his sheepshearers to Timnath, and his friend Hirah the Adullamite.

[104]

SUPPRESSION OF ADAMITES IN AMSTERDAM

The Adamites were a religious sect that practiced nudism in common worship. They originated in North Africa in the second and third centuries A.D. In time, they spread through Europe.

Dutch: c. 1700

And it was told Tamar, saying, Behold thy father in law goeth up to Timnath to shear his sheep.

And she put her widow's garments off from her, and covered her with a veil, and wrapped herself, and sat in an open place, which is by the way to Timnath; for she saw that Shelah was grown, and she was not given unto him to wife.

When Judah saw her, he thought her to be a harlot; because she had covered her face.

And he turned unto her by the way, and said, Go to, I pray thee, let me come in unto thee: (for he knew not that she was his daughter in law). And she said, What wilt thou give me, that thou mayest come in unto me?

And he said, I will send thee a kid from the flock. And she said, Wilt thou give me a pledge, till thou send it?

And he said, What pledge shall I give thee? And she said, Thy signet, and thy bracelets, and thy staff that is in thine hand. And he gave it to her, and came in unto her, and she was conceived by him.

And she arose and went away, and laid by her veil from her, and put on the garments of her widowhood.

And Judah sent the kid by the hand of his friend the Adulammite, to receive his pledge from the woman's hand: but he found her not.

Then he asked the men of that place, saying, Where is the harlot, that was openly by the wayside? And they said, There was no harlot in this place.

And he returned to Judah, and said, I cannot find her; and also the men of the place said, that there was no harlot in this place.

And Judah said, Let her take it to her, lest we be shamed: behold, I sent this kid, and thou hast not found her.

And it came to pass about three months after, that it was told Judah, saying, Tamar thy daughter in law hath played the harlot; and also, behold, she is with child by whoredom. And Judah said, Bring her forth, and let her be burnt.

When she was brought forth, she sent to her father in law, saying, By the man, whose these are, am I with child: and she said, Discern, I pray thee, whose are these, the signet, and bracelet, and staff.

And Judah acknowledged them, and said, She hath been more righteous than I; because that I gave her not to Shelah my son. And he knew her again no more.

H. E. W.

[105]

Zosimus offers a cloak to Mary the Egyptian.

Dominique Papety
Musée de Montpellier

Homosexuality

Homosexuality

Homosexuality is an aberration that can be traced back to the earliest antiquity. Even the god Apollo himself, in the traditional Greek mythology, has twenty male favorites. In the first century B.C., in Rome, a special festival, dedicated to this deviation, was celebrated annually on April 23. Ancient literature is pervaded by the homosexual concept, notably in the Satyricon, the Roman picaresque novel by Petronius Arbiter, a voluptuary attached to the court of the Emperor Nero. The locus classicus, however, on the subject is the philosopher Plato's dialogue entitled The Symposium.

SYMPOSIUM

In good truth, Eryximachus, said Aristophanes, I have it in my mind to speak in some other way than you and Pausanias have spoken. For to me men appear to be utterly insensible of the power of Love. Since, being sensible of it, they would have instituted most important sacred rites, and (built) altars, and made to him the greatest sacrifices; nor, as now would any thing of this kind have occurred, at a time when it ought to have occurred the least. For he is, of all the gods, the most friendly to man, the aider of man, and the healer of those (wounds) which, being healed, there would be the greatest happiness to the human race. I will, therefore, endeavour to explain to you his power, and you shall be the teacher of it to others. But you must first learn the nature of man, and what sufferings it has undergone. For our nature of old was not the same as it is now. In the first place, there were three kinds of human beings, not as at present, only two, male and female; but there was also a third common to both of those; the name only of which now remains, it has itself disappeared. It was then [one] man-woman, whose form and name partook of and was common to

both the male and the female. But it is now nothing but a name, given by way of reproach. In the next place, the entire form of every individual of the human race was rounded, having the back and sides as in a circle. It had four hands, and legs equal in number to the hands; and two faces upon the circular neck, alike in every way, and one head on both the faces placed opposite, and four ears, and two kinds of sexual organs, and from these it is easy to conjecture how all the other parts were (doubled). They walked, as now, upright, whithersoever they pleased. And when it made haste to run, it did, in the manner of tumblers, who after turning their legs (upward) in a circle, place them accurately in an upright position, support itself on its eight limbs, and afterwards turn itself over quickly in a circle. Now these three and such kinds of beings existed on this account, because the male kind was the produce originally of the sun, the female of the earth, and that which partook of the other two, of the moon; for the moon partakes of both the others (the sun and the earth). The bodies thus were round, and the manner of their running was circular, through their being like their parents. They were terrible in force and strength and had high aspirations, and they made an attempt against the gods, and what Homer says of Ephialtus and Otus, was told of them likewise; that they attempted to ascend to heaven with the view of attacking the gods. Upon which Jupiter and the other gods consulted together what they should do to them; but they were in a difficulty. They had not the mind to destroy them by making the race to disappear with the thunderbolt, as they did the giants; for then the honours and the holy rites paid them by that race would have been extinct, nor yet could they suffer them to act wantonly. At length Jupiter, on reflection, said, I seem to myself to have a plan, so that men may exist, and still be stopt by becoming weaker from their unbridled licentiousness. For now, said he, I will divide each of them into two; and they will at the same time become weaker, and at the same time more useful to us, through their becoming more in number; and they shall walk upright upon two legs; but if they shall think fit to behave licentiously, and are not willing to keep quiet, I will again, said he, divide them, each into two, so that they shall go upon one leg, hopping. So saying, he cut men into two parts, as people cut medlars when about to pickle them, or as they cut eggs with hairs. But whomsoever he cut, he ordered Apollo to turn the face and the half of the neck to that part where the section had taken place, in order that the man might, on seeing the cutting off, be better behaved than before, and he ordered him to heal the other parts. And he (Apollo) turned the face; and pulling the skin together on every side like a contracted purse, over that which is now called the belly, he did, after making a single orifice, tie up (the skin) at the middle of the belly, now called the navel. He then smoothed the greater part of the remainder of the wrinkles of the skin, and jointed the breast, having an instrument such as shoemakers use when they smooth wrinkles of the leather on the last. But he left a few wrinkles on the belly and navel as a memorial of their original suffering. Now when their nature had been bisected, each half perceived with a longing its other self; and throwing their arms around each other and becoming entwined, they had a great desire to grow together, but they died through famine and idleness. And when one of these halves died, and the other was left, the surviving half sought another, and was entwined with it, whether it met with the half of a whole woman, (which half we now call a woman,) or with (the half of a whole) man. And thus they were in the act of perishing. But Jupiter in pity devised another plan, and placed the organs of generation in front, for hitherto they had been on the outside, and they begot and bred, not with one another, but with the earth, like grasshoppers. And therefore he changed them to the front; and by them he caused the generation to be with each other, from the female through the male, on this account, that should a male meet with a female, they might in the embrace at one time generate, and the race be thus propagated; but if at another time a male met with a male, a surfeit might take place from the connexion, and that they might cease and turn themselves to their business, and attend to the other affairs of life. From this (period) has been implanted by nature in mankind a mutual love, which is the bringer together of their ancient nature, and which endeavours to make one out of two, and to heal the nature of man. Each of us then is but the counterpart of a human creature, as having been cut like the Psettae from one into two. Hence

each one is in search of his counterpart. As many men then as are sections of the form common to men, which was then called Man-Woman, are lovers of women; and from this race are sprung the majority of adulterers: and on the other hand, as many women as are addicted to the love of men, and are adulteresses, are sprung from the same race. But such women as are sections of the female, do not pay much attention to men, but turn themselves rather to women; and from this race are the (Lesbian) courtesans. Such as are sections of the male form, follow the males: and whilst they are young, being fragments of men, they love men and are delighted in being with them; and these are the best of boys and youths, as being the most manly in their disposition. Yet some say, indeed, they are shameless. But in this they say false; for it is not through shamelessness, but through assurance, and a manly temper and manly look, that they embrace what resembles themselves. And of this there is a great proof. For when they are full grown, such alone turn out men as regards political affairs: but when they have become men, they feel a love for young persons, and do not turn their thoughts to marriage and child-getting naturally, but are led by the force of custom and law, although it would be sufficient for them to continue to live unmarried. Altogether then such a person is both a lover of youths and a lover of those who love him, and ever embraces what is from the same race as himself. Now, whenever the lover of youths, and every one else, meet with that very thing, the half of himself, they are both smitten with a friendship in a wondrous manner, and (attracted) by an intimacy and love, and are unwilling to be separated from each other for even, so to say, a brief period. And these are they, who continue to live together through life; and yet they could not tell what they wish to take place to themselves from each other; for it does not seem to be sexual intercourse, that the one should, for the sake of that, be delighted with the company of the other, and (seek it) with so much trouble; but the soul of each being evidently desirous of something else, which it is unable to tell, it divines what it wishes, and hints at it. And if while they are lying down in the same place, Vulcan were to stand over them with his tools in his hand, and ask them "What is it do ye, mortals, desire to take place, the one by the other?" and if, finding them in a difficulty, were he to demand them again, "Do ye desire this, to be as much as possible in the same place with each other, so as never, by night or day, to be apart from each other? for if ye long for this, I am willing to melt you down together, and to mould you into the same mass, so that ye two may become one, and as long as ye live, may live both of you in common, as one person; and when ye die, may, having died in common, remain for ever in Hades." On

ANDROGYNOUS ANGEL

Byzantium discussed the sex of angels. Comment adds,
however, that the angelic character was androgynous.

Czanara

hearing this not a single person, I know that, would refuse, nor would he appear to wish for any thing else;
but (every one) would in reality conceive he had heard
that which he had long ago wished for, and that having
come into the company of, and being melted with, his
beloved, he would out of two become one. And of this
the cause is, that this was our original nature. We were
once whole. To the desire then and pursuit of this whole,
the name of Love is given. And we were, as I said,
formerly one. But now, for our iniquity, we have been cut
in twain by the deity, and have been made, like the
Arcadians by the Lacedaemonians, to dwell asunder.
There is therefore a fear, that, unless we are well-
behaved towards the gods, we shall be again cleft in
twain, and go about with our noses split down, as those

have, who are modelled on pillars in profile, and become,
as it were, pebbles cut through and rubbed smooth. On
this account then, it is meet to exhort every man to
behave in all things piously towards the gods, that we
may on the one hand escape from the ills, and on the
other obtain the good, to which Love is our guide and
general; to whom let no one act in opposition. For he
who acts in opposition, is an enemy to the gods. But by
becoming friends and being reconciled to the god, we
shall, what few of those now living do, find and meet with
our beloved, the halves of ourselves. And let not Eryximachus take me up, and ridicule my speech, as if I meant
Pausanias and Agatho. For perhaps they are amongst
such, (the fortunate few,) and are both of them males in
nature. I say then of all in general, both men and women,

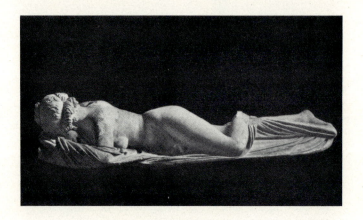

HERMAPHRODITE

The hermaphrodite, a physiological synthesis of Hermes and Aphrodite, combining male and female principles.
Thermes Museum, Rome

that the whole of our race would be happy, if we worked out Love perfectly; and if each were to meet with his beloved, having returned to his original nature. If this then be the best, it necessarily follows, that of the things now present, that which is nearest to this is the best; and that is, to meet with youthful objects of love that are naturally suited to one's ideas. In celebrating then the deity who is the cause of this fitness, we should justly celebrate Love; who both at the present time benefits us the most, by leading us to our own; and for hereafter gives us the greatest hopes, that, if we pay the debt of piety to the gods, he will restore us to our original nature, and, by healing us, render us happy.

Such, Eryximachus, said he, is my speech, in behalf of Love, of a different kind from yours.

Thereupon all the company was in an uproar, and ordered him to enter and recline on a couch, and Agatho too invited him. And he (Alcibiades) came, led by his attendants; and at the same time taking off the fillets, as if about to bind them (on Agatho), he did not see Socrates, who was before his eyes, but sat down by Agatho, and between him and Socrates: for Socrates had made way for him that he might sit down; and sitting down he embraced Agatho, and bound the fillet on him. Thereupon said Agatho, Slaves, unloose the sandals of Alcibiades, that he may recline as the third among us. By all means, said Alcibiades; but, who is this third person our fellow-drinker? and at the same time turning round, he beheld Socrates; and on seeing him, he started up and exclaimed, O Hercules! what is this? What ho Socrates? are you again sitting here in ambush against me, just as you are wont to do, and to appear suddenly, where I least expected you would be. And why are you reclining here? and not with Aristophanes, or any other person who is, and wishes to be a source of merriment? But you have contrived to sit near the most beautiful of those within. Then said Socrates. See, Agatho, if you can assist me; for the love of this man here is to me no trifling matter; since from the time when I fell in love with him, I am no longer permitted either to look at, or speak to, any beautiful person; or he is, through jealousy and envy, practising strange devices, and abuses me, and scarcely keeps off his hands? See therefore that he does not do something now, but do you reconcile us; or, should he attempt to do any violence, do you assist me: for I greatly

SAPPHO AND THE MUSES

National Museum, Syracuse

fear the madness of this man, and his strong feeling of love.—But, said Alcibiades, there shall be no reconciliation between you and me. For I will by and by revenge myself upon you for this. But for the present, Agatho, said he, give me some of the fillets, that I may bind them on the wonderful head of this man and he may not find fault with me because I have bound the fillets on you, but not on him, who vanquishes all men in discourse, not only lately as you have done, but at all times, upon all subjects. And at the same time, taking some of the fillets, he bound them upon Socrates, and laid himself down. When he had laid himself down, he said, Let things be; for you appear to me to be sober; this you must not be allowed, but you must drink; for so it has been agreed. I therefore elect myself the chairman until you have drunk enough. But, Agatho, let some one bring a beaker, if there is a large one; or rather, there is no need; but bring hither, boy, said he, that wine cooler, which seems to hold more than eight kotylae. Having filled it, he first drank it off himself; and afterwards ordered them to pour out of it for Socrates, and stated at the same time, This stratagem of mine, gentlemen, is of no avail against Socra-

tes; for, let him drink as much as any one may command, he will not be a bit the more intoxicated. Socrates then, when the boy had poured out the wine drank it off. And Eryximachus said, What shall we do, Alcibiades? Shall we neither say nor sing over the cup, but drink really like those who are thirsty? To this Alcibiades replied, Hail, Eryximachus! thou best of men, sprung from the best and most temperate of fathers. And hail thou too, said Eryximachus. But what shall we do? Whatever you may order; for you we must obey. For

A man of physic has 'gainst many others
A worth.

Order then what you will. Hear then, said Eryximachus. Before you came in, it was determined that every one, beginning at the right hand, should in turn make a speech in praise of Love, to the best of his ability. All the rest of us, therefore, have spoken; and it is just, since you have not spoken, but have been drinking, that you too should make a speech; and, when you have spoken, order Socrates to do whatever you please, and he too order the person on his right hand, and so with respect to the rest.

[113]

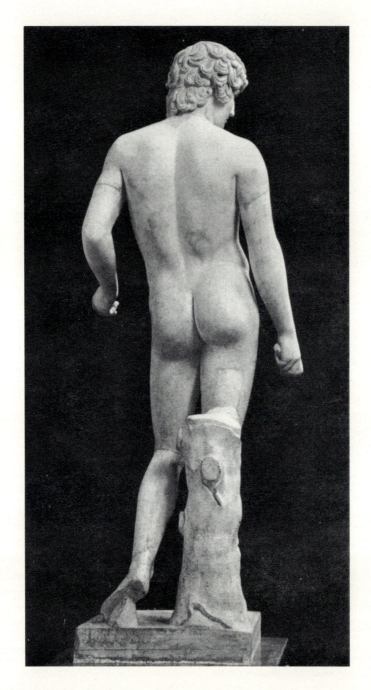

ANTINOUS

Noted for his beauty, Antinous, a favorite of the Roman Emperor Hadrian (76-138 A.D.) was drowned during a trip on the Nile. The Emperor had him deified and in his memory founded the city of Antinoopolis in Egypt. Coins were struck bearing Antinous' image, and busts and statues commemorated him.

Marble Group
National Museum, Naples

[114]

Alcibiades then said, You say well, Eryximachus; but it is not fair to compare a drunken man against a sober one in their speeches. But, O happy man, does Socrates persuade you with respect to what he has just now said? Or do you know that every thing is the contrary to what he has said? For he it is, who, when I in his presence praise any one, except himself, whether god or man, will not keep his hands from me. Will you not speak fair words? said Socrates. By Neptune, said Alcibiades, say nothing against this; for I will praise no other person, while you are present. Do so then, said Eryximachus; if you will, praise Socrates. How say you? rejoined Alcibiades. Does it seen good to you, Eryximachus, that I should do so? Must I fall upon this man, and revenge myself before you? Ho, sir, said Socrates, what have you in mind? Will you praise me so as to make me ridiculous? or what will you do? I will speak the truth. But see whether you will permit me. Nay, said Socrates, I both permit, and command you to speak the truth. I will do it instantly, said Alcibiades. But however do you act thus; if I assert any thing not true, lay hold of me while speaking if you will, and say that I am telling a falsehood; for I shall not willingly tell a lie. And do not wonder if I speak as if recollecting one thing after another; for it is not easy for a man in my state to enumerate readily, and in succession, your strange behaviour. I will then endeavour, gentlemen, to praise Socrates in this way by means of images. He indeed will perhaps imagine that I am turning him into ridicule; but the image will be for the sake of what is true, and not ridiculous.

I say, then, that Socrates is most like the figures of Silenus that are seated in the workshops of statuaries, which the artists have made, holding reeds or flutes; but which, when they are opened down the middle, appear to contain within them statues of the gods. And I again say, that he resembles the satyr Marsyas. Now that in your outward form, Socrates, you resemble these things, even you yourself will not deny; but that you resemble them likewise in other points, hear in the next place. You are saucy in deeds; or are you not? For, if you do not acknowledge it, I will bring witnesses to the fact. Are you not also a piper much more wonderful than Marsyas? For he charmed men through instruments, by a power proceeding from the mouth; and he (charms) even now, when any one plays his melodies. For what Olympus played, I call the melodies of Marsyas, who taught him. Now his melodies, whether a good male flute-player plays them, or a bad female one, alone cause a person to be spell-bound, and point out, through their being divine, those that stand in need of the gods and the mysteries; but you in this respect alone differ from him, that you effect the very same thing by naked words without instruments. We therefore, when we hear another person, although a good speaker himself, pronouncing the speeches of others, not a single hearer, so to say, pays any regard to them; but when any one hears you, or your discourses spoken by another, although he is a wretched speaker, yet, whether a woman or a man or a lad is the auditor, we are astonished and spell-bound. I therefore, gentlemen, unless I seemed to be very much in liquor, would tell you upon oath what I have suffered by the discourses of this man, and am suffering even now. For when I hear him, my heart leaps much more than that of the Corybantes; and my tears flow forth through his discourses. I see too many others suffering in the very same way. But when I hear Pericles, and other excellent orators, I think indeed that they speak well, but I suffer nothing of this kind; nor is my soul agitated with tumult, nor is it indignant, as if I were in a servile state. But by this Marsyas here I am often so affected, that it appears to me I ought not to live, while I am in such a state. You will not, Socrates, say that this is not true. And even now I feel conscious that, were I willing to lend him my ears, I could not bear it, but should suffer in the very same way. For he would compel me to confess, that, being yet very deficient, I neglect my own affairs, but attend to those of the Athenians. By violence therefore restraining myself as to my ears, I depart from him, flying, as it were, from the Syrens, lest I should sit there by him until I grew old. And towards him alone of all men, I suffer that, which no one would think to be in me, to be ashamed of any one. [But I am abashed before him alone.] For I feel conscious of my inability to deny that what he exhorts me to do ought not to be done; but when I depart from him, I am (conscious) of being overcome by the honour (I receive) from the multitude. I therefore run away from and avoid him; and when I see him, I am ashamed for what I had consented to do. And often, indeed, I would gladly see him no longer amongst men: and yet again, if this should happen, I well know I should be afflicted still more; so that I know not what to do with this man. And from the melodies indeed of this Satyr in such a manner both I and many others have suffered.

Hear too from me on other points, how like he is to what I have compared him, and what a wonderful power he possesses. For be well assured, that not one of you knows him; but I will lay him open, since I have begun (to speak.) You see then that he is disposed in a very amatory manner towards beautiful persons; and that he is always about them and struck with them; but on the other hand, he is ignorant of every thing and knows nothing how his figure is. Is not this Silenus-like? For he is invested with this externally like a carved Silenus; but when he is opened inwardly, with temperance how great, think you, fellow-tipplers, is he filled? Know too, that if any person is beautiful, he regards him not, but despises him to such an extent as no one would suppose; nor if he is wealthy, or possesses any other honour amongst those who are considered by the multitude as blessed; but he holds all these possessions to be nothing worth, and that we too are of no account. He passes likewise the whole of life indulging in irony and jests against mankind; but when he is serious and is opened, I know not whether any one (of you) has seen the images within; but I once saw them, and they appeared to me to be so divine and golden, and all-beautiful and wonderful, that I (thought) I must

the way that lovers are wont to speak to their beloved in private; and I was (highly) delighted (with the expectation). Nothing however of this kind very much took place; but after conversing somewhat and passing the day with me as usual, he went away. Then I challenged him to contend with me in the naked exercises, and I did contend as if about to effect something by this means. He engaged therefore naked, and had a tussle frequently against me, no one being present. But why need I mention this? Nothing more took place. But when I accomplished noth-

LESBIAN LOVE

Lesbianism or tribadism is the female perversion corresponding to homosexuality. The arch-priestess of Lesbianism was the Greek poetess Sappho of Lesbos, who belongs in the sixth century B.C.

Toulouse-Lautrec (1864-1901)

in a short time do whatever Socrates ordained. Conceiving too that he paid great attention to my beauty, I considered this as a god-send, and a piece of wondrous good fortune for myself, since by gratifying Socrates it would be in my power to hear from him all that he knew. For I prided myself on my beauty marvellously. With these thoughts in my head, although I had previously been never accustomed to be in his company without an attendant, on that occasion I sent the page away and remained with him alone; for I must state the whole truth, and do you give me your attention; and if I am telling a falsehood, do you, Socrates, confute me. I was, gentlemen, alone with him alone; and I thought he would immediately converse with me in

ing at all by this means, I determined to attack the man with all my might, nor to let him off; since I had put my hand to the task. But you must now know what is the affair. Accordingly I invited him to supper, artlessly laying a plot as a lover does against his beloved. Even to this he did not quickly give ear. In time, however, he was over-persuaded. But when he came for the first time, he wished, as soon as he had supped, to go away; and I, feeling ashamed, let him go. Having laid however again a plot, after supper I had a conversation with him far into the night; and when he wished to go away, I pretended it was late, and I compelled him to stay. He reposed, therefore, in a couch close to mine, and on which he had supped; and no other person besides us slept in the house. Thus far in my story it would be well to state to any one; but what is to come, you would not have heard me telling, unless, in the first place, according to the proverb,

> Wine, with children, or without,
> Does a tale of truth let out;

and in the second place, it seems to me to be unjust in him who comes to praise a person, to leave in obscurity a proud deed of Socrates. Moreover, the suffering of him, who has been bitten by a viper, possesses likewise myself.

imachuses, Pausaniases, Aristodemuses, Aristophaneses. —But why need I say, Socrates himself, and whoever forms the rest (of the company). For all of you have partaken with me of the madness and Bacchic fury of philosophy; and on this account you shall all hear. For you will pardon what was done then, and is said now. But let the domestics, and if there is any other profane and rude person present, place upon their ears gates of very great size. When therefore the lamp was extinguished, and the servants had gone out, it seemed to me that I ought not to

TWO WOMEN

Aristide Maillol (1861-1944)
Bibliotheque Nationale, Paris

For they say that the person so suffering is unwilling to tell what it is, except to those who have been bitten, as being alone about to know and to pardon him, should he dare to do and say every thing from excess of pain. I say it then, having been bitten by something still more painful. For it is the most painful of all, by which a person can be bitten, in heart or soul, or whatever else it is meet to call it, [bitten and wounded,] namely, by discourses in philosophy; which are wont to give out something more acute than that from the viper, when they (the discourses) lay hold of a young person with a not badly-disposed soul, and cause him to do and say any thing whatever. And looking, moreover, at the Phaedruses, Agathos, Eryx-

employ words of many meanings towards him, but tell him freely what was in my thoughts. And nudging him I said, Socrates, are you asleep? Not yet, he replied. Do you know then on what I am determined? What is it particularly? said he. You seem to me, said I, the only lover worthy of myself; and yet you appear to feel a dread to have a recollection towards me. But, as I am thus affected, I think it very silly for me not to gratify you both in this point, and in any thing else of which you may be in want, whether it be my own property, or that of my friends: for nothing is to me of greater moment than to become the best of men: and for this I think there is no person a more competent assister than yourself; and I should feel a much greater shame before the wise, in not gratifying such a man, than before the [many and the] unwise by gratifying him. Socrates, having heard me, said, very ironically, and very much after his usual manner, My dear Alcibiades, you seem to be in reality a man of no common mark, if what you say concerning me happens to be true, and there is in me a certain power, through which you can become better. But what boundless beauty could you see in me, and vastly superior to the fine form in yourself, if, on beholding it, you endeavour to have dealings with me, and to exchange beauty for beauty. You have surely an idea of possessing more than I do; for you endeavour to obtain the truth of beautiful things instead of the reputation, and you conceive that you will in reality exchange brass for gold. But, O blessed man, think better of it, nor let me lie hid from you, as being nothing. The power of intellectual vision begins then to see acutely, when that of the eye loses its acmé. You however are still far off from this. And I, having heard him replied. As regards myself the facts are so; of which not one has been stated otherwise than as I conceive myself. But do you counsel me in what you may consider to be best both for you and me. In this, said he, you say well: for in the time to come let us consult together, and we will do what appears to be the best for us, both with respect to these and other matters. Having thus heard and spoken, and sent as it were arrows, I thought that he was wounded; and I rose up, and not suffering him to speak any more, I wrapped myself round with this garment, (for it was winter,) and lying down under the old cloak of this man, I threw my arms around the truly divine and wonderful man, and lay there the whole night. And in this again, Socrates, you will not say that I am telling a falsehood. But though I acted in this manner, yet he was victorious, and despised, and jeered at, and even insulted my beauty. And yet I fancied it was something, men and judges, for judges you are, of the haughtiness of Socrates. For by the gods and goddesses, rest assured that I rose from Socrates no otherwise than if I had slept with my father, or my elder brother.

THE SYMPOSIUM
Plato

SLEEP
The perversion of tribadism was rife in antiquity.

Gustave Courbet (1819-1877)
Petit Palais, Paris

[119]

Immorality-Renaissance Style

Immorality-Renaissance Style

The relation of the various peoples of the earth to the supreme interests of life, to God, virtue, and immortality, may be investigated up to a certain point, but can never be compared to one another with absolute strictness and certainty. The more plainly in these matters our evidence seems to speak, the more carefully must we refrain from unqualified assumptions and rash generalizations.

This remark is especially true with regard to our judgment on questions of morality. It may be possible to indicate many contrasts and shades of difference among different nations, but to strike the balance of the whole is not given to human insight. The ultimate truth with respect to the character, the conscience, and the guilt of a people remains for ever a secret; if only for the reason that its defects have another side, where they reappear as peculiarities or even as virtues. We must leave those who find a pleasure in passing sweeping censures on whole nations, to do so as they like. The peoples of Europe can maltreat, but happily not judge one another. A great nation, interwoven by its civilization, its achievements, and its fortunes with the whole life of the modern world, can afford to ignore both its advocates and its accusers. It lives on with or without the approval of theorists.

Accordingly, what here follows is no judgment, but rather a string of marginal notes, suggested by a study of the Italian Renaissance extending over some years. The value to be attached to them is all the more qualified as they mostly touch on the life of the upper classes, with respect to which we are far better informed in Italy than in any other country in Europe at that period. But though both fame and infamy sound louder here than elsewhere, we are not helped thereby in forming an adequate moral estimate of the people.

What eye can pierce the depths in which the character and fate of nations are determined? — in which that which is inborn and that which has been experienced combine to form a new whole and a fresh nature? — in which even those intellectual capacities, which at first sight we should take to be most original, are in fact evolved late and slowly? Who can tell if the Italian before the thirteenth century possessed that flexible activity and certainty in his whole being — that play of power in shaping whatever subject he dealt with in word or in form, which was peculiar to him later? And if no answer can be found to these questions, how can we possibly judge of the infinite and infinitely intricate channels through which character and intellect are incessantly pouring their influence one upon the other. A tribunal there is for each one of us, whose voice is our conscience; but let us have done with these generalities about nations. For the people that seem to be most sick the cure may be at hand; and one that appears to be healthy may bear within it the ripening germs of death, which the hour of danger will bring forth from their hiding-place.

At the beginning of the sixteenth century, when the civilization of the Renaissance had reached its highest pitch, and at the same time the political ruin of the nation seemed inevitable, there were not wanting serious thinkers who saw a connexion between this ruin and the prevalent immorality. It was not one of those methodistical moralists who in every age think themselves called to declaim against the wickedness of the time, but it was Macchiavelli, who, in one of his most well-considered works, said openly: 'We Italians are irreligious and corrupt above others.' Another man had perhaps said, 'We are individually highly developed; we have outgrown the limits of morality and religion which were natural to us in our undeveloped state, and we despise outward law, because our rulers are illegitimate, and their judges and officers wicked men.' Macchiavelli adds, 'because the Church and her representatives set us the worst example.'

Shall we add also, 'because the influence exercised by

antiquity was in this respect unfavourable'? The statement can only be received with many qualifications. It may possibly be true of the humanists, especially as regards the profligacy of their lives. Of the rest it may perhaps be said with some approach to accuracy, that, after they became familiar with antiquity, they substituted for holiness — the Christian ideal of life — the cultus of historical greatness. We can understand, therefore, how easily they would be tempted to consider those faults and vices to be matters of indifference, in spite of which their heroes were great. They were probably scarcely conscious of this themselves, for if we are summoned to quote any statement of doctrine on this subject, we are again forced to appeal to humanists like Paolo Giovio, who excuses the perjury of Giangaleaz-zo Visconti, through which he was enabled to found an empire, by the example of Julius Caesar. The great Florentine historians and statesmen never stoop to these slavish quotations, and what seems antique in their deeds and their judgments is so because the nature of their political life necessarily fostered in them a mode of thought which has some analogy with that of antiquity.

Nevertheless, it cannot be denied that Italy at the beginning of the sixteenth century found itself in the midst of a grave moral crisis, out of which the best men saw hardly any escape.

Let us begin by saying a few words about that moral force which was then the strongest bulwark against evil. The highly gifted men of that day thought to find it in the sentiment of honour. This is that enigmatic mixture of conscience and egoism which often survives in the modern man after he has lost, whether by his own fault or not, faith, love, and hope. This sense of honour is compatible with much selfishness and great vices, and may be the victim of astonishing illusions; yet, nevertheless, all the noble elements that are left in the wreck of a character may gather around it, and from this fountain may draw new strength. It has become, in a far wider sense than is commonly believed, a decisive test of conduct in the minds of the cultivated Europeans of our own day, and many of those who yet hold faithfully by religion and morality are unconsciously guided by this feeling in the gravest decisions of their lives.

It lies without the limits of our task to show how the men of antiquity also experienced this feeling in a peculiar form, and how, afterwards, in the Middle Ages, a special sense of honour became the mark of a particular class. Nor can we here dispute with those who hold that conscience, rather than honour, is the motive power. It would indeed be better and nobler if it were so; but since it must be granted that even our worthier resolutions result from 'a conscience more or less dimmed by selfishness,' it is better to call the mixture by its right name. It is certainly not always easy, in treating of the Italian of this period, to distinguish this sense of honour from the passion for fame, into which, indeed, it easily passes. Yet the two sentiments are essentially different.

There is no lack of witnesses on this subject. One who speaks plainly may here be quoted as a representative of the rest. We read in the recently-published 'Aphorisms' of Guicciardini: 'He who esteems honour highly, succeeds in all that he undertakes, since he fears neither trouble, danger, nor expense; I have found it so in my own case, and may say it and write it; vain and dead are the deeds of men which have not this as their motive.' It is necessary to add that, from what is known of the life of the writer, he can here be only speaking of honour, and not of fame. Rabelais has put the matter more clearly than perhaps any Italian. We quote him, indeed, unwillingly in these pages. What the great, baroque Frenchman gives us, is a picture of what the Renaissance would be without form and without beauty. But his description of an ideal state of things in the Thelemite monastery is decisive as historical evidence. In speaking of his gentlemen and ladies of the Order of Free Will, he tells us as follows:—

'En leur reigle n'estoit que ceste clause: Fay ce que vouldras. Parce que gens liberes, bien nayz, bien instruictz, conversans en compaignies honnestes, ont par nature ung instinct et aguillon qui toujours les poulse à faitz vertueux, et retire de vice; lequel ilz nommoyent honneur.'

This is that same faith in the goodness of human nature which inspired the men of the second half of the eighteenth century, and helped to prepare the way for the French Revolution. Among the Italians, too, each man appeals to this noble instinct within him, and though with regard to the people as a whole — chiefly in consequence of the national disasters — judgments of a more pessimistic sort became prevalent, the importance of this sense of honour must still be rated highly. If the boundless development of individuality, stronger than the will of the individual, be the work of a historical providence, not less so is the opposing force which then manifested itself in Italy. How often, and against what passionate attacks of selfishness it won the day, we cannot tell, and therefore no human judgment can estimate with certainty the absolute moral value of the nation.

A force which we must constantly take into account in judging of the morality of the more highly-developed Italian of this period is that of the imagination. It gives to his virtues and vices a peculiar colour, and under its influence his unbridled egoism shows itself in its most terrible shape.

The force of his imagination explains, for example, the fact that he was the first gambler on a large scale in modern times. Pictures of future wealth and enjoyment rose in such

Court life in France in the Age of Catherine de Mèdici. Music, dining and amorous dalliance proceeded while war, destruction and pestilence ravaged the land.

Theodor Bernard (1521 1592)

LEDA AND THE SWAN

Tintoretto (1518-1594)
Uffizi Gallery, Florence

life-like colours before his eyes, that he was ready to hazard everything to reach them. The Mohammedan nations would doubtless have anticipated him in this respect, had not the Koran, from the beginning, set up the prohibition against gambling as a chief safeguard of public morals, and directed the imagination of its followers to the search after buried treasures. In Italy, the passion for play reached an intensity which often threatened or altogether broke up the existence of the gambler. Florence had already, at the end of the fourteenth century, its Casanova — a certain Buonaccorso Pitti, who, in the course of his incessant journeys as merchant, political agent, diplomatist and professional gambler, won and lost sums so enormous that none but princes like the Dukes of Brabant, Bavaria, and Savoy, were able to compete with him. That great lottery-bank, which was called the Court of Rome, accustomed people to a need of excitement, which found its satisfaction in games of hazard during the intervals between one intrigue and another. We read, for example, how Franceschetto Cybò, in two games with the Cardinal Raffaello Riario, lost no less than 14,000 ducats, and afterwards complained to the Pope that his opponent had cheated him. Italy has since that time been the home of the lottery.

It was to the imagination of the Italians that the peculiar character of their vengeance was due. The sense of justice was, indeed, one and the same throughout Europe, and any violation of it, so long as no punishment was inflicted, must have been felt in the same manner. But other nations, though they found it no easier to forgive, nevertheless forgot more easily, while the Italian imagination kept the picture of the wrong alive with frightful vividness. The fact that, according to the popular morality, the avenging of blood is a duty — a duty often performed in a way to make us shudder — gives to this passion a peculiar and still firmer basis. The government and the tribunals recognise its existence and justification, and only attempt to keep it within certain limits. Even among the peasantry, we read of Thyestean banquets and mutual assassination on the widest scale. Let us look at an instance.

In the district of Aquapendente three boys were watching cattle, and one of them said: 'Let us find out the way how people are hung.' While one was sitting on the shoulders of the other, and the third, after fastening the rope round the neck of the first, was tying it to an oak, a wolf came, and the two who were free ran away and left the other hanging. Afterwards they found him dead, and buried him. On the Sunday his father came to bring him bread, and one of the two confessed what had happened, and showed him the grave. The old man then killed him with a knife, cut him up, brought away the liver, and entertained the boy's father with it at home. After dinner, he told him whose liver it was. Here-upon began a series of reciprocal murders between the two families, and within a month thirty-six person were killed, women as well as men.

And such 'vendette,' handed down from father to son, and extending to friends and distant relations, were not limited to the lower classes, but reached to the highest. The chronicles and novels of the period are full of such instances, especially of vengeance taken for the violation of women. The classic land for these feuds was Romagna, where the 'vendetta' was interwoven with intrigues and party division of every conceivable sort. The popular legends present an awful picture of the savagery into which this brave and energetic people had relapsed. We are told, for instance, of a nobleman at Ravenna, who had got all his enemies together in a tower, and might have burned them; instead of which he let them out, embraced them, and entertained them sumptuously; whereupon shame drove them mad, and they conspired against him. Pious and saintly monks exhorted unceasingly to reconciliation, but they can scarcely have done more than restrain to a certain extent the feuds already established; their influence hardly prevented the growth of new ones. The novelists sometimes describe to us this effect of religion — how sentiments of generosity and forgiveness were suddenly awakened, and then again paralysed by the force of what had once been done and could never be undone. The Pope himself was not always lucky as a peace-maker. 'Pope Paul II, desired that the quarrel between Antonio Caffarello and the family of Alberino should cease, and ordered Giovanni Alberino and Antonio Caffarello to come before him, and bade them kiss one another, and promised them a fine of 2,000 ducats in case they renewed this strife, and two days after Antonio was stabbed by the same Giacomo Alberino, son of Giovanni, who had wounded him once before; and the Pope was full of anger, and confiscated the goods of Alberino, and destroyed his houses, and banished father and son from Rome.' The oaths and ceremonies by which reconciled enemies attempted to guard themselves against a relapse, are sometimes utterly horrible. When the parties of the 'Nove' and the 'Popolari' met and kissed one another by twos in the cathedral at Siena on Christmas Eve, 1494, an oath was read by which all salvation in time and eternity was denied to the future violator of the treaty — 'an oath more astonishing and dreadful than had ever yet been heard.' The last consolations of religion in the hour of death were to turn to the damnation of the man who should break it. It is clear, however, that such a ceremony rather represents the despairing mood of the mediators than offers any real guarantee of peace, inasmuch as the truest reconciliation is just that one which has least need of it.

This personal need of vengeance felt by the cultivated and highly placed Italian, resting on the solid basis of an analogous popular custom, naturally displays itself under a thousand different aspects, and receives the unqualified approval of public opinion, as reflected in the works of the novelists. All are at one on the point, that, in the case of those injuries and insults for which Italian justice offered no redress, and all the more in the case of those against which no human law can ever adequately provide, each man is free to take the law into his own hands. Only there must be art in the vengeance, and the satisfaction must be compounded of the material injury and moral humiliation of the offender. A mere brutal, clumsy triumph of force was held by public opinion to be no satisfaction. The whole man with his sense of fame and of scorn, not only his fist, must be victorious.

The Italian of that time shrank, it is true, from no dissimulation in order to attain his ends, but was wholly free from hypocrisy in matters of principle. In these he attempted to deceive neither himself nor others. Accordingly, revenge was declared with perfect frankness to be a necessity of human nature. Cool-headed people declared that it was then most worthy of praise, when it was disengaged from passion, and worked simply from motives of expedience, 'in order that other men may learn to leave us unharmed.' Yet such instances must have formed only a small minority in comparison with those in which passion sought an outlet. This sort of revenge differs clearly from the avenging of blood, which has been already spoken of; while the latter keeps more or less within the limits of retaliation — the 'jus talionis' — the former necessarily goes much farther, not only requiring the sanction of the sense of justice, but craving admiration, and even striving to get the laugh on its own side.

Here lies the reason why men were willing to wait so long for their revenge. A 'bella vendetta' demanded as a rule a combination of circumstances for which it was necessary to wait patiently. The gradual ripening of such opportunities is described by the novelists with heartfelt delight.

There is no need to discuss the morality of actions in which plaintiff and judge are one and the same person. If this Italian thirst for vengeance is to be palliated at all, it must be by proving the existence of a corresponding national virtue, namely gratitude. The same form of imagination which retains and magnifies wrong once suffered, might be expected also to keep alive the memory of kindness received. It is not possible, however, to prove this with regard to the nation as a whole, though traces of it may be seen in the Italian character of to-day. The gratitude shown by the inferior classes for kind treatment, and the good memory of the upper for politeness in social life, are instances of this.

This connexion between the imagination and the moral qualities of the Italian repeats itself continually. If, never-

theless, we find more cold calculation in cases where the Northerner rather follows his impulses, the reason is that individual development in Italy was not only more marked and earlier in point of time, but also far more frequent. Where this is the case in other countries, the results are also analogous. We find, for example, that the early emancipation of the young from domestic and paternal authority is common to North America with Italy. Later on, in the more generous natures, a tie of freer affection grows up between parents and children.

It is in fact a matter of extreme difficulty to judge fairly of other nations in the sphere of character and feeling. In these respects a people may be developed highly, and yet in a manner so strange that a foreigner is utterly unable to understand it. Perhaps all the nations of the West are in this point equally favoured.

But where the imagination has exercised the most powerful and despotic influence on morals is in the illicit intercourse of the two sexes. It is well known that prostitution was freely practised in the Middle Ages, before the appearance of syphilis. A discussion, however, on these questions does not belong to our present work. What seems characteristic of Italy at this time, is that here marriage and its rights were more often and more deliberately trampled under foot than anywhere else. The girls of the higher classes were carefully secluded, and of them we do not speak. All passion was directed to the married women.

Under these circumstances it is remarkable that, so far as we know, there was no diminution in the number of marriages, and that family life by no means underwent that disorganization which a similar state of things would have produced in the North. Men wished to live as they pleased, but by no means to renounce the family, even when they were not sure that it was all their own. Nor did the race sink, either physically or mentally, on this account; for that apparent intellectual decline which showed itself towards the middle of the sixteenth century may be certainly accounted for by political and ecclesiastical causes, even if we are not to assume that the circle of achievements possible to the Renaissance had been completed. Notwithstanding their profligacy, the Italians continued to be, physically and mentally, one of the healthiest and best-born populations in Europe, and have retained this position, with improved morals, down to our own time.

When we come to look more closely at the ethics of love at the time of the Renaissance, we are struck by a remarkable contrast. The novelists and comic poets give us to understand that love consists only in sensual enjoyment, and that to win this, all means, tragic or comic, are not only permitted, but are interesting in proportion to their audacity and unscrupulousness. But if we turn to the best of the lyric poets and writers of dialogues, we find in them a deep

RUSTIC CONCERT

Giorgione (c. 1478-1511)
Louvre, Paris

[129]

and spiritual passion of the noblest kind, whose last and highest expression is a revival of the ancient belief in an original unity of souls in the Divine Being. And both modes of feeling were then genuine, and could co-exist in the same individual. It is not exactly a matter of glory, but it is a fact, that in the cultivated man of modern times, this sentiment can be not merely unconsciously present in both its highest and lowest stages, but may thus manifest itself openly, and even artistically. The modern man, like the man of antiquity, is in this respect too a microcosm, which the mediaeval mind was not and could not be.

To begin with the morality of the novelists. They treat, chiefly, as we have said, of married women, and consequently of adultery.

The opinion mentioned above of the equality of the two sexes is of great importance in relation to this subject. The highly developed and cultivated woman disposes of herself with a freedom unknown in Northern countries; and her unfaithfulness does not break up her life in the same terrible manner, so long as no outward consequence follows from it. The husband's claim on her fidelity has not that firm foundation which it acquires in the North through the poetry and passion of courtship and betrothal. After the briefest acquaintance with her future husband, the young wife quits the convent or the paternal roof to enter upon a world in which her character begins rapidly to develop. The rights of the husband are for this reason conditional, and even the man who regards them in the light of a 'jus quaesitum' thinks only of the outward conditions of the contract, not of the affections. The beautiful young wife of an old man sends back the presents and letters of a youthful lover, in the firm resolve to keep her honour (honesta). 'But she rejoices in the love of the youth for the sake of his great excellence; and she perceives that a noble woman may love a man of merit without loss to her honour.' But the way is short from such a distinction to a complete surrender.

The latter seems indeed as good as justified, when there is unfaithfulness on the part of the husband. The woman, conscious of her own dignity, feels this not only as a pain, but also as a humiliation and deceit, and sets to work, often with the calmest consciousness of what she is about, to devise the vengeance which the husband deserves. Her tact must decide as to the measure of punishment which is suited to the particular case. The deepest wound, for example, may prepare the way for a reconciliation and a peaceful life in the future, if only it remains secret. The novelists, who themselves undergo such experiences or invent them according to the spirit of the age, are full of admiration when the vengeance is skilfully adapted to the particular case, in fact, when it is a work of art. As a matter of course, the husband never at bottom recognises this

right of retaliation, and only submits to it from fear or prudence. Where these motives are absent, where his wife's unfaithfulness exposes him or may expose him to the derision of outsiders, the affair becomes tragical, and not seldom ends in murder or other vengeance of a violent sort. It is characteristic of the real motive from which these deeds arise, that not only the husbands, but the brothers and the father of the woman feel themselves not only justified in taking vengeance, but bound to take it. Jealousy, therefore, has nothing to do with the matter, moral reprobation but little; the real reason is the wish to spoil the triumph of others. 'Nowadays,' says Bandello, 'we see a woman poison her husband to gratify her lusts, thinking that a widow may do whatever she desires. Another, fearing the discovery of an illicit amour, has her husband murdered by her lover. And though fathers, brothers, and husbands arise to extirpate the shame with poison, with the sword, and by every other means, women still continue to follow their passions, careless of their honour and their lives.' Another time, in a milder strain, he exclaims: 'Would that we were not daily forced to hear that one man has murdered his wife because he suspected her of infidelity; that another has killed his daughter, on account of a secret marriage; that a third has caused his sister to be murdered, because she would not marry as he wished! It is great cruelty that we claim the right to do whatever we list, and will not suffer women to do the same. If they do anything which does not please us, there we are at once with cords and daggers and poison. What folly it is of men to suppose their own and their house's honour depends on the appetite of a woman!' The tragedy in which such affairs commonly ended was so well known that the novelist looked on the threatened gallant as a dead man, even while he went about alive and merry. The physician and lute-player Antonio Bologna had made a secret marriage with the widowed Duchess of Amalfi, of the house of Aragon. Soon afterwards her brother succeeded in securing both her and her children, and murdered them in a castle. Antonia, ignorant of their fate, and still cherishing the hope of seeing them again, was staying at Milan, closely watched by hired assassins, and one day in the society of Ippolita Sforza sang to the lute the story of his misfortunes. A friend of the house, Delio, 'told the story up to this point to Scipione Atellano, and added that he would make it the subject of a novel, as he was sure that Antonio would be murdered.' The manner in which this took place, almost under the eyes of Delio and Atellano, is thrillingly described by Bandello.

Nevertheless, the novelists habitually show a sympathy for all the ingenious, comic, and cunning features which may happen to attend adultery. They describe with delight how the lover manages to hide himself in the house, all the

THE JUDGMENT OF PARIS

Nikolaus Manuel (1484-1530)

HOLY ROMAN EMPEROR SIGISMUND
Sigismund (1361-1437) was notorious for his erotic excesses.

means and devices by which he communicates with his mistress, the boxes with cushions and sweetmeats in which he can be hidden and carried out of danger. The deceived husband is described sometimes as a fool to be laughed at, sometimes as a bloodthirsty avenger of his honour; there is no third situation except when the woman is painted as wicked and cruel, and the husband or lover is the innocent victim. It may be remarked, however, that narratives of the latter kind are not strictly speaking novels, but rather warning examples taken from real life.

When in the course of the sixteenth century Italian life fell more and more under Spanish influence, the violence of the means to which jealousy had recourse perhaps increased. But this new phase must be distinguished from the punishment of infidelity which existed before, and which was founded in the spirit of the Renaissance itself. As the influence of Spain declined, these excesses of jealousy declined also, till towards the close of the seventeenth century they had wholly disappeared, and their place was taken by that indifference which regarded the 'Cicisbeo' as an indispensable figure in every household, and took no offense at one or two supernumerary lovers ('Patiti').

But who can undertake to compare the vast sum of wickedness which all these facts imply, with what happened in other countries? Was the marriage-tie, for instance, really more sacred in France during the fifteenth century than in Italy? The 'fabliaux' and farces would lead us to doubt it, and rather incline us to think that unfaithfulness was equally common, though its tragic consequences were less frequent, because the individual was less developed and his claims were less consciously felt than in Italy. More evidence, however, in favour of the Germanic peoples lies in the fact of the social freedom enjoyed among them by girls and women, which impressed Italian travellers so pleasantly in England and in the Netherlands. And yet we must not attach too much importance to this fact. Unfaithfulness was doubtless very frequent, and in certain cases led to a sanguinary vengeance. We have only to remember how the northern princes of that time dealt with their wives on the first suspicion of infidelity.

But it was not merely the sensual desire, not merely the vulgar appetite of the ordinary man, which trespassed upon forbidden ground among the Italians of that day, but also the passion of the best and noblest; and this, not only because the unmarried girl did not appear in society, but also because the man, in proportion to the completeness of his own nature, felt himself most strongly attracted by the woman whom marriage had developed. These are the men who struck the loftiest notes of lyrical poetry, and who have attempted in their treatises and dialogues to give us an idealised image of the devouring passion —'l'amor divino.' When they complain of the cruelty of the winged god, they are not only thinking of the coyness or hard-heartedness of the beloved one, but also of the unlawfulness of the passion itself. They seek to raise themselves above this painful consciousness by that spiritualisation of love which found a support in the Platonic doctrine of the soul, and of which

Pietro Bembo is the most famous representative. His thoughts on this subject are set forth by himself in the third book of the 'Asolani,' and indirectly by Castiglione, who puts in his mouth the splendid speech with which the fourth book of the 'Cortigiano' concludes; neither of these writers was a Stoic in his conduct, but at that time it meant something to be at once a famous and a good man, and this praise must be accorded to both of them; their contemporaries took what these men said to be a true expression of their feeling, and we have not the right to despise it as affectation. Those who take the trouble to study the speech in the 'Cortigiano' will see how poor an idea of it can be given by an extract. There were then living in Italy several distinguished women, who owed their celebrity chiefly to relations of this kind, such as Giulia Gonzaga, Veronica da Coreggio, and, above all, Vittoria Colonna. The land of profligates and scoffers respected these women and this sort of love — and what more can be said in their favour? We cannot tell how far vanity had to do with the matter, how far Vittoria was flattered to hear around her the sublimated utterances of hopeless love from the most famous men in Italy. If the thing was here and there a fashion it was still no trifling praise for Vittoria that she, at least,

THE FAVORITE LOVER
Louis Leopold Boilly (1761-1845)
Victoria and Albert Museum, London

[133]

never went out of fashion, and in her latest years produced the most profound impressions. It was long before other countries had anything similar to show.

In the imagination then, which governed this people more than any other, lies one general reason why the course of every passion was violent, and why the means used for the gratification of passion were often criminal. There is a violence which cannot control itself because it is born of weakness; but in Italy what we find is the corruption of powerful natures. Sometimes this corruption assumes a colossal shape, and crime seems to acquire almost a personal existence of its own.

The restraints of which men were conscious were but few. Each individual, even among the lowest of the people, felt himself inwardly emancipated from the control of the State and its police, whose title to respect was illegitimate, and itself founded on violence; and no man believed any longer in the justice of the law. When a murder was committed, the sympathies of the people, before the circumstances of the case were known, ranged themselves instinctively on the side of the murderer. A proud, manly bearing before and at the execution excited such admiration that the narrator often forgets to tell us for what offence the criminal was put to death. But when we add to this inward contempt of law and to the countless grudges and enmities which called for satisfaction, the impunity which crime enjoyed during times of political disturbance, we can only wonder that the state and society were not utterly dissolved. Crises of this kind occurred at Naples during the transition from the Aragonese to the French and Spanish rule, and at Milan, on the repeated expulsions and returns of the Sforzas; at such times those men who have never in their hearts recognised the bonds of law and society, come forward and give free play to their instincts of murder and rapine. Let us take, by way of example, a picture drawn from a humbler sphere.

When the Duchy of Milan was suffering from the disorders which followed the death of Giangaleazzo Sforza, about the year 1480, all safety came to an end in the provincial cities. This was the case in Parma, where the Milanese Governor, terrified by threats of murder, and after vainly offering rewards for the discovery of the offenders, consented to throw open the gaols and let loose the most abandoned criminals. Burglary, the demolition of houses, shameless offences against decency, public assassination and murders, especially of Jews, were events of everyday occurrence. At first the authors of these deeds prowled about singly, and masked; soon large gangs of armed men went to work every night without disguise. Threatening letters, satires, and scandalous jests circulated freely; and a sonnet in ridicule of the Government seems to have roused its

indignation far more than the frightful condition of the city. In many churches the sacred vessels with the host were stolen, and this fact is characteristic of the temper which prompted these outrages. It is impossible to say what would happen now in any country of the world, if the government and police ceased to act, and yet hindered by their presence the establishment of a provisional authority; but what then occurred in Italy wears a character of its own, through the great share which personal hatred and revenge had in it. The impression, indeed, which Italy at this period makes on us is, that even in quiet times great crimes were commoner than in other countries. We may, it is true, be misled by the fact that we have far fuller details on such matters here than elsewhere, and that the same force of imagination, which gives a special character to crimes actually committed, causes much to be invented which never really happened. The amount of violence was perhaps as great elsewhere. It is hard to say for certain, whether in the year 1500 men were any safer, whether human life was after all better protected, in powerful, wealthy Germany, with its robber knights, extortionate beggars, and daring highwaymen. But one thing is certain, that premeditated crimes, committed professionally and for hire by third parties, occurred in Italy with great and appalling frequency.

So far as regards brigandage, Italy, especially in the more fortunate provinces, such as Tuscany, was certainly not more, and probably less, troubled than the countries of the North. But the figures which do meet us are characteristic of the country. It would be hard, for instance, to find elsewhere the case of a priest, gradually driven by passion from one excess to another, till at last he came to head a band of robbers. That age offers us this example among others. On August 12, 1495, the priest Don Niccolò de' Pelegati of Figarolo was shut up in an iron cage outside the tower of San Giuliano at Ferrara. He had twice celebrated his first mass; the first time he had the same day committed murder, but afterwards received absolution at Rome; he then killed four people and married two wives, with whom he travelled about. He afterwards took part in many assassinations, violated women, carried others away by force, plundered far and wide, and infested the territory of Ferrara with a band of followers in uniform, extorting food and shelter by every sort of violence. When we think of what all this implies, the mass of guilt on the head of this one man is something tremendous. The clergy and monks had many privileges and little supervision, and among them were doubtless plenty of murderers and other malefactors — but hardly a second Pelegati. It is another matter, though by no means creditable, when ruined characters sheltered themselves in the cowl in order to escape the arm of the law, like the corsair whom Massuccio knew in a convent at Naples. What the real truth was with regard to Pope John XIII,

FAITHLESSNESS
The artist has here produced an illustration for Ovid's
Metamorphoses. *The symbolism of the scale is to be noted.*
Plighted troth, in those Renaissance times, was as light as a
feather, and equally unenduring.
Hubert Goltzius (1558-1617)

in this respect, is not known with certainty.

The age of the famous brigand chief did not begin till later, in the seventeenth century, when the political strife of Guelph and Ghibelline, of Frenchman and Spaniard, no longer agitated the country. The robber then took the place of the partisan.

In certain districts of Italy, where civilization had made little progress, the country people were disposed to murder any stranger who fell into their hands. This was especially the case in the more remote parts of the Kingdom of Naples, where the barbarism dated probably from the days of the Roman 'latifundia,' and when the stranger and the enemy ('hospes' and 'hostis') were in all good faith held to be one and the same. These people were far from being irreligious. A herdsman once appeared in great trouble at

the confessional, avowing that, while making cheese during Lent, a few drops of milk had found their way into his mouth. The confessor, skilled in the customs of the country, discovered in the course of his examination that the penitent and his friends were in the practice of robbing and murdering travellers, but that, through the force of habit, this usage gave rise to no twinges of conscience within them. We have already mentioned to what a degree of barbarism the peasants elsewhere could sink in times of political confusion.

A worse symptom than brigandage of the morality of that time was the frequency of paid assassination. In that respect Naples was admitted to stand at the head of all the cities of Italy. 'Nothing,' says Pontano, 'is cheaper here than human life.' But other districts could also show a terrible list of these crimes. It is hard, of course, to classify them according to the motives by which they were prompted, since political expediency, personal hatred, party hostility, fear, and revenge, all play into one another. It is no small honour to the Florentines, the most highly-developed people of Italy, that offences of this kind occurred more rarely among them than anywhere else, perhaps because there was a justice at hand for legitimate grievances which was recognised by all, or because the higher culture of the individual gave him different views as to the right of men to interfere with the decrees of fate. In Florence, if anywhere, men were able to feel the incalculable consequences of a deed of blood, and to understand how insecure the author of a so-called profitable crime is of any true and lasting gain. After the fall of Florentine liberty, assassination, especially by hired agents, seems to have rapidly increased, and continued till the government of Cosimo I had attained such strength that the police were at last able to repress it.

Elsewhere in Italy paid crimes were probably more or less frequent in proportion to the number of powerful and solvent buyers. Impossible as it is to make any statistical estimate of their amount, yet if only a fraction of the deaths which public report attributed to violence were really murders, the crimes must have been terribly frequent. The worst example of all was set by princes and governments, who without the faintest scruple reckoned murder as one of the instruments of their power. And this, without being in the same category with Caesar Borgia. The Sforzas, the Aragonese monarchs, the Republic of Venice, and later on, the agents of Charles V resorted to it whenever it suited their purpose. The imagination of the people at last became so accustomed to facts of this kind, that the death of any powerful man was seldom or never attributed to natural causes. There were certainly absurd notions current with regard to the effect of various poisons. There may be some truth in the story of that terrible white powder used by the Borgias, which did its work at the end of a definite period and it is possible that it was really a 'vennenum atterminatum' which the Prince of Salerno handed to the Cardinal of Aragon, with the words: 'In a few days you will die, because your father, King Ferrante, wished to trample upon us all.' But the poisoned letter which Caterina Riario sent to Pope Alexander VI. would hardly have caused his death even if he had read it; and when Alfonso the Great was warned by his physicians not to read in the 'Livy' which Cosimo de' Medici had presented to him, he told them with justice not to talk like fools. Nor can that poison with which the secretary of Piccinino wished to anoint the sedan-chair of Pius II., have affected any other organ than the imagination. The proportion which mineral and vegetable poisons bore to one another, cannot be ascertained precisely. The poison with which the painter Rosso Fiorentino

destroyed himself (1541) was evidently a powerful acid, which it would have been impossible to administer to another person without his knowledge. The secret use of weapons, especially of the dagger, in the service of powerful individuals, was habitual in Milan, Naples, and other cities. Indeed, among the crowds of armed retainers who were necessary for the personal safety of the great, and who lived in idleness, it was natural that outbreaks of this mania for blood should from time to time occur. Many a deed of horror would never have been committed, had not the master known that he needed but to give a sign to one or other of his followers.

Among the means used for the secret destruction of others — so far, that is, as the intention goes — we find magic, practised, however, sparingly. Where 'maleficii,' 'malie,' and so forth, are mentioned, they appear rather as a means of heaping up additional terror on the head of some hated enemy. At the courts of France and England in the fourteenth and fifteenth centuries, magic, practised with a view to the death of an opponent, plays a far more important part than in Italy.

In this country, finally, where individuality of every sort attained its highest development, we find instances of that ideal and absolute wickedness which delights in crimes for their own sake, and not as means to an end, or at any rate as means to ends for which our psychology has no measure.

Among these appalling figures we may first notice certain of the 'Condottieri,' such as Braccio di Montone, Tiberto Brandolino, and that Werner von Urslingen whose silver hauberk bore the inscription: 'The enemy of God, of pity and of mercy.' This class of men offers us some of the earliest instances of criminals deliberately repudiating every moral restraint. Yet we shall be more reserved in our judgment of them when we remember that the worst part of their guilt — in the estimate of those who record it — lay in their defiance of spiritual threats and penalties, and that to this fact is due that air of horror with which they are represented as surrounded. In the case of Braccio, the hatred of the Church went so far that he was infuriated at the sight of monks at their psalms, and had thrown them down from the top of a tower; but at the same time 'he was loyal to his soldiers and a great general.' As a rule, the crimes of the 'Condottieri' were committed for the sake of some definite advantage, and must be attributed to a position in which men could not fail to be demoralised. Even their apparently gratuitous cruelty had commonly a purpose, if it were only to strike terror. The barbarities of the House of Aragon, as we have seen, were mainly due to fear and to the desire for vengeance. The thirst for blood on its own account, the devilish delight in destruction, is most clearly exemplified in the case of the Spaniard Caesar

ALLEGORY OF LOVE

Angelo Bronzino (1500-1572)
National Gallery, London

Borgia, whose cruelties were certainly out of all proportion to the end which he had in view. In Sigismondo Malatesta, tyrant of Rimini, the same disinterested love of evil may also be detected. It is not only the Court of Rome, but the verdict of history, which convicts him of murder, rape, adultery, incest, sacrilege, perjury and treason, committed not once but often. The most shocking crime of all — the unnatural attempt on his own son Roberto, who frustrated it with his drawn dagger,— may have been the result, not merely of moral corruption, but perhaps of some magical or astrological superstition. The same conjecture has been made to account for the rape of the Bishop of Fano by Pierluigi Farnese of Parma, son of Paul III.

If we now attempt to sum up the principal features in the Italian character of that time, as we know it from a study of the life of the upper classes, we shall obtain something like the following result. The fundamental vice of this character was at the same time a condition of its greatness, namely, excessive individualism. The individual first inwardly casts off the authority of a state which, as a fact, is in most cases tyrannical and illegitimate, and what he thinks and does is, rightly or wrongly, now called treason. The sight of victorious egoism in others drives him to defend his own right by his own arm. And, while thinking to restore his inward equilibrium, he falls, through the vengeance which he executes, into the hands of the powers of darkness. His love, too, turns mostly for satisfaction to another individuality equally developed, namely, to his neighbour's wife. In face of all objective facts, of laws and restraints of whatever kind, he retains the feeling of his own sovereignty and in each single instance forms his decision independently, according as honour or interest, passion or calculation, revenge or renunciation, gain the upper hand in his own mind.

If therefore egoism in its wider as well as narrower sense is the root and fountain of all evil, the more highly developed Italian was for this reason more inclined to wickedness than the member of other nations at that time.

But this individual development did not come upon him through any fault of his own, but rather through an historical necessity. It did not come upon him alone, but also, and chiefly by means of Italian culture, upon the other nations of Europe, and has constituted since then the higher atmosphere which they breathe. In itself it is neither good nor bad, but necessary; within it has grown up a modern standard of good and evil — a sense of moral responsibility — which is essentially different from that which was familiar to the Middle Ages.

But the Italian of the Renaissance had to bear the first mighty surging of a new age. Through his gifts and his passions, he has become the most characteristic representative of all the heights and all the depths of his time. By the side of profound corruption appeared human personalities of the noblest harmony, and an artistic splendour which shed upon the life of man a lustre which neither antiquity nor mediaevalism either could or would bestow upon it.

THE CIVILIZATION OF THE RENAISSANCE IN ITALY.
Jacob Burckhardt

Erotologists

Jealousy inflicts horrible punishment upon those possessed by it.

Lucas Cranach (1472-1553)
Art Gallery, Weimar

Erotologists

Every age has its commentators, analysts and critics. In the field of erotology, that comprehends all humanity at all levels and in every stage of intellectual, social, and emotional development, there is a notable roster of names of physicians and alchemists, philosophers, poets, travelers, anthropologists who have devoted themselves to the study of this physiological phase. They have compiled erotic manuals. They have analyzed the amatory mores of men and women. They have expounded, soberly or exultantly, the basic physiological urges. Others have through translations brought into the public view obscure but revelatory treatises and handbooks. In some cases the purpose of publication was almost exclusively literary: in others, especially in the medical profession, the intention has been both expository and therapeutic enlightenment and sane and balanced counsel.

Among the various names of such personalities are the following:

AHMAD BIN SULAYMAN: Arab author of the Book of Age-Rejuvenation in the Power of Concupiscence. This treatise deals with various phases of sexology, along with specific recommendations for strengthening and maintaining amatory vigor.

ALBERTUS MAGNUS (1193-1280): One of the outstanding savants of the Middle Ages. Albertus Magnus studied in Padua and Bologna, and became a professor of theology at the University of Paris. His extensive knowledge and wide interests gave him the designation of Doctor Universalis. Apart from his formal philosophical speculations, he studied cosmology and physics and experimental science. In 1223 he entered the Dominican Order and became Bishop of Ratisbon. One of his pupils was Thomas Aquinas. Through his chemical studies Albertus acquired the reputation of an occultist. In one of his works, De Secretis Mulierum, he deals with the erotic theme.

ASHBEE, SIR HENRY SPENCER (1834-1900): English bibliophile. Under the pseudonym of Pisanus Fraxi he privately published a number of erotic bibliographies: Index Librorum Prohibitorum. Being Notes, Bio - Biblio - Iconographical and critical on Curious and Uncommon Books. London: c. 1877.

Centuria Librorum Absconditorum. Published in London c. 1880.

Catena Librorum Tacendorum. Published in London c. 1880. Ashbee left his books to the British Museum and his engravings to the South Kensington Museum.

BELL, T. A nineteenth century English physician who wrote Kalogynomia: The Laws of Female Beauty. This is a comprehensive sexological text that deals with amatory practices, perversions, female characteristics and defects. It was published in London in 1821.

BLOCH, IWAN (1872-1922): Noted German sexologist who sometimes wrote under the pseudonym of Dr. Eugen Dühren. Among his works are a History of English Morals, published in London by Aldor in 1936: and The Sexual Life of Our Times, published in London by Rebman, in 1908.

BURTON, SIR RICHARD (1821-1890): He was an English explorer, Orientalist, and anthropologist. He saw military service, in India, held diplomatic posts: penetrated into the holy city of Mecca, at great personal hazard, in the guise of a Pathan. He explored large tracts of Africa. Of all his experiences he wrote voluminously. As a linguist, he was interested in the tongues of Asia and as an anthropologist probed into the mores of strange tribes. His researches included many monographs on Oriental customs, particularly of an erotic nature. Burton's translation of The Arabian Nights is remarkable for its extensive anthropological commentary. He also translated a number of Oriental erotic manuals, notably the Kama Sutra.

CALCAGNINUS, CAELIUS: A medieval writer, mentioned by the sixteenth century Spanish demonographer Martin Delrio. Author of a treatise on erotic practices, entitled De Amatoria Magia.

CLAUDER, GABRIEL: A German physician who in 1661 published a dissertation on philtres. From a medical and also a historical viewpoint he discusses various types of potions: some designed as poisons, and others of presumed erotic attributes.

CLEARCHUS: Clearchus was a Greek writer of Soli, in Cyprus, who belongs in the third century B.C. He is the author of Erotica, a treatise that expounded on the nature of love. His postulates and analyses were accompanied by mythological and historical illustrations. There are fragments of the monograph still extant, in the citations and references of later writers.

DAVENPORT, JOHN: Author of two books of essays on intimate anthropological and sexual subjects. The title of one series is Aphrodisiacs and Anti-Aphrodisiacs. The other is Curiositates Eroticae Physiologiae; Or Tabooed Subjects freely Treated in Six Essays, viz.; Generation; Chastity; Marriage; Circumcision; Eunuchism; Hermaphrodism. Privately Printed. London, 1875.

DEMETRIUS: Demetrius of Phalerum was a Greek peripatetic philosopher of the fourth century B.C. He was the author of an amatory study, that is no longer extant, entitled Eroticus.

DE SADE, MARQUIS (1745-1814): A French novelist and erotologist. De Sade was notorious for his own personal and licentious life and for the scatological and lewd nature of his writings. His works investigate, in the most lavish and prurient detail, all kinds of sexual perversions, from incest and adultery to anthropophagy as an amatory stimulant. Among his novels are Les 120 Journées de Sodome, Juliette, Justine, Le Petit Fils d'Hercule.

From the Marquis de Sade is derived the term sadism, to denote an abnormality involving amatory pleasure through the infliction of pain.

DOCTOR OF MEDICINE: An early study of sexological problems and their social impacts appeared under the title of The Elements of Social Science or Physical, Sexual and Natural Religion, with a solution of the Social Problem. By a Doctor of Medicine. The author remained anonymous. The book itself was published in London by Edward Truelove, at 256 High Holborn.

ELLIS, HAVELOCK (1859-1939): An English pioneer in sexology, Ellis was a physician and a psychologist as well. Tremendously influential in promoting new public attitude toward amatory and physiological problems. Among his notable works are Man and Woman, published in London in 1930: and Studies in the Psychology of Sex, in four volumes: published in New York by Random House, 1936.

EROTIC MANUALS: Among Hindu erotic manuals, written originally in Sanskrit and later translated, most frequently into Hindi, are the following:

Ratirahasya — The Secrets of Love: by the poet Kukoka.

Panchasakya — The Five Arrows, a poem in some 600 verses. By Jyotirisha.

Rasmanjari — The Sprout of Love, by the poet Bhanudatta.

Smara Pradipa — The Light of Love, consisting of 400 verses. By the poet Gunakara.

Ratimanjari — The Garland of Love. By the poet Jayadeva.

FREUD, SIGMUND (1856-1939): Freud was an Austrian neurologist whose researches developed into the establishment of psychoanalysis. He postulated the value and significance of the unconscious, particularly the dream state: and the concept of repressed desires, notably of a sexual nature.

GALOPIN, AUGUSTE: A French physician who produced a study of the osphresiological reactions of perfumes on amatory tendencies. The monograph, published in Paris in 1889, is entitled Le Parfum de la Femme et Le Sens Olfactif dans l'Amour.

A brief but similar study of the same type was made by Lafcadio Hearn. The ancient Greek dramatist Aristophanes realized this relationship and in his Lysistrata he refers to the subject in a sexual context. Emile Zola in his novels La Terre and Germinal treats the theme from a fictional angle. A Rebours and Là-Bas, both by J. K. Huysmans, likewise contain frequent references to the impact of natural and concocted aromas on the sexual consciousness.

HAGG: Abdul Hagg Effendi is the Turkish author of the Bah-Nameh: The Book of Delight. It is a compilation of erotic tales containing aphrodisiac suggestions. Under the title of Le Livre de Volupté it was translated into French and published in Brussels in 1878.

HALEBY, OMAR: This Arab medical writer had a wide reputation in Islamic countries. In his recommendations of the use of erotic stimulants he was consistent with the practice that permitted polygamy and a multiplicity of concubines and slaves.

HIRSCHFELD, MAGNUS (1868-1935): German physician and sexologist. He specialized in psychological problems involving sexual features. He was also founder of the Sexual Research Institute of Berlin, in 1918. With Havelock Ellis, he promoted many marriage and sexual reforms.

IBN H'AZM: Muhammed Ali ibn H'azm al Andalusi was an Hispano-Arab. In the tenth century he composed an erotic treatise known as The Risala. Scholar, poet, and statesman, Ibn H'azm spent his childhood in a harem in Cordova. There he was initiated into the amatory practices

In "Vanity and Allegory of Music," the artists represent the dominance of woman, her power of subjugation.

Hans Baldung Grien (1484-1545)
Alte Pinakothek, Munich

VENUS AND ADONIS

Abraham Janssens (1575-1632)
Art Gallery, Vienna

of the feminine contingent. The Risala, written in exile in old age, is a survey of love that is both speculative and earthy, devout and scabrous. It contains anecdotes of contemporary libertines and personal encounters. An English version, by A. R. Nykl, appeared in Paris in 1931. A French rendering, under the title of Le Collier du Pigeon, by Léon Bercher, was published in Algiers in 1949.

JACOBUS: Dr. Jacobus X is the pseudonymous author of a unique conspectus entitled Untrodden Fields of Anthropology. It has been suggested that the name of the author was Dr. Jacobus Sutor. The French edition, published in Paris in 1893, and again in 1896 and 1898, is the original of the English translation.

The author, in any case. was a French army surgeon who saw service in Cochin-China, in Oceania, Tonkin, Cambodia, the West Indies, and the United States. His observations deal, in a large measure, with the sexual practices of the Orient.

JALAL AD-DIN AS-SIYUTI: The putative author of an Arabic erotic handbook entitled Kitab al-Izah fi'llm al-Nikah b-t-w-al - Kamal: The Book of Exposition of the Science of Coition. The material treats, in intimate detail, a variety of erotic practices, but the tone is free from lewdness or ribaldry. On the contrary, there is implicit in the entire exposition a sense of reverence for the cosmic force that controls all human situations, spiritual, material, and functional. An English rendering was published at the beginning of the twentieth century in Paris.

KALYANAMALLA: Hindu author of a Sanskrit erotic guide known as Ananga - Ranga. This is a course in amatory techniques, feminine ways of embellishment and heightening allurement by means of drugs, incense, magic incantations, ointments, cosmetics. An English version exists in the translation by the Orientalist Sir Richard Burton. It was privately printed in 1885, for the Kamashastra Society of London and Benares, in Cosmopoli, the cryptic designation for London.

KINSEY, A. C. (1894-1956): American zoologist who gained national and international publicity by his studies in sexual mores. The volumes appeared as Sexual Behavior in the Human Male, and Sexual Behavior in the Human Female, published in 1948 and 1953 respectively.

KSHEMENDRA: Hindu author of Samayamatrika, a study of a harlot's progress and ultimate decline.

LIEBAULT, JEAN (c. 1535-1596): French sexologist. He was attached to the Faculty of Medicine in Paris. He wrote, originally in Latin and then in a French translation in 1582, an encyclopedia of contemporary sexual knowledge entitled Thrésor des Remèdes Secrets pour les Maladies des Femmes.

The work contains recomendations on erotic stimuli in harmony with psychological or organic conditions. He discusses at great length the types of food, spices, personal hygiene, behavior, conversation and thoughts that are conducive to amatory reinforcements.

MARANON, GREGORIO (1887-1960): Spanish physician. Associated with Paul Ehrlich in Germany. He made important discoveries in sexual hormones. Professor of Endocrinology in Madrid. Wrote an essay on Don Juan and the origin of the legend. Also wrote on sexual questions, notably The Evolution of Sexuality in the Intersexual States: published in 1930.

MULLER, JOHANNES: In 1689 Muller published a doctoral dissertation entitled De Febre Amatoria. He examines particularly the sexual mores of women. With respect to amatory provocations, he discusses aphrodisiac and anaphrodisiac items, emphasizing the amatory stimulation produced by the euphoria attendant on rich foods.

NEFZAWI: Sheikh al-Iman abu Abd-Allah al-Nefzawi lived in Southern Tunisia in the sixteenth century. He is the author of The Perfumed Garden, a manual of erotic devices and procedures that, despite the revelations on sexual matters, was produced, as the author himself asserts, in no lascivious or prurient spirit. The contents range from sexual rites and medical treatment to a kind of exposé of female wiles in their erotic life. The manual belongs among the notable Oriental treatises. It was translated into English by the Orientalist Sir Richard Burton.

OVID: Publius Ovidius Naso (43 B.C. - c. 17 A.D.) was a prolific Roman poet whose popular reputation has rested during the centuries on his erotic pieces: The Ars Amatoria, a guide in amatory diversions: The Remedium Amoris, although nominally an apologetic recantation of the previous work, deals with the same theme: The Amores, a series of love poems.

In Rome, Ovid associated with the dominant social circles of the Imperial Court. Later in life, he was banished, the traditional explanation being the publication of a poem that displeased the Emperor Augustus. The place of Ovid's permanent exile was Tomis, a frontier outpost on the Euxine Sea.

SACHER-MASOCH, LEOPOLD VON (1835-1895): Austrian novelist whose works described a sexual abnormality involving erotic pleasure through infliction on oneself of pain or acts of cruelty. The perversion itself is now known as Masochism. The Venus in Furs describes the condition intimately. So with his Les Batteuses d'Hommes.

SINIBALDUS, JOHANNES BENEDICT: Italian professor of medicine. In 1642, in Rome, he published his Geneanthropoeia. This is a comprehensive textbook, written in Latin, that virtually constitutes a course in sexology and anatomy. Sinibaldus devotes considerable space to the subject of erotic stimulation, from the historical and academic viewpoint, and at the same time he gives warnings against excessive amatory practice.

STEKEL, WILHELM (1868-1940): Stekel, a friend of Freud, was a noted Viennese psychiatrist who wrote voluminously on sexual perversions, aberrations, physiological deficiencies, neurotic conditions, and in general on men and women as erotic beings.

VELDE, VAN DE, THEODOR: Contemporary Dutch physician who produced in 1928 The Ideal Marriage, a monumental treatise that has been translated into many European and Oriental languages.

VATSAYAYANA: Hindu author of an erotic handbook entitled Kama Sutra. The manual contains advice, elaborately detailed, designed for men and women, on the acquisition of amatory attraction and the means of maintaining or restoring potency. The contents range over the selection of foods, osphresiological hints, cosmetics, and philtres. The sobriety and the formal restraint, the advice to the suppliant postulate, as the introductory chapters indicate, an intelligent and prudent person, attending to Dharma and Artha, and attending to Kama also, who, by not becoming a slave to his passion, will obtain success in all his undertakings. The author thus virtually recommends an Aristotelian middle course, a golden mean that leans to neither extreme. The work was translated from the Sanskrit by Sir Richard Burton in 1883.

VENETTE, NICOLAS: A French physician of the seventeenth century. Author of a Tableau de l'Amour Conjugal: a discussion of amatory relationships, accompanied by advice on remedial techniques and on necessary physiological restraints.

H. E. W.

Crimes of Passion

Crimes of Passion

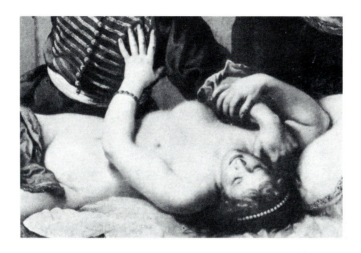

TARQUINIUS AND LUCRETIA
The Roman legend ran that Lucretia, wife of Tarquinius, was outraged by Sextus. After revealing the crime to her husband, she took her own life.
Cagnacci
S. Luca Gallery, Rome

An analysis of crimes of passion disproves yet another of the many popular fallacies regarding women. The inferiority of the weaker sex to the other in this respect is not so much numerical as that the female offenders differ from the genuine type of the male criminal in their nature. which has more analogy with the born female delinquent on the one hand and the occasional criminal on the other. But crimes of passion have, nevertheless, much in common in both sexes.

Naturally, as among men, so among women, the offenders are chiefly young.

Rarer, yet not exceptional, are the cases in which crimes of passion resulting from love have been committed at an age comparatively advanced, by women in whom youth and sexuality have a shorter cycle.

It is remarkable that female offenders of this class have also some masculine traits of disposition; such, for instance, as the love of firearms.

Finally, many women, contrary to the usual tendencies of their sex, occupy themselves with politics and become religious and political martyrs.

Sometimes the female offenders of this description take a strange pleasure in dressing themselves as men. It is true that masculine qualities are not always found in criminals alone, as is proved by the instance of Mrs. Carlyle, certainly the purest and most angelic of women, who yet as a child climbed walls and gates and loved to box with her schoolboy companions, from whom she got usually less than she gave.

In the women who commit crimes of passion there is great intensity of feeling. Indeed, their affections are infinitely more ardent than those of normal women, and they never show the absence of domestic sentiments which we noted in the born criminal.

The infanticides — who are mostly criminal from passion — are, according to Cère, almost the only female of-

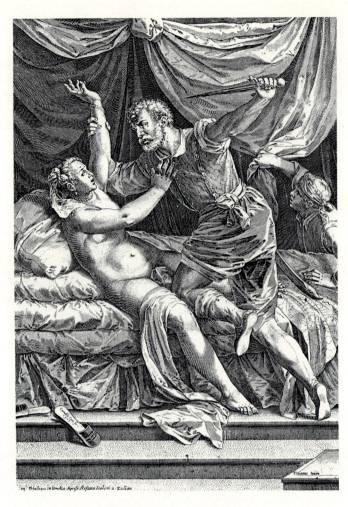

RAPE OF LUCRETIA
The ancient Roman legend recounts that Lucretia, wife of
Tarquinius, was assaulted by Sextus.

Titian (1477-1576)

fenders who, when married in the penal settlements, become excellent mothers of families.

The passion which most often betrays such women as we have described into crime is love. Strangers to the coldness of the normal woman, they love with all the intensity of Héloïse, and take a real delight in sacrificing themselves for the man they adore, and for whom they are ready to violate prejudices, custom, and even social laws.

Vinci for her lover sacrificed the long hair which was her only beauty.

Jamais sent her soldier-lover money and gifts, although she had to support herself and two children by her toil. Dumaire was disinterestedly but passionately in love with Picart, whom she assisted by paying for his studies, never demanding that he would marry her if only she might continue to live with him.

This intensity of love explains why almost all such women have formed illicit connections without being, for that reason, impure. Virginity and marriage are social institutions adapted, like all customs and institutions, to the average type — that is to say, in this case, to the sexual coldness of the normal woman. But our offenders love too passionately to submit to such laws. They are like Héloïse, who refused to marry Abelard for fear of injuring him, and declared herself proud to be called his mistress.

The greater number of infanticides are to be ascribed originally to an imprudent passion which overrides respect for social usage. Grandpré gives an instance in the infanticide who in a short time fell hopelessly in love with a stranger who had come to her neighborhood during the summer season, and whom she met in the country roads.

From this point of view, then, the woman whom passion

[150]

*The King of the Ethiopians abusing his Power as related in
a story by Voltaire.*

Moitte

betrays into crime is very different from the born offender who violates the laws of chastity from lust and love of pleasure and idleness. But all such good and passionate women have a fatal propensity to love bad men, and they fall into the power of frivolous and fickle, sometimes depraved lovers, who not only abandon them when tired of them, but often add to the cruelty of betrayal the still greater cruelty of scorn and calumny.

To all these causes we must add the unjust scorn of the world which visits on the woman what it calls her sin, but which is only an excess of love, dangerous in a society where the dominating force is egotism. Derision, and often the inhuman severity of relations, add to a sorrow which is already profound. Jamais, for instance, was repulsed by her dying father, who would not receive her last kiss; and Provensal was the recipient of a letter from her brother,

who reproached her with having dishonored her family and become a stranger to it.

Such impelling causes are secondary in the cases which we have been considering, but become the principal motive of crime in infanticides, who are, however, also moved by a kind of desire to revenge themselves on the child for the infidelity of the father.

Statistics prove unmistakably all that we have advanced by showing that illegitimate births and infanticides are in inverse, and not as might be expected, in direct ratio; that is to say, that infanticide is most frequent in districts where, illegitimate births being rarest, they are regarded with most severity.

More rarely than the other causes which we have detailed, the incentive to crime is some injury inflicted on the woman's maternal or domestic affections.

[151]

A centaur, a creature partly human and partly equine, bibulous and lustful, is represented as carrying off a young Lapith girl.

Olympia Museum, Greece

One is disposed to wonder at first at the rarity of offences committed through maternal love, since that is woman's strongest sentiment. But maternity is, so to speak, a moral prophylactic against crime and evil; for a mother hesitates to commit an offence which might separate her temporarily or permanently from her child. The idea of such a risk leads her to forgive injuries inflicted on the child himself rather than resort to violent means of revenge; and she will urge the child to forgiveness in preference to losing him as she might do if he resented his wrongs.

Moreover, maternity is pre-eminently a physiological function; while criminality, even when induced by passion, is pathological; and it is rare for the two things to be confounded.

Maternity is an intense normal feeling, and cannot therefore become a perturbing element; but the case with love is different.

In the normal woman love is weak, and only becomes intense when it has reached the stage of a pathological phenomenon.

There is yet another restraining factor which accounts for the small number of crimes arising out of maternal passion. A woman regards her child as a part of herself, providing for him and resenting in her own person the injuries inflicted on him, especially while he is little and cannot provide for himself. But when the child grows up and can look after himself, he separates from his mother, and she, while following his actions, his struggles and attempts, with affectionate interest, no longer feels bound to interfere as protectress or avenger. A wrong to her child will grieve her profoundly, but it will no longer excite her as in his infancy. To a certain degree, in short, she recalls the behavior of female animals who abandon their little ones as soon as they can fly or walk alone.

And if a crime committed out of maternal love is possible only when the children are small, for this very reason it must be rare, since an infant not having entered upon the struggle for life has few enemies, and is exposed to few injuries or persecutions. Almost the only person against whom they have to be protected or revenged is a bad or careless father, and he fortunately is not a very common phenomenon, elementary duty to his family not being the relation in which the civilized male shows himself most frequently wanting.

It is a singular fact that connected, and sometimes even confounded into a whole with maternal love, is that pas-

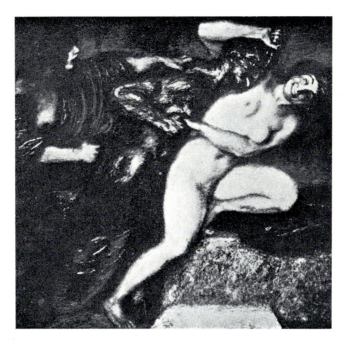

LUST

Franz von Stuck (1863-1928)

sion for dress which we found so characteristic of the born criminal.

Up to this point the analogy between male and female criminals from passion has been nearly perfect, but we have now to consider certain characteristics which, while essential to the type of the male offender, are only found in some women. Such, for instance, is the almost instantaneous explosion of vindictiveness following on the provocation. Madame Guérin, hearing that her husband was at Versailles with his mistress, flew there and stabbed him. Madame Daru, on being threatened, together with her children, more seriously than usual one evening by her drunken husband, waited till he was asleep, then thrust a knife into his heart. Spinetti cut her lover's throat immediately on his making the proposition which we have already described.

Only in some women, again, does sincere and violent remorse follow on their crime.

The women are as a rule not previously quite immaculate. Often they have bad traits which contrast with the exaggerated goodness of the male criminal, and cause them to approximate on the one hand to the born criminal, and on the other to the occasional criminal. Frequently they brood for months and years over their resentment, which is even

susceptible of alternations of forbearance and even liking towards their victim.

That is to say, that often premeditation in the woman is longer than in the man; it is also colder and more cunning, so that the crime is executed with an ability and a gloating which in the deed of pure passion are psychologically impossible. Nor does sincere penitence always follow the offence; on the contrary, there is often exultation; and rarely does the offender commit suicide.

Dav .... was seduced by a sergeant whom she passionately loved, and who had promised to marry her. He deserted her when she was pregnant, and she threw vitriol over him.

Now here was no cocotte or prostitute, who alleges desertion as the cause of a vengeance to which she has been really moved by egotism. Here is a girl who had been gravely injured, and in whose offence passion was a strong factor.

Nevertheless, there are in the case certain particulars opposed to the crime of pure impulse. Before seduction she threatened her lover with death should he desert her, thus showing that theoretically she had already conceived the deed before anything had happened to provoke it. Also she sought out her lover in a low masked ball to which she went accompanied by another man, thus showing some lightness of conduct; and finally she chose vitriol as her weapon, because, as she declared, she wished her victim to feel all the pain of death; and, so far from evincing remorse, she eagerly asked the prison doctors if the man was dead.

Equally balanced between the two sorts of crime (that ascribable to impulse and that proper to the born delinquent) is the deed of the girl Santa, who three times at a distance of months endeavored to wound her most unworthy lover (who had seduced and abandoned her), and finally did kill him with a knife.

In all these cases, then, we find not the sudden fury of passion which blinds even a good man and transforms him temporarily into a homicide, but a slower and more tenacious feeling, which produces a ferment of cruel instincts and allows time for reflection in preparing and calculating the details of the crime. It may be said, in answer to this, that the women we have described are naturally very good; and it is true that they differ but little from normal women. But this apparent contradiction diminishes when we reflect that the normal woman is deficient in moral sense, and possessed of slight criminal tendencies, such as vindictiveness, jealousy, envy, malignity, which are usually neutralized by less sensibility and less intensity of passion. Let a woman, normal in all else, be slightly more excitable than usual, or let a perfectly normal woman be exposed to grave provocations, and these criminal tendencies which are physiologically latent will take the upper hand. But then the woman does not become a criminal through the intensity of her passions (these being colder in her), but through the explosion of a latent tendency to crime which an occasion has set free. That is to say, a normal or quasi-normal woman may commit a crime of passion without being a typical criminal from impulse. Her passions are weaker (than the man's), yet strong enough to drive her to a criminal act when some outrage to her dearest feelings sets free her latent tendencies to crime. Her deed then is ascribable partly to passion and partly to an innate depravity, which yet does not detract from the fact that the offender is generally a good and even a very good woman.

We see, then, that passion alone would not be sufficient to produce a crime, but must be reinforced by suggestion. This only means in other words that suggestion is necessary in the case of women whose criminal tendencies are more latent, but for that reason profounder and more tenacious. A man who commits a crime when driven to it by strong passion, may have a great natural repugnance to the offence, which is momentarily suffocated by feeling; but a person who, even when under the influence of passion, is induced by suggestion to commit a deed of blood — that is, with leisure to calculate and to feel a horror of the action demanded — must have a lower degree of organic repulsion to crime. The latent fund of wickedness existing in the normal woman renders possible a hybrid form of criminal impulse which admits also of complicity.

Egotistic criminal impulses prove even better that crimes of passion must be the effect of a slow fermentation of the wickedness latent in the normal woman. There is a class of pure, good, affectionate women in whom the only motive for their crime is the egotistical sentiment of jealousy bred in them, by illness, accident, etc. Their offence may be regarded as originating partly in passion; but it lacks a grave cause, and is also entirely unprovoked by the victim; thus showing an analogy with the deeds of the born criminal.

THE FEMALE OFFENDER
Caesar Lombroso.

IN FLAGRANTE DELICTO

Jules Garnier (1847-1889)

Mormonism

BRIGHAM YOUNG

Brigham Young (1801-1877), the American Mormon leader, proclaimed polygamy as a tenet of Mormonism and practiced polygamy himself. He was indicted on this charge, but not convicted.

Daguerreotype: 1850

[158]

Mormonism

The Mormons are an American religious sect, consisting of six groups, founded by Joseph Smith in 1830. Mormons are also known as Latter Day Saints. The members encountered great opposition because of their principles, particularly their advocacy of polygamy. After the death of Smith, his successor, Brigham Young, published, in 1852, his doctrine of 'celestial marriage' and polygamy. Young and the Mormon leaders generally practiced plural marriage. Polygamy was publicly disavowed by the Mormons in 1890.

H. E. W.

This cartoon, published after the death of Brigham Young, the Mormon leader, is a commentary on Mormon polygamy.

ENTRANCE INTO POLYGAMY

JOSEPH SMITH

Joseph Smith (1805-1844) was the founder of the poly-gamous Mormon Church.

Contemporary Engraving

Fetishism

Madame Tallien and Josephine are dancing in puris naturalibus *before the Revolutionary Barras and the screened Napoleon.*

James Gillray (1757-1815)
Dusseldorf

Fetishism

Fetishism is a term applied to a perversion involving a sexual association with some object. The expression orignated with the French psychologist and neurologist Alfred Binet. Fetishism never appears among women.

The fetishist obtains sexual consummation onanistically by means of a visual, palpable symbol. This symbol may take the form of some item of clothing, a shoe, a hat, a stocking, hair or nails of the female concerned. The sight of an object belonging to this female, or contact with the article, or actual possession, produces the erotic stimulus.

H. E. W.

OBELISK
The monolithic sculpture in Frogner Park, Oslo. A symbolism of human conflict and effort toward spiritual heights.

THE KISS

Auguste Rodin (1840-1917)

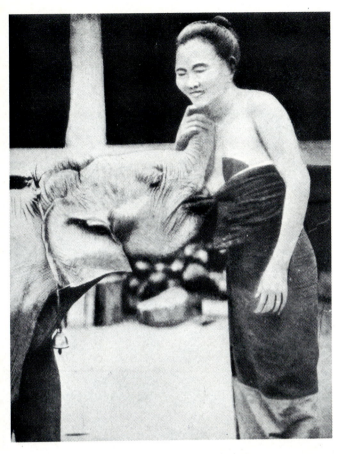

SIAMESE WOMAN SUCKLING YOUNG ELEPHANT

*Lactation, involving humans and animals, has been known
since antique legends, and is confirmed in factual instances.*
— Retzenshein

SIMON AND VERA

*The theme of woman suckling an invalid was not rare in
medieval legend.*

Rubens (1577-1640)

A strange anthropological phenomenon among tribal communities. Functional contrivances in use among Hindu ascetics.

Satan can be frightened away by exposure of the body.

Jean H. Fragonard (1732-1806)
École des Beaux-Arts, Paris

Phallic Symbolism

A Japanese instrumentarium for sexual practices.
Archives
Institute of Sexual Research, Berlin

Phallic Symbolism

The phallic symbol has historically been pervasive among all nations. And phallic worship, dedicated to the ultimate cosmic procreative force, has been a significant factor in the mores of antiquity, in Greece and the Middle East, throughout Asia and Africa, in the islands of the Pacific Ocean, down through the Renaissance and implicitly, if by more subtle and erotic indirection, as far as these contemporary times. Aristophanes, the Greek comedy writer, bases one of his major plays on this theme and on the importance of phallic power. And although the phallic rites associated with the Dionysiac cult of antiquity are no longer practiced, the concept of phallic dominance is still in flourishing ascendance.

PHALLICISM

The classic scholar whose studies have hardly exceeded the limits prescribed in the curriculum of the universities, and the biblical student whose explorations of the Hebrew Scriptures have not led him beyond the field of exegesis and theological pursuit, are ill-prepared to hear of a larger world than Greece, Rome, and Palestine, or of an archaic time which almost remands the annals of those countries into the domain of modern history. Olympian Zeus with his college of associate deities, afterward Latinized into Jupiter and his divine subordinates, and the Lord alone with his ten thousands of sacred ones, comprise their idea of the supernal world and its divinities. Beyond, they recognize a vague and misty chaos of mythologies, which, not accurately understanding, they superciliously affect to despise. Whoever would be really intelligent, must boldly explore that chaos, voyaging through the "outer world" away from Troy and Greece, as far as Ulysses went, and from biblical scenes to the very heart of the ancient empires. There is no occasion for terror, like that displayed by the mariners who sailed with Columbus into the unknown ocean. Wherever man is to be found, like instincts, passions, hopes, and ambitions will attest a common kindred. Each person's life is in some manner repeated in that of his fellows, and every human soul is a mirror in which other souls, as well as future and former events, reflect their image.

It is more than probable that the diversified customs institutions, and religions of the several nations of the world are less dissimilar in their origin than is often imagined. The differences uprose in the progress of time, the shifting scenes of climate, condition, and event. But the original ideas of existence, and the laws which pertain to all created things, are pretty much the same among the various tribes of mankind. The religions, philosophical systems and symbolisms, are outgrowths,— the aspirations of thinking and reverential men to solve and express in suitable form the facts which underlie and constitute all things.

We should therefore approach the subject of human faith and worship with candor, modesty, and respect. Men's beliefs are entitled to so much. The unwitting individual may be astonished at beholding men, the masters of the science and thought of their time, adoring gods that are represented as drunken and adulterous, and admitting extravagant stories and scandalous narrations among their religious verities. In his simplicity he may conceive that he has a right to contemn, and even to scoff at, such prodigious infatuation. But the infatuation and absurdity are only apparent. There is a fuller, profounder meaning, which sanctifies the emblems and legends which ignorant and superficial men denounce. M. Rénan speaks justly as well as eloquently: "It is sacrilege, in a religious light, this making sport of symbols consecrated by Time, wherein, too, man had deposited his first views of the divine world."

Religions were never cunningly devised by priests, or

ambitious leaders, for the purpose of enabling them to hold the human mind in abject bondage. Nor did they come into existence, full-grown, like Athené, the Jove-born; nor were they constructed from the lessons of sages or even of prophets. They were born, like men, not mature but infantile; the body and life as a single entity, without a definite evolving of the interior, symbolized idea, yet containing all potentially; so that time and growth were required to enable the intelligent mind to distinguish rightly between the form and the substance which it envelops and shadows forth. When this substance, like the human soul, has fully developed, the external forms and symbols become of little value, and are cast off and rejected like chaff from the wheat. Yet for the sake of their use they are to be valued and respected. The well-thinking medical student never indulges in ribald hilarity at or in the presence of the corpse which he dissects, from reverence for the human soul that was once its tenant. But religious symbols lose their sacredness when they are employed to supplant the idea which alone had rendered them valuable.

Let there be no contempt, then, for the Children of the Mist, who love to gaze backward into the past to ascertain what man has been, and to look within to learn what he is and ought to be. They are not prophets without inspiration, or apostles that have no mission. Behind the veil is the Shekinah; only the anointed have authority to lift aside the curtain.

Modern science somewhat audaciously has endeavored to set aside the time-honored traditions of a Golden Age. We do not undertake to controvert the new doctrine, so necessary to establish the recently-traced relationships between men and monkeys. The same social law which allows every man to choose his own company, can be extended perhaps to the selection of his kindred.

But, so far as we are able to perceive, there have been cycles of human development, analogous to the geological periods, that have been accomplished upon the earth. Men, nations, and civilizations, like the seasons, have passed over the great theatre of existence. We have often only the traces of them in a few remains of language, maufacture, and religion. Much is lost save to conjecture. Judging from our later observations of human progress, there must have been a long term of discipline that schooled them; yet, perhaps, it was the divine intuition and instinct implanted in them that enabled them to achieve so much. It is not possible, however, to extend researches back far enough to ascertain. We are not equal to the task of describing the fossils of a perished world. We are compelled to read the archaic history through the forms and mysteries of religion, and the peculiarities of language, rather than in the pages of the annalist. The amber of mythology has served to preserve to us the most of what is to be learned on these topics.

The primitive religion of mankind is perhaps only to be ascertained when we know accurately their original habitats. But this, like the gilded butterfly, eludes our search. India, Persia, Babylonia, Syria, Phoenicia, Egypt, were but colonies. The Vendidad indicates a country north of the river Oxus; and Sir William Jones, adopting the story of the learned Sufi, Mohsan Fani, declared his belief that a powerful monarchy once existed there long before the Assyrian empire; the history of which was engrafted upon that of the Hindoos, who colonized the country between the river Indus and the Bay of Bengal. In conformity with the views of this writer, Sir William accordingly describes the primeval religion of Iran and the Aryan peoples as consisting of "a firm belief that One Supreme God made the world by his power and continually governed it by his providence: — a pious fear, love, and adoration of him; — a due reverence for parents and aged persons; a paternal affection for the whole human species, and a compassionate tenderness even for the brute creation."

But, however much of truth there may be in this description, it evidently relates only to the blonde races. We see plainly enough the engrafting in "history," or rather legends, in many other countries, as well as among the Brahmins of India. The Hebrew records, tracing their patriarchs to Egypt and Assyria, are probably no exception. The Garden of Eden appears to have been well known to the king of Tyre (Ezekiel xxviii. 13-16), who is styled "the anointed cherub;" the Assyrian is also described (xxxi. 3-18) as a cedar in Lebanon, "fair by the multitude of his branches, so that all the trees of Eden that were in the garden of God envied him;" and Pharaoh, king of Egypt, is also assured that he shall "be brought down with the trees of Eden into the nether parts of the earth." From that region Abraham is reputed to have emigrated, and its traditions are probably therefore consecrated as religious legends.

If we had time and space to follow this subject, we might be able to show that in the period when the Hebrew patriarch is supposed to have removed from the region of the Upper Euphrates, revolutions were occurring there which changed the structure of society. "Your fathers," said Joshua to the assembled Israelites, "your fathers dwelt on the other side of the flood in old time, even Terah, the father of Abraham and the father of Nahor; and they served other gods." The Persian legend of "Airyana-vaeja, of the good creation which Anra-mainyas (Ahriman) full of death filled with evils," and the Hebrew story of the garden of Eden which was by the headwaters of the Oxus, Tigris, and Euphrates, where dwelt the man and the woman till the successful invasion of the Serpent, indicate the Great Religious War of which traditions exist in the principal countries of ancient time. It occurred between the nations of the East and the nations of the West, the Iranians and Turanians, the Solar and Lunar nations, the Lingacitas and the Yonijas, those who venerated images and religious symbols and those who discarded them. Vast bodies of men were compelled to abandon their homes, many of them skilled in the arts of civilization and war. Tribes and dynasties emigrated to escape slavery and destruction; and other climates received and cherished those who had been deemed unworthy to live. These events are superimposed upon the history of every people. Whether the migration mentioned by Juno of the *gens inimica,* the Trojans, from Troy to Italy, bearing its political genius and conquered divinities, depicts any actual occurrence, we do not undertake to say; but convulsions did take place, by which peoples once living as one nation, the Hindoos and Persians, Greeks and Romans, Germans and Slavs, were divided from each other and removed to other regions. The Ethiopian or Hamitic races underwent a like overturning and dispersion, probably from their contests with the blonde invaders of the North. Thus, the second chapter of Genesis describes the river Pison, as compassing the land of Ethiopia or Cush, which was evidently situated upon the Erythraean or Arabian Sea. The people of this region appear to have occupied or colonized India, Babylonia, Arabia, Syria, Egypt, and other countries of the West. They were the builder-race *par excellence;* and carried civilization, architecture, mathematical science, their arts and political institutions wherever they went. Their artisans, doubtless, erected the temples and pyramids of Egypt, India, and Babylon; excavated the mountain of Ellora, the islands of Salsette and Elephanta, the artificial caves of Bamian, the rocks of Petra and the hypogea of Egypt; built the houses of Ad in Arabia, the Cyclopean structures of India, Arabia, and the more western countries; constructed ships for the navigation of the seas and oceans, and devised the art of sculpture. Mathematics and astronomy, alphabetical as well as hieroglyphical writing, and many other sciences, perhaps those which have been *discovered* in later times, were possessed and cultivated by these "blameless Aethiopians, most ancient of men."

The Hebrew Scriptures, which have been regarded as especially the oracles of religious truth, develop the fact, as has been already suggested, of a close resemblance of the earlier Israelites with the surrounding nations. Their great progenitor, Abraham, is described as emigrating from the region of Chaldea, at the junction of the Tigris and Euphrates, in the character of a dissenter from the religion of that country. Yet he and his immediate descendants appear to have at least employed the same religious symbols and forms of worship as the people of Canaan and Phoenicia, who are recorded to have already occupied Palestine. He erected altars wherever he made a residence; and "planted a grove" or pillar in Beer-sheba, as a religious emblem.

He is also represented as conducting his son to the land of Moriah, to immolate him as a sacrifice to the Deity, as was sometimes done by the Phoenicians: and as was afterwards authorized in the Mosaic law. One of the *suffets,* or judges, Jephthah the Gileadite, in like manner sacrificed his own daughter at Mizpeh; and the place where Abraham built his altar was afterwards selected as the site for the temple of Solomon. Jacob is twice mentioned as setting up a pillar, calling the place Beth-el, and as making libations. On the occasion also of forming a treaty of amity with his father-in-law, Laban, the Syrian, he erected a pillar and directed his brethren to pile up a cairn, or heap of stones; to which were applied the names Galeed, or circle, and Mizpeh, or pillar. Monoliths, or "great stones," appear to have been as common in Palestine as in other countries, and the cairns and circles (gilgals) were equally so, as well as the mounds or "high places." The *suffets,* or "judges," and the kings, maintained them till Hezekiah. Samuel the prophet worshipped at a high place at Ramah, and Solomon at the "great stone," or high place in Gibeon. There were also priests, and we suspect *kadeshim,* stationed at them. At Mizpeh, probably at the pillar, was a seat of government of the Israelites; and Joshua set up a pillar under the oak of Shechem, by the sanctuary. Jephthah the judge made his residence at the former place, and his daughter, the Iphigenia of the Book of Judges, was immolated there. Samuel was also inaugurated there as *suffet* of Israel. There were other "great stones" mentioned, as Abel, Bethshemesh or Heliopolis; Ezel, where David met with Jonathan; and Ebenezer, erected by Samuel on the occasion of a victory over the Philistines.

But Hezekiah appears to have changed the entire Hebrew religious policy. He removed the Hermaic or Dionysiac statues, and the conical omphalic emblems of Venus-Ashtoreth; overthrew the mounds and altars, and broke in pieces the serpent of brass made by Moses, to which the people had burned incense "unto those days." Josiah afterwards also promulgated the law of Moses, and was equally iconoclastic. He removed the paraphernalia of the worship of the sun, destroyed the image of Semel, or Hermes, expelled the *kadeshim,* or consecrated men and women, from the cloisters of the Temple, and destroyed the statues and emblems of Venus and Adonis.

We have suggested that Abraham was represented in the character of a dissenter from the worship prevailing at "Ur of the Khasdim." As remarked on a subsequent page by Mr. Wake, "that some great *religious* movement, ascribed by tradition to Abraham, did take place among the Semites at an early date, is undoubted." It may have been the "Great Religious War." The religion of the patriarchs appears to have had some affinity with that of the Persians, in so much that some writers intimate an identity of origin.

This was certainly the case at a later period. Other peoples were also driven to emigration. Many Scythian nations abandoned their former seats. The Phoenicians left their country on the Erythrean Sea, and emigrated to the shores of the Mediterranean. The Pali, or shepherds on the Indus, removed to the west. A part of the population of Asiatic Ethiopia, or Beluchistan, it is supposed, also emigrated.

INFLUENCE OF THE PHALLIC IDEA
A. Wilder, M.D. (1875)

HUMAN NATURE is the same in all climes; and the workings of this same human nature are almost identical in the different stages of its growth. Hence similar and analogous ideas, beliefs, and superstitious practices are frequently evolved independently among different peoples. These are the result of suggestions arising spontaneously in the human mind at certain stages of its development, and which seem almost universal.

As a remarkable instance of this, I have drawn up the following sketch of phallic worship, which was one of those beliefs or superstitious practices which have sprung up independently, and which seems to have extensively prevailed among many nations.

It will acquire additional interest when it is considered that it is the most ancient of the superstitions of the human race, that it has prevailed more or less among all known people in ancient times, and that it has been handed down even to a very late and Christian period.

In the earlier ages the operations of nature made a stronger impression on the minds of men. Those ideas, springing from the constant observation of the mode of acting in nature, were consequently more readily suggested to the minds of all races of men in the primitive ages.

Two causes must have forcibly struck the minds of men in those early periods when observant of the operations of nature, one the generative power, and the other the productive, the active and passive causes. This double mode of production visible in nature must have given rise to comparisons with the mode of proceeding in the generation of animals, in which two causes concur, the one active and the other passive, the one male and the other female, the one as father, the other as mother. These ideas were doubtless suggested independently and spontaneously in different countries; for the human mind is so constituted that the same objects and the same operation of nature will suggest like ideas in the minds of men of all races, however widely apart.

Nature to the early man was not brute matter, but a being invested with his own personality, and endowed with the same feelings, passions, and performing the same actions. He could only conceive the course of nature from the analogy to his own actions. Generation, begetting — production, bringing forth — were thus his ideas of cause and effect. The earth was looked upon as the mould of nature, as the recipient of seeds, the nurse of what was produced in its bosom; the sky was the fecundating and fertilizing power. An analogy was suggested in the union of the male and female. These comparisons are found in ancient writers. "The sky," Plutarch says, "appeared to men to perform the functions of a father, as the earth those of a mother. The sky was the father, for it cast seed into the bosom of the earth, which in receiving them became fruitful and brought forth, and was the mother."

Columella has related, in his treatise on agriculture, the loves of nature, or the marriage of heaven and earth, which takes place in the spring of the year.

Three phases in the representation of the phallus should be distinguished; first, when it was the object of reverence and religious worship; secondly, when it was used as a protecting power against evil influences of various kinds, and as a charm or amulet against envy and the evil eye, as at the postern gate at Alatri and at Pompeii, and as frequently occurs in amulets of porcelain found in Egypt, and of bronze in Italy; thirdly, when it was the result of mere licentiousness and dissolute morals. Another cause also contributed to its reverence and frequent representation — the natural desire of women among all races, barbarous as well as civilized, to be the fruitful mother of children — especially as, among some people, women were esteemed according to the number of children they bore, and as, among the Mohammedans of the present day, it is sinful not to contribute to the population; as a symbol, therefore, of prolificacy, and as the bestower of offspring, the phallus became an object of reverence and especial worship among women. At Pompeii was found a gold ring, with the representation of the phallus on its bezel, supposed to have been worn by a barren woman. To propitiate the deity and to obtain offspring, offerings of this symbol were made in Roman temples by women, and this custom has been retained in modern times at Isernia, near Naples. Stone offerings of phalli are also made at the present day in a Buddhist temple in Peking, and for the same object Mohammedan women kiss with reverence the organ of generation of an idiot or saint. In India this worship has found its most extensive development. There young girls who are anxious for husbands, and married women who are desirous of progeny, are ardent worshippers of Siva; and his symbol, the lingam, is sometimes exhibited in enormous proportions.

In the sixteenth century, St. Foutin in the south of France, St. Ters at Antwerp, and in the last century Saints Cosmo and Damiano at Isernia, near Naples, were worshipped for the same purpose by young girls and barren women.

Sir Gardner Wilkinson records similar superstitious practices at the present day at Ekhmin in Egypt. The superstitions of the natives here ascribed the same properties to a stone in one of the sheikh's tombs, and likewise to that of the temple of Pan, which the statues of the god of generation, the patron deity of Panopolis (Ekhmim), were formerly believed to have possessed; and the modern women of Ekhmim, with similar hopes and equal credulity, offer their vows to these relics for a numerous progeny.

We may conclude with the following passage from Captain Burton, which exhibits similar customs among a rude and barbarous people of the present day: "Among all barbarians whose primal want is progeny, we observe a greater or less development of the phallic worship. In Dahomé it is uncomfortably prominent. Every street from Whydah to the capital is adorned with the symbol, and the old ones are not removed. The Dahoman Priapus is a clay figure, of any size between a giant and the pigmy, crouched upon the ground, as if contemplating its own attributes. The head is sometimes a wooden block rudely carved, more often dried mud, and the eyes and teeth are supplied by cowries. The tree of life is anointed with palm-oil, which drips into a pot or a shard placed below it, and the would-be mother of children prays that the great god Legba will make her fertile."

PHALLIC WORSHIP.
H. M. Westropp. 1875

It will not be necessary for me to give details of the rites by which the phallic superstition is distinguished, as they may be found in the works of Dulaure, Payne Knight, and other writers. I shall refer to them, therefore, only so far as may be required for the due understanding of the subject to be considered — *the influence of the phallic idea in the religions of antiquity*. The first step in the inquiry is to ascertain the origin of the superstition in question. Faber ingeniously referred to a primitive universal belief in a great father, the curious connection seen to exist between nearly all non-Christian mythologies, and he saw in phallic worship a degradation of this belief. Such an explanation as this is, however, not satisfactory, since, not only does it require the assumption of a primitive divine revelation, but proof is still wanting that all peoples have, or ever had, any such notion of a great parent of mankind as that supposed to have been revealed. And yet there is a valuable germ of truth in this hypothesis. The phallic superstition is founded essentially in the family idea. Captain Richard Burton recognized this truth when he asserted that "amongst all barbarians whose primal want is progeny, we observe a greater or less development of the phallic worship." This view, however, is imperfect. There must have been something more than a mere desire for progeny

to lead primitive man to view the generative process with the peculiar feelings embodied in this superstition. We are, in fact, here taken to the root of all religions — awe at the mysterious and unknown. That which the uncultured mind cannot understand is viewed with dread or veneration, as it may be, and the object presenting the mysterious phenomenon may itself be worshipped as a fetish, or the residence of a presiding spirit. But there is nothing more mysterious than the phenomena of generation, and nothing more important than the final result of the generative act. Reflection on this result would naturally cause that which led to it to be invested with a certain degree of superstitious significance. The feeling generated would have a double object, as it had a double origin — wonder at the phenomenon itself and a perception of the value of its consequences. The former, which is the most simple, would lead to a veneration for the organs whose operation conduced to the phenomena — hence the superstitious practices connected with the phallus and the yoni among primitive peoples. In this, moreover, we have the explanation of numerous curious facts observed among eastern peoples. Such is the respect shown by women for the generative organ of dervishes and fakirs. Such also is the Semitic custom referred to in the Hebrew Scriptures as "the putting of the hand under the thigh," which is explained by the Talmudists to be the touching of that part of the body which is sealed and made holy by circumcision: a custom which was, up to a recent date, still in use among the Arabs as the most solemn guarantee of truthfulness.

The second phase of the phallic superstition is that which arises from a perception of the value of the consequences of the act of generation. The distinction between this and the preceding phase is that, while the one has relation to the organs engaged, the other refers more particularly to the chief agent. Thus, the father of the family is venerated as the generator; this authority is founded altogether on the act and consequences of generation. We thus see the fundamental importance, as well as the phallic origin, of the family idea. From this has sprung the social organization of all primitive peoples.

An instance in point may be derived from Mr. Hunter's account of the Santals of Bengal. He says that the classification of this interesting people among themselves depends, "not upon social rank or occupation, but upon the family basis." This is shown by the character of the six great ceremonies in a Santal's life, which are: "admission into the family; admission into the tribe; admission into the race; union of his own tribe with another by marriage; formal dismission from the living race by incremation; lastly, a reunion with the departed fathers."

We may judge from this of the character of certain customs which are widespread among primitive peoples, and the phallic origin of which has long been lost sight of. The value set on the results of the generative act would naturally make the arrival at the age of puberty an event of peculiar significance. Hence, we find various ceremonies performed among primitive, and even among civilized, peoples at this period of life. Often when the youth arrives at manhood other rites are performed to mark the significance of the event.

Marriage, too, derives an importance from its consequences which otherwise it would not possess. Thus, among many peoples it is attended with certain ceremonies denoting its object, or, at least, marking it as an event of peculiar significance in the life of the individual, or even in the history of the tribe. The marriage ceremonial is especially fitted for the use of phallic rites or symbolism; the former, among semi-civilized peoples, often being simply the act of consummation itself, which appears to be looked on as part of the ceremony. The symbolism we have ourselves retained to the present day in the wedding-ring, which must have had a phallic origin, if, as appears probable, it originated in the Samothracian mysteries. Nor does the influence of the phallic idea end with life. The veneration entertained for the father of the family as the "generator," led in time to peculiar care being taken of the bodies of the dead; and, finally, to the worship of ancestors, which, under one form or another, distinguished all the civilized nations of antiquity, as it does even now most of the peoples of the heathen world.

SERPENT SYMBOLISM ASSOCIATED WITH PHALLIC WORSHIP.

That we have, in the Mosaic account of the "fall," a phallic legend, is evident from other considerations connected with the narrative. The most important relate to the introduction of the serpent on the scene, and the position it takes as the inciting cause of the sinful act. We are here reminded of the passage already quoted from Clemens Alexandrinus, who tells us that the serpent was the special symbol of the worship of Bacchus. Now, this animal holds a very curious place in the religions of the civilized peoples of antiquity. Although, in consequence of the influence of later thought, it came to be treated as the personification of evil, and as such appears in the Hebrew legend of the fall, yet before this the serpent was the symbol of wisdom and healing. In the latter capacity it appears even in connection with the exodus from Egypt. It is, however, in its character as a symbol of wisdom that it more especially claims our attention, although these ideas are intimately connected — the power of healing being merely a phase of wisdom. From the earliest times of which we have any historical notice, the serpent has been connected with the gods of wisdom. This animal was the especial symbol of *Thoth* or *Taaut*, a primeval deity of Syro-Egyptian mythology, and of all those gods, such as *Hermes* and *Seth*, who can be con-

nected with him. This is true also of the third member of the primitive Chaldean triad, *Héa* or *Hoa*. According to Sir Henry Rawlinson, the most important titles of this deity refer "to his functions as the source of all knowledge and science." Not only is he "the intelligent fish," but his name may be read as signifying both "life" and a "serpent," and he may be considered as "figured by the great serpent which occupies so conspicuous a place among the symbols of the gods on the black stones recording Babylonian benefactions." The serpent was also the symbol of the Egyptian *Kneph*, who resembled the *Sophia* of the Gnostics, the Divine Wisdom. This animal, moreover, was the *Agathodaemon* of the religions of antiquity — the giver of happiness and good fortune. It was in these capacities, rather than as having a phallic significance, that the serpent was associated with the sungods, the Chaldean *Bel*, the Grecian *Apollo*, and the Semitic *Seth*.

But whence originated the idea of the wisdom of the serpent which led to its connection with the legend of the "fall"? This may, perhaps, be explained by other facts which show also the nature of the wisdom here intended. Thus, in the annals of the Mexicans, the first woman, whose name was translated by the old Spanish writers *"the woman of our flesh,"* is always represented as accompanied by a great male serpent. This serpent is the Sun-god *Tonacatl-coatl*, the principal deity of the Mexican pantheon; and the goddess-mother of primitive man is called *Cihua-Cohuatl*, which signifies *woman of the serpent*. According to this legend, which agrees with that of other American tribes, a serpent must have been the father of the human race. This notion can be explained only on the supposition that the serpent was thought to have had at one time a human form. In the Hebrew legend the tempter speaks; and "the old serpent having two feet," of Persian mythology, is none other than the evil spirit Ahriman himself. The fact is that the serpent was only a symbol, or at most an embodiment, of the spirit which it represented, as we see from the belief of certain African and American tribes, which probably preserves the primitive form of this supposition. Serpents are looked upon by these peoples as embodiments of their departed ancestors, and an analogous notion is entertained by various Hindu tribes. No doubt the noiseless movement and the activity of the serpent, combined with its peculiar gaze and marvellous power of fascination, led to its being viewed as a spirit-embodiment, and hence also as the possessor of wisdom. In the spirit-character ascribed to the serpent, we have the explanation of the association of its worship with human sacrifice noted by Mr. Fergusson — this sacrifice being really connected with the worship of ancestors.

It is evident, moreover, that we may find here the origin of the idea of evil sometimes associated with the ser-

HERCULES AND OMPHALE
Omphale, the Lydian queen, has set Hercules to women's work.

Bartolomaeus Spranger
Kunsthistorisches Museum, Vienna

[175]

pent-god. The Kafir and the Hindu, although he treats with respect any serpent which may visit his dwelling, yet entertains a suspicion of his visitant. It may, perhaps, be the embodiment of an *evil* spirit, or for some reason or other it may desire to injure *him*. Mr. Fergusson states that "the chief characteristic of the serpents throughout the east in all ages seems to have been their power over the wind and rain," which they gave or withheld according to their good or ill-will towards man. This notion is curiously confirmed by the title given by the Egyptians to the Semitic god *Seti (Seth) - Typhon,* which was the name of the Phoenician evil principle, and also of a destructive wind, thus having a curious analogy with the "typhoon" of the Chinese seas. When the notion of a duality in nature was developed, there would be no difficulty in applying it to the symbols or embodiments by which the idea of wisdom was represented in the animal world. Thus, there came to be, not only good, but also bad, serpents, both of which are referred to in the narrative of the Hebrew exodus, but still more clearly in the struggle between the good and the bad serpents of Persian mythology, which symbolized Ormuzd, or Mithra, and the evil spirit Ahriman. So far as I can discover, the serpent-symbol has not a *direct* phallic reference, nor, after all, is its attribute of wisdom the most essential. The idea most intimately associated with this animal was *life,* not present, but future, and ultimately, no doubt, *eternal.* Thus the snake *Bai* was figured as guardian of the doorways of those chambers of Egyptian tombs which represented the mansions of heaven. A sacred serpent appears to have been kept in all the Egyptian temples, and we are told that "many of the subjects, in the tombs of the kings at Thebes in particular, show the importance it was thought to enjoy in a future state." The use of crowns formed of the asp, or sacred *Thermuthis,* given to sovereigns, and divinities, particularly to Isis, the goddess of life and healing, was, doubtless, intended to symbolize eternal life. This notion is quite consistent with the ideas entertained by the Phoenicians as to the serpent, which they supposed to have the quality "of putting off its old age, and assuming a second youth."

THE PHALLIC IDEA
G. S. Wake. 1875.

Prostitution

Prostitution

THE HISTORY OF PROSTITUTION

Prostitution, which is co-eval with man's first erotic consciousness, evolved into religious and social directions. The ancient hierodouloi, the temple prostitutes, acquired hieratic and sacrosanct attributes in Greece and Egypt, in Babylonia and India: while the growth of urban life and stabilized society created, in regard to prostitution, a domestic, social, national and finally global problem.

In Rome prostitution was an established fact. There were, in a wide sense, two types of harlot or meretrix. There were those who were recognized officially, had to register, and pay the meretricium tax for the licentia stupri. The other class consisted of clandestine lupae — she-wolves — unregistered, who lived nowhere in particular, merely wandering through the streets, posing on the steps of monuments, halting at public benches, near aqueducts, in the vicinity of tombstones. They were termed erratica scrota.

For registered lupae there were touts, admissarii, who accosted prospective customers in public thoroughfares and offered to guide them.

Cryptic lupae were euphemistically called dancers, saltatrices, or flute-players, fidicinae, or tibicinae, lyre-players. They were the bonae meretrices, the delictae and pretiosae — invited to dinners, kept in the higher social levels.

The practice was so prevalent, so accepted, that there are no fewer than twenty-five synonyms for the meretrix. Amica, a mistress, is frequent in the poets: so too is domina. Isidore of Seville calls them, generically, fornicatrices. Lupa, actually a she-wolf, is associated with the nurse of Romulus, named Acca Larentia. She was a favorite prostitute of Faustulus' fellow shepherds. The dwelling of the lupa was the lupanar, the lair. Meretrix itself is strictly a professional harlot who takes merx, payment. Moecha, of Greek origin, means an adulteress. The poets use pellex as a synonym for a kept woman, a concubine, a mistress.

The comic poet Plautus uses the term prostibula. These prostibulae were again designated by a specific term relating to their status, their character, their mores within their occupation. An alicaria frequented the mills. One who waited for a client at home was known as a caserita. The copa was a kind of serving maid attached to inns. Foraria was one who frequented public thoroughfares. A night hag was noctuvigila. One who associated with foreigners or who was herself of foreign origin was called peregrina. Proseda sat in wait, in public.

Other terms include: cuadrantaria, one whose favors are very cheap — a 'quarter' of the coin called the as. Vaga wanders the streets. Scrantia, scratta, scratia are generic terms. Scortum is a harlot. Scortillum is a diminutive of the same term.

Before passing to the subject of prostitution in Greece, a glance at Egypt, and those nations of Asia which seem to have preceded Greece in civilization, may not be out of place.

Egypt was famous for her courtesans before the time of Herodotus. Egyptian blood runs warm; girls are nubile at ten. Under the Pharaohs, if ancient writers are to be believed, there existed a general laxity of moral principle, especially among young females. Their religion was only too suggestive. The deities Isis and Osiris were the types of the sexes. A statue of the latter, a male image, made of gold, was carried by the maidens at festivals, and worshiped by the whole people. Nor were the rites of Isis more

[179]

modest. "At the festival at Bubastis," says Herodotus, "men and women go thither in boats on the Nile, and when the boats approach a city they are run close to the shore. A frantic contest then begins between the women of the city and those in the boats, each abusing the other in the most opprobrious language, and the women in the boats conclude the performance by lascivious dances, in the most undisguised manner, in sight of the people, and to the sound of flutes and other musical instruments." There is little reason to doubt that the temples, like those of Baal, were houses of prostitution on an extensive scale. Herodotus remarks significantly that a law in Egypt forbade

spread throughout Europe, and was much celebrated in Greece. Rhadopis, a Thracian by birth, led the life of a prostitute in Egypt with such success, that she not only bought her own freedom from the slavedealer who had taken her there on speculation, but, if the Egyptians are to be believed, built a pyramid with her savings. A large portion of her story is doubtless mythical, but enough remains to warrant the opinion that she was, though a prostitute, a wealthy and highly considered person.

In Chaldaea, too, religion at first connived at, and then commanded prostitution. Every Babylonian female was obliged by law to prostitute herself once in her life in the

SYMPOSIUM
Alcibiades, the Greek statesman and friend of Socrates, is represented among the hetairae. An ancient Greek symposium was an occasion for intellectual, literary discussion, accompanied by moderate eating and drinking. Flute-girls and hired female entertainers furnished music and dance.
Hellenistic Relief
National Museum, Naples

sexual intercourse within the walls of a temple, and exacted of both sexes that intercourse should be followed by ablution before the temple was entered.

Where piety required such sacrifices, it is not surprising that public morals were loose. It was not considered wholly shameful for an Egyptian to make his living by the hire of his daughter's person, and a king is mentioned who resorted to this plan in order to discover a thief. Such was the astonishing appetite of the men, that young and beautiful women were never delivered to the embalmer until they had been dead some days, a miserable wretch having been detected in the act of defiling a recently-deceased virgin! Of course, in such a society, there was no disgrace in being a prostitute. The city of Naucratis owed its wealth and fame to the beauty of its courtesans, whose reputation

temple of the Chaldaean Venus, whose name was Mylitta. Herodotus appears to have seen the park and grounds in which this singular sacrifice was made. They were constantly filled with women with strings bound round their hair. Once inside the place, no woman could leave it until she had paid her debt, and had deposited on the altar of the goddess the fee received from her lover. Some, who were plain, remained there as long as three years; but, as the grounds were always filled with a troop of voluptuaries in search of pleasure, the young, the beautiful, the highborn seldom needed to remain over a few minutes. This strange custom is mentioned by the prophet Baruch, who introduces one of the women reproaching her neighbor that she had not been deemed worthy of having her girdle of cord burst asunder by any man. Similar statements are made by Strabo and other ancient writers. At the time of Alexander the Great the demoralization had reached a climax. Babylonian banquets were scenes of unheard-of infamies. When the meal began, the women sat modestly enough in presence of their fathers and husbands; but, as the wine went round, they lost all restraint, threw off one garment after another, and enacted scenes of glaring immodesty. And these were the ladies of the best families.

The Mylitta of Chaldaea became Astarte in Phoenicia, at Carthage, and in Syria. Nothing was changed but the name; the voluptuous rites were identical. In addition to the forced prostitution in the temples, however, the Phoenicians

successors in empire, the early Persians. Their Venus was named Mithra, in honor of whom festivals were given at which human nature was horribly outraged. Fathers and daughters, sons and mothers, husbands and wives sat together at the table, while voluptuous dances and music inflamed their senses, and when the wine had done its work, a promiscuous combat of sensuality began which lasted all night. Details of such scenes must be left to other works, and veiled in a learned tongue.

The Greek mythology supposes obviously a relaxed state of public morals. What period in the history of the nation it may be assumed to reflect is, however, by no means

These sculptured figures, with the caption To The Four Sisters, *were on display in a Roman lupanar.*
State Museum, Berlin

and most of their colonies maintained for many years the practice of requiring their maidens to bestow their favors on any strangers who visited the country. Commercial interest, no doubt, had some share in promoting so scandalous a custom. On the high shores of Phoenicia, as at Carthage and in the island of Cyprus, the traveler sailing past in his boat could see beautiful girls, arrayed in light garments, stretching inviting arms to him.

Originally the sum paid by the lover was offered to the goddess, but latterly the girls kept it, and it served to enhance their value in the matrimonial market. In some places the girl was free if she chose to abandon her hair to the goddess, but Lucian notes that this was an uncommonly rare occurrence.

Very similar were the customs of the Lydians and their

certain. It is not reasonable to suppose that the Homeric poems were composed for immodest audiences, and it would perhaps be fairer to lay the blame of the mythological indecencies at the door of the age which polished and improved upon them, rather than of that which is entitled to the credit of their conception in the rough.

Our first reliable information regarding the morals of the Greek women, passing over, for the present, the legislation ascribed to Lycurgus, is found in the ordinances of Solon. Draco is supposed to have affixed the penalty of death indiscriminately to rape, seduction, and adultery. It has been conjectured that the safety-valve used at that time, ordinary prostitution being unknown, was a system of religious prostitution in the temples, borrowed from and analogous to the plan already described. This, however, is mere conjecture.

Solon, while softening the rigors of the Draconian code, by law formally established houses of prostitution at Athens, and filled them with female slaves. They were called *Dicteria*, and the female tenants *Dicteriades*. Bought with the public money, and bound by law to satisfy the demands of all who visited them, they were in fact public servants, and their wretched gains were a legitimate source of revenue to the state. Prostitution became a state monopoly, and so profitable that, even in Solon's lifetime, a superb temple, dedicated to Venus the courtesan, was built out of the fund accruing from this source. The fee charged, however, appears to have been small. In Solon's time, the Dicteriades were kept widely apart from the Athenian women of repute. They were not allowed to mix in religious ceremonies or to enter the temples. When they appeared in the streets they were obliged to wear a particular costume as a badge of infamy. They forfeited what rights of citizenship they may have possessed in virtue of their birth. A procurer or procuress who had been instrumental in introducing a free-born Athenian girl to the Dicterion incurred the penalty of death. Nor was the law content with branding with infamy prostitutes and their accomplices alone. Their children were bastards; that is to say, they could not inherit property, they could not associate with other youths, they could not acquire the right of citizenship without performing some signal act of bravery, they could not address the people in the public assemblies. Finally, to complete their ignominy, they were exempt from the sacred duty of maintaining their parents in old age.

These regulations, for which Solon obtained the praise of Athenian philosophers, were not long maintained in force. Tradition imputed to the profligacy of the Pisistratidae a relaxation of the laws concerning prostitutes. It was believed that the sons of Pisistratus not only gave to the Dicteriades the freedom of the city, but allotted to them seats at banquets beside the most respectable matrons, and, on certain days each year, turned them into their father's beautiful gardens, and let loose upon them the whole petulance of the Athenian youth. The law against procuresses was modified, a fine being substituted for death. "About the same time," says the scandalous Greek chronicle, "the death-penalty for adultery was also commuted for scourging."

Still, notwithstanding this falling off, it would appear that Athens was more moral than her neighbors, Corinth and Sparta. The former, then the most flourishing sea-port of Greece, was filled with a very low class of prostitutes. No laws regulated the subject. Any female who chose could open house for the accommodation of travelers and seamen, and, though Corinth was yet far from the proverbial celebrity it afterward obtained for its prostitutes, there is no doubt they bore a fearful proportion to the aggregate population of the port. At Sparta the case was different. In the system of legislation which bears the name of Lycurgus, the individual was sacrificed to the state: the female to the male. Women were educated for the sole purpose of bearing robust children. Virgins were allowed to wrestle publicly with men. Girls were habited in a robe open at the skirts, which only partially concealed the person in walking, whence the Spartan women acquired an uncomplimentary name. A Spartan husband was authorized to lend his wife to any handsome man for the purpose of begetting children. That these laws, the skillfully contrived appeals to the sensual appetites, and the constant spectacle of nude charms, must have led to a general profligacy among the female sex, is quite obvious. Aristotle affirms positively that the Spartan women openly committed the grossest acts of debauchery. Hence it may be inferred that prostitutes by profession were unnecessary at Sparta, at all events until a late period of its history.

After the Persian wars, the subject of Athenian prostitution is revealed in a clearer light. As a reaction from the looseness of the age of the Pisistratidae, the Solonian laws were reaffirmed and their severity heightened. It has been imagined, from certain obscure passages in Greek authors, that the courtesans formed several corporations, each of which was responsible for the acts of all its members. They were liable to vexatious prosecutions for such acts as inciting men to commit crime, ruining thoughtless youths, fomenting treason against the state, or committing impiety. Against such charges it was rarely possible to establish a sound defense. If the accuser was positive, the Areopagus, notoriously biased against courtesans, unhesitatingly condemned the culprit to death, or imposed on her corporation a heavy fine. In this way, says an old author, the state frequently contrived to get back from these women the money they obtained from their lovers. Before the famous case of Phryne, they were wholly at the mercy of their profligate associates. A man only needed to threaten an accusation of impiety or the like to obtain a receipt in full. Phryne, so long the favorite of the Athenians, was thus accused of various vague offenses by a common informer named Euthias. Her friend Bacchis fortunately persuaded Hyperides, the orator, to undertake her case, and he softened the judges by exhibiting her marvelous beauty in a moment of affected passion. "Henceforth," says the hetaira Bacchis to Myrrhina, "our profits are secured by law."

At this time, that is to say, at the height of Athenian prosperity, there were four classes of women who led dissolute lives at Athens. The highest in rank and repute were the *Hetairae*, or kept women, who lived in the best part of the city, and exercised no small influence over the manners and even the politics of the state. Next came the *Auletrides*, or flute-players, who were dancers as well. They were usually foreigners, bearing some resemblance to the opera-

TEMPLE PROSTITUTION
*In antiquity, in Greece, Rome, Egypt, and the Middle
East, temple prostitution was associated with divine rituals.
In Greece the prostitutes were known as hierodouloi.*
Temple of Cybele
Drawing of Nazarine School: c. 1820

dancers of the last century, and they combined the most unblushing debauchery with their special calling. The lowest class of prostitutes were the *Dicteriades,* already mentioned. They were originally bound to reside at the Piraeus, the seaport of Athens, some four miles from the city, and were forbidden to walk out by day, or to offend the eyes of the public by open indecency. Lastly came the *Concubines,* who were slaves owned by rich men with the knowledge and consent of their wives, serving equally the passions of their master and the caprices of their mistress. These all paid a tax to the state, called *Pornikon Telos,* which was farmed out to speculators, who levied it with proverbial harshness upon the unfortunate women. In the time of Pericles the revenue from this source was large.

All classes, too, wore garments of many colors. The law originally specified "flowered robes" as the costume of courtesans; but this leading to difficulties, a further enactment prohibited prostitutes from wearing precious stuffs, such as scarlet or purple, or jewels. Thenceforth the custom,

which appears to have been general throughout the Greek cities and colonies, prescribed cheap robes, with flowers or stripes of many colors embroidered or painted on them. To this a part of the women added garlands of roses. It was lawful in some cities for courtesans to wear light, transparent garments; but at Sparta, as may be imagined, the reverse was the rule, semi-nudity being the badge of virtuous women.

Perhaps the most singular of the marks by which a Greek courtesan was known was her hair. It is said that no law prescribed the habit; if so, it must have been a sort of *esprit de corps* which led all courtesans to dye their hair of a flaxen or blonde color. Allusions to this custom abound in the light literature of Greece. Frequently a flaxen wig was substituted for the dyed locks. At a very late period in the history of Greece, modest women followed the fashion of sporting golden hair. This forms one of the subjects of reprimand addressed to the women of Greece by the early Christian preachers.

[183]

THE DICTERIADES, OR COMMON PROSTITUTES OF ATHENS

This class approaches more nearly than any other to the prostitutes of our day, the main difference being that the former were bound by law to prostitute themselves when required to do so, on the payment of the fixed sum, and that they were not allowed to leave the state. Their home. as mentioned already, was properly at the port of Piraeus. An open square in front of the citadel was their usual haunt. It was surrounded with booths, where petty trade or gambling was carried on by day. At nightfall the prostitutes swarmed into the square. Some were noisy and obscene; others quiet, and armed with affected modesty. When a man passed on his way from the port to the city, the troop assailed him. If he resisted, coarse abuse was lavished on him. If he yielded, there was the temple of Venus the Courtesan close by, and there was the wall of Themistocles, under the friendly shelter of either of which the bargain could be consummated. Were the customer nice, the great dicterion was not far distant, and a score or more of smaller rivals were even nearer at hand, as a well-known sign was there to testify.

The Dicteria were under the control of the municipal police. The door was open night and day, a bright curtain protecting the inmates from the eye of the passer-by; and in the better class of establishments, a fierce dog, chained in the vestibule, served as sentinel. At the curtain sat an old woman, often a Thessalian and a pretended witch, who received the money before admitting visitors. Originally the fee was an obolus — about three cents; but this attempt to regulate the value of a variable merchandise was soon abandoned. Within, at night, the sounds of music, revelry, and dancing might be constantly heard. The visitor was not kept in suspense. The curtain passed, he was in full view of the dicteriades, standing, sitting, or lying about the room; some engaged in smoothing their blonde hair, some in conversation, some anointing themselves with perfumery. The legal principle with regard to the dicteriades appears to have been that they should conceal nothing; no doubt in contrast to the irregular prostitutes, of whom something will be said presently. There was no rule, however, forbidding the wearing of garments in the dicterion, but the common practice appears to have been to dispense with them, or to wear a light scarf thrown over the person. This custom was observed by day as well as by night, and a visitor has described the girls in a large dicterion as standing in a row, in broad daylight, without any robes or covering.

It seems that in later times any speculator had a right to set up a dicterion on paying the tax to the state. An Athenian forfeited his right of citizenship by so doing; but,

as a popular establishment was very lucrative, avaricious men frequently embarked in the business under an assumed name. Comic writers have lashed these wretches severely. On paying the tax to the state regularly, the *pornobosceion*, or master of the house, acquired certain rights. The dicterion was an inviolable asylum, no husband being allowed to pursue his wife, or the wife her husband, or the creditor his debtor, within its walls. Public decency requires, says Demosthenes, that men shall not be exposed in houses of prostitution. It was not, however, considered wholly shameful to frequent such places.

There appear to have been attached to these dicteria schools of prostitution, where young women were initiated into the most disgusting practices by females who had themselves acquired them in the same manner. Alexis vigorously describes the frauds taught in these places, while there is a shocking significance in an expression of Athenaeus — "You will be well satisfied with the performance of the women in the dicteria."

Besides these regular dicteriades, there were at Athens, as there have been in every large city, a number of women who exercised the calling of prostitutes, without properly belonging to any of the recognized classes. They were sometimes called free dicteriades, sometimes she-wolves, and also cheap hetairae. Some were native Athenians who had been seduced and abandoned, and who, led by stings of conscience and idleness to pursue their career, had still an invincible repugnance to adopt the flowered robe and yellow hair of the regular courtesan. They roamed the Piraeus, and even the streets of Athens, after dark, eking out a miserable subsistence by the hardest of trades, and haunting the dark recesses of old houses or the shade of trees. Others, again, were old hetairae whose charms had faded, and who sought a scanty subsistence where they were not known, and shrank from encountering the eye of a lover where the friendly shade of night would not hide the ravages of time. Others were the servants of hotels and taverns, who were always expected to serve the caprices of visitors.

All of these led a most miserable life. Now and then we hear of one or two of them meeting a rich and inexperienced traveler, after which the heroine of the exploit naturally ascended to the rank of hetaira; but, in general, their customers were the lowest of the port people — sailors, fishermen, farm-servants. Their price was a meal, a fish, a handful of fruit, or a bottle of wine. One poor creature, who belonged to no class in particular, but acquired some celebrity by being kept by the orator Ithatocles, was named Didrachma because she offered the favors to the public generally for two drachmas, about thirty-five cents.

Perhaps the most curious fact in reference to these prostitutes is the singular predominance of old women among them. It appears to have been adopted as an invariable rule for this sort of courtesans to paint their faces with a thick ointment, and it is even said that the great painters of Greece did not disdain to beguile their leisure hours by thus improving upon nature. Of course, under this disguise, it was impossible to distinguish a young face from an old one. An aged prostitute thus bedizened would place herself at an open window with a sprig of myrtle in her hand, with which she would beckon to people in the street. When a customer was found, a servant would open the door and conduct him in silence to the chamber of her mistress. Before entering he paid the sum demanded, when he found himself in a room lighted only by a feeble glimmer passing through the curtain, which now hung down over the window. In such a twilight the most venerable old woman could not be distinguished from a Venus.

THE AULETRIDES, OR FLUTE-PLAYERS

Female flute-players were a common accompaniment to an Athenian banquet. The flute, which in modern times is played by men, was rarely seen in male hands in Greece. Though the fable ascribed its invention to the god Pan, and its development to the mythical king Midas, it was monopolized at a very early period by women, who consoled themselves for the ravages it wrought in their beauty by the power of fascination it imparted among a people intensely musical. Flute-playing soon became an essential rite in the service of certain deities. Ceres was invariably worshiped to the sound of the flute. And when the Athenians had once tried the experiment of listening to flute-players after dinner, they never would dine in company without them.

Thebes appears to have been the native city of the earliest famous flute-players, but before long the superior beauty of the Asiatic girls — Ionians and Phrygians — drove their Theban rivals out of the field. Dancing was combined with flute-playing, and in this art the Asiatics bore the palm from the world. During the golden days of Greece, numbers of beautiful girls were every year imported into Athens from Miletus and the other Ionic ports in Asia Minor, just as in more modern times a similar trade was carried on between Trebizond and Constantinople.

An Athenian hired his flute-players as a modern European noble hires his band. They charged so much for their musical performances, reserving the right of accepting presents in the course of the evening. Some were singers as well as performers. At each course a new air was played, increasing in tenderness and expression as the wine circulated. It is stated that the sounds of a good flute-concert excited people to such a state of phrensy that they would take off their rings and jeweled ornaments to throw them to the performers: those who have witnessed a triumphant operatic soirée can readily believe the statement. But the fair artists did not wholly rely on their music for their success. The performer danced while she played, accompanying every note with a harmonious movement of the body. There is no doubt these dances were in the highest degree immoral and lascivious. Athenaeus tells a story of an embassy from Arcadia waiting upon King Antigonus, and being invited to dinner. After the hunger of the venerable guests was appeased, Phrygian flute-players were introduced. They were draped in semi-transparent veils, arranged with much coquetry. At the given signal they began to play and dance, balancing themselves alternately on each foot, and gradually increasing the rapidity of their movements. As the performance went on, the dancers uncovered their heads, then their busts; lastly, they threw the veils aside altogether, and stood before the wondering ambassadors with only a short tunic around the loins. In this state they danced so indecently that the aged Arcadians, excited beyond control, forgot where they were, and rushed upon them. The king laughed; the courtiers were shocked at such ill-breeding, but the dancers discharged the sacred duty of hospitality.

A flute-player who had achieved a success of this kind was enabled to conclude a lucrative bargain for other performances. We find allusions to fees as high as two talents (say $2500) and fifty pieces of gold, though these were evidently unusual charges. Many of the most fashionable flute-players were slaves who had been brought to Greece by speculators. They were commonly sold by auction at the dinner-table, when their owner judged that the enthusiasm of the guests had attained the highest point. An anecdote is told of one of the most esteemed names in Greek philosophy in reference to this strange custom. He was dining with a party of young men, when a youthful flute-player was introduced. She crept to the philosopher's feet, and seemed to shelter herself from insult under the shadow of his venerable beard; but he, a disciple of Zeno, spurned her, and burst forth into a strain of moralizing. Piqued by the affront, the girl rose, and played and danced with inimitable grace and pruriency. At the close of the performance her owner put her up to auction, and one of the first bidders was the philosopher. She was adjudged to another, however, and the white-haired sage so far forgot his principles as to engage in a fierce conflict with the victor for the possession of the prize. Hand to hand battles on these occasions were common in the best society at Athens, and a flute-player in fashion made a boast of the riots she had caused. Of the fortunes realized by successful artists in this line, an idea may be formed from the gorgeous presents made to the Delphian oracle by flute-players, and from the fact that the finest houses at Alexandria were inscribed with the names of famous Greek auletrides.

As might be inferred from the character of their dances, the auletrides were capable of every infamy. Constantly breathing an atmosphere of debauchery, and accustomed to the daily spectacle of nudities, they naturally attained a pitch of amorous exaltation of which we, at the present day, can hardly form an idea. They kept a cherished festival in honor of Venus Peribasia, which was originally established by Cypselus of Corinth. At that ceremony all the great flute-players of Greece assembled to celebrate their calling. Men were not usually allowed to be present, a regulation prompted perhaps by modesty, as the judgment of Paris was renewed at the festival, and prizes were awarded for every description of beauty. The ceremony was often mentioned as the Callipygian games; and a sketch of a scene which took place at one of these reunions, contained in a letter from a famous flute-player, justifies the appellation. The banquet lasted from dark till dawn, with wines, perfumes, delicate viands, songs, and music. An after-scene was a dispute between two of the guests as to their respective beauty. A trial was demanded by the company, and a long and graphic account is given of the exhibition, but modern tastes will not allow us to transcribe the details.

A knowledge of these scandalous scenes, it may be briefly observed, would be worse than useless, were it not that they illustrate the life of Greek courtesans; and, being performed under the sanction of religion and the law, they throw no inconsiderable light on the real character of Greek society. Their value may be best apprehended by trying to realize what the effect would be if similar scenes occurred annually in some public edifice in our large cities, under the auspices of the police, with the approval of the clergy, and with the full knowledge of the best female society.

It has been suggested that these festivals were originated by, or gave rise to, those enormous aberrations of the Greek female mind known to the ancients as Lesbian love. There is, no doubt, grave reason to believe something of the kind. Indeed, Lucian affirms that, while avarice prompted common pleasures, taste and feeling inclined the flute-players toward their own sex. On so repulsive a theme it is unnecessary to enlarge.

Many flute-players seem to have been susceptible of lasting affections. In the remains we have of the erotic works of the Greeks, several names are mentioned as those of successful flute-players whose gains were consumed by exacting lovers. It does not appear that they often, or ever, married. The most famous of all the flute-players was Lamia, who, after being the delight of Alexandria and of King Ptolemy for some fifteen or twenty years, was taken with the city by Demetrius of Macedon, and raised to the rank of his mistress. She was forty years of age at this time, yet her skill was such that she ruled despotically her dissolute lover, and left a memorable name in Greek history. The ancients asserted that she owed her name, Lamia, which means a sort of vampire or bloodsucker, to the most

loathsome depravities. Her power was so great that, when Demetrius levied a tax of some $250,000 on the city of Athens, he gave the whole to her, to buy her soap, as he said. The Athenians revenged themselves by saying that Lamia's person must be very dirty, since she needed so much soap to wash it. But they soon found it to their interest to build a temple in her honor, and deify her under the name of Venus Lamia.

THE HETAIRAE, OR KEPT WOMEN

The Hetairae were by far the most important class of women in Greece. They filled so large a place in society that virtuous females were entirely thrown into the shade, and it must have been quite possible for a chaste Athenian girl, endowed with ambition, to look up to them, and covet their splendid infamy. An Athenian matron was expected to live at home. She was not allowed to be present at the games or the theatres; she was bound, when she appeared in public, to be veiled, and to hasten whither she was going without delay; she received no education, and could not share the elevated thoughts or ideas of her husband; she had no right to claim any warmth of affection from him, though he possessed entire control over her.

Now, to judge of the position into which this social system thrust the female sex, one must glance at the mythology, or, to speak more correctly, at the religious faith of the Greek people. It has been conjectured that they derived their idea of Venus from the East. However this be, Venus was certainly one of the earliest goddesses to whom their homage was paid. Solon erected opposite his dicterion a temple where there were two statues: one of the goddess, the other of a nymph, Pitho, who presided over persuasion; and the attitudes and execution of the statues were such that they explained the character without inscription. At this temple a festival was held on the fourth of each month, to which all the men of Athens were invited. But Venus Pandemos soon made way for newer and more barefaced rivals. Twenty temples were raised in various cities of Greece to Venus the Courtesan. In one author we find allusion made to Venus Mucheia, or the Venus of houses of ill-fame. Another celebrates Venus Castina, or the goddess of indecency. Others honor Venus Scotia, the patroness of darkness; and Venus Derceto, the guardian deity of street-walkers. More famous still was Venus Divaricatrix, whose surname, derived, it is said by a father of the Church, *a divaricatis cruribus,* must be left in a learned tongue. And still more renowned was Venus Callipyge, whose statue is at this day one of the choice ornaments of one of the best European collections of antiquities. It owed its charm to the marvelous beauty of the limbs, and was understood to have been designed from two Syracusan sisters, whose extraordinary symmetry in this particular had been noticed by a

THE SIGN

The digital sign made by one of the women is known in French as la figue. It was the ancient gesture of invitation.

Antoine Wiertz (1806-1865)

countryman who surprised them while bathing. All these Venuses had temples, and sacrifices, and priestesses. Their worship was naturally analogous to their name, and consistent with their history. Their devotees were every man in Greece. Yet it was in this society, trained to such spectacles, and nurtured in such a creed, that matrons and maidens were taught to lead a life of purity, seclusion, and self-sacrifice.

The consequence was obvious. While ignorance and forcible restraint prevented the women from generally breaking loose, the men grew more and more addicted to the society of hetairae, and more liable to regard their wives as mere articles of furniture. Nor was the anomaly without effect upon the kept women. They alone of their sex saw the plays of Menander and Aristophanes; they alone had the *entrée* of the studio of Phidias and Apelles; they alone heard Socrates reason, and discussed politics with Pericles; they alone shared in the intellectual movement of Greece. No women but hetairae drove through the streets with uncovered face and gorgeous apparel. None but they mingled in the assemblages of great men at the Pnyx or the Stoa. None but they could gather round them of an evening the choicest spirits of the day, and elicit, in the freedom of unrestrained intercourse, wit and wisdom, flashing fancy and burning eloquence. No wonder that the Hetairae should have filled so prominent a part in Greek society! And how small a compensation to virtuous women to know that their rivals could not stand by the altar when sacrifice was offered; could not give birth to a citizen!

There are many reasons besides these why the contest was unequal. Tradition reported several occasions on which hetairae had rendered signal service to the state. Leaena, for instance, the mistress of Harmodius, had bitten off her tongue rather than reveal the names of her fellow-conspirators. Recollections like these more than nullified the nominal brand of the law. Again, every wise legislator saw the necessity of encouraging any form of rational intercourse, in order to arrest the startling progress which the most degrading of enormities was making in Greece. When Alcibiades was openly courted by the first philosophers and statesmen, it was virtue to applaud Aspasia. And besides, it can not be questioned, in view of the Greek memoirs we possess, that many of the leading hetairae were women of remarkable mind, as well as unusual attractions. Indeed, the leading trait in their history is their intellectuality, as contrasted with other classes of dissolute women in antiquity. That trait can be best illustrated by referring to the lives of a few of the more celebrated hetairae.

A Milesian prostitute, named Thargelia, accompanied Xerxes on his invasion of Greece. Some idea may be formed of the position in society occupied by prostitutes from the fact that Xerxes employed this woman as nego-

tiator with the court of Thessaly, just as in later times modern ministers have used duchesses. Thargelia married the King of Thessaly.

Fired by her success, another Milesian girl, named Aspasia, established herself at Athens. She set up a house of prostitution, and peopled it with the most lovely girls of the Ionic cities. But wherein she differed from her rivals and predecessors was the prominence she gave to intellect in her establishment. She lectured publicly, among her girls and their visitors, on rhetoric and philosophy, and with such marked ability that she counted among her patrons and lovers the first men of Greece, including Socrates, Alcibiades, and Pericles. The last divorced his wife in order to marry her, and was accused of allowing her to govern Athens, then at the height of its power and prosperity. She is said to have incited the war against Samos; and the principal cause of that against Megara was believed to have been the rape, by citizens of Megara, of two of Aspasia's girls. What a wonderful light these facts throw on Greek society!

Enraged beyond control at her success, the virtuous women of Athens rose against her. She was publicly insulted at the theatre; was attacked in the street: and, as a last resort, was accused of impiety before the Areopagus. Pericles, then in the decline of his power, and unable to save his friends Phidias and Anaxagoras, appeared as her advocate. But on such an occasion his eloquence failed him. He could only seize his beloved wife in his arms, press her to his breast, and burst into tears in presence of the court. The appeal succeeded; possibly the judges made allowance for popular prejudice; at all events, Aspasia was acquitted and restored to society. She lived to be the delight of a flour merchant, under whose roof her lectures on philosophy were continued with undiminished success to the day of her death.

Her friend, and the inheritor of her mantle, Hipparchia, led an equally remarkable life. She was an Athenian by birth, and of good family, but, having heard the Cynic Crates speak, she declared to her parents that nothing would restrain her from yielding herself to him. She kept her word, and became the philosopher's mistress, in spite of his dirt, his poverty, and his grossness. She is reported to have acquired great reputation as a practical professor of the cynic philosophy. Having engaged one day in a fierce discussion with a somewhat brutal philosopher of a rival sect, the latter, by way of answer to a question she put, violently exposed her person before the whole assembly. "Well," said she, coolly, "what does that prove?" This woman was one of the most voluminous and esteemed authors of her day.

Bacchis, the mistress of the orator Hyperides, illustrates the character of the Athenian kept woman from another point of view. She was extremely beautiful, and gifted with a sweet disposition. One of her early admirers had presented her with a necklace of enormous value. The first ladies of Athens, and even foreign women of rank, coveted the precious trinket in vain. She was in the height of her fame and charms when she heard the orator Hyperides plead. Smitten on the spot, she became his mistress, and observed a fidelity toward him which was neither usual with her class, nor reciprocated by her lover. On one occasion, a rival announced that the price of her complaisance would be the possession of the necklace of Bacchis. The lover had the meanness to ask for it, and Bacchis gave it without a word.

doned him to keep a sort of *table d'hôte* for the wit and fashion of Athens. The "best society" gathered around her board, and at the close of the meal she sold herself by auction. Athenaeus has chronicled a number of her witty and sarcastic sayings, adding that the grace of her elocution imparted a singular charm to every thing she said. Her protegée, Gnathenion, grew up in time to receive the mantle which age was wresting from the shoulders of Gnathena. An anecdote is preserved which throws some light upon the profits of the calling of hetairae. At the temple of Venus, Gnathena and her protegée met an old Persian satrap, richly clothed in purple, who was struck

PUNISHMENT OF HARLOTS
Cutting of the hair was a common punishment of prostitutes. This practice was carried out in France as late as the Second World War, in the case of female collaborators with the Nazis.

French copperplate: 18th century
Anonymous

Again: when all Athens knew that she was the mistress of Hyperides, an officious friend came to tell her that her lover was at that moment making love to another woman. Bacchis received the announcement tranquilly. "What do you intend to do?" asked her visitor, with impetuosity. "To wait for him," was the meek answer. She died very young, and her lover partially atoned for his ill treatment by pronouncing a splendid oration over her remains. Very few passages in Greek literature are marked by such eloquent tenderness and genuine feeling as this fragment of Hyperides.

Gnathena, and her heir and successor, Gnathenion, were famous in their day as wits; the biography of the first was written in verse by the poet Machon. She began life as the mistress of the comic poet Diphilus, but soon aban-

with the beauty of the latter, and demanded her price. Gnathena answered, a thousand drachmas (about two hundred dollars). The satrap exclaimed at such extortion, and offered five hundred, observing that he would return again. "At your age," maliciously retorted Gnathena, "once is too much," and turned on her heel. In her old age it appears that Gnathena was reduced to the disgraceful calling which the Greeks termed *hippopornos*.

But the fame of these hetairae is eclipsed by that of the only two kept women who can rank with Aspasia—Lais and Phryne.

Lais was a Sicilian by birth. Like the Empress Catharine of Russia, she was taken prisoner when her native city was captured, and sold as a slave. The painter Apelles saw her carrying water from a well, and, struck with the beauty of her figure, he bought her, and trained her in his own house. This, again, is a striking picture. Fancy a leading modern painter deliberately training a prostitute! It is to be presumed that Apelles gathered round him the best society in Greece. Lais, when her education was complete, was as remarkable for wit and information as for her matchless figure and lovely face. Her master freed her, and established her at Corinth, then in the height of its prosperity, and the largest commercial emporium of Greece.

Corinth and the Corinthian prostitutes deserve particular notice. It appears that almost every house in the place was, in fact, a house of prostitution. There were regular schools where the art of debauchery was taught, and frequent importations of young girls from Lesbos, Phoenicia, and the Aegean Islands supplied them with pupils. Ancient erotic writers are full of allusions to the danger of visiting Corinth; the proverb, *Non cuivis homini contingit adire Corinthum*, which most moderns have erroneously conceived to refer to Lais alone, was, in fact, an adage justified by the experience of merchants and sailors. It would be incorrect, however, to compare Corinth with modern sea-ports, where the natural demands of sailors require a cheap supply of women. The first-class hetairae of Corinth charged as high as a talent (say $1000) for a single night's company, and $200 appears to have been no unusual fee. For the common sailors, the commercial shrewdness of the Corinthians had established a temple to Venus, containing a thousand young slaves, who were obliged to prostitute themselves for a single obolus (a cent).

It was in this metropolis of prostitution that Lais commenced business. She soon rose to the first rank in her trade. Her capriciousness gave additional value to her charms. Even money could not purchase her when it was her whim not to yield. She refused $2000 from the orator Demosthenes, who had actually turned his property into money to lay it at her feet; but she yielded gratuitously to the muddy, ragged cynic Diogenes, and graciously shared the patrimony of the philosopher Aristippus. To the latter, who occupied no mean rank in Greek society, a remark was made to the effect that he ought to debar his mistress from promiscuous intercourse for his own sake. He replied phlegmatically, "Would you object to live in a house or sail in a ship because others had just preceded you in the one or the other?" Xenocrates, the disciple of Plato, resisted Lais successfully. She had made a wager that she would overcome his stoical coldness. Rushing into his house one evening in affected terror, she besought an asylum, as she said thieves had chased her. The philosopher sternly bade her fear nothing. She sat silent till Xenocrates went to bed; then, throwing off her dress, and revealing all her wonderful beauty, she placed herself at his side.

He gruffly submitted to this encroachment. Growing bolder, she threw her arms round him, caressed him, and exhausted her arts of fascination, but Xenocrates remained unmoved. "I wagered," she cried, "to rouse a man, not a statue;" and, springing from the couch, she resumed her dress and disappeared.

The people of Corinth desired to possess her statue, and, having spent her money in embellishing the city, perhaps she was entitled to this mark of respect. Myron, the sculptor, was deputed to model her charms. He was old and gray; but so fascinating was her beauty, that at his second visit he laid at her feet all the savings of his life. The haughty courtesan spurned him. He went away, placed himself in the hands of a skillful perfumer, had his hair and beard dyed, and his appearance rejuvenated. Then he renewed his suit. "My poor friend," said Lais, with a bitter smile, "you are asking what I refused yesterday to your father."

In old age Lais had leisure to repent of her caprices. She had spent her money as fast as she made it, and she retained her calling long after her charms had vanished. Epicrates has drawn a melancholy picture of a drunken old woman wandering over the quay at Corinth, and seeking to sell for three cents what had once been considered cheap at a thousand dollars. Such was the end of Lais.

Phryne was more fortunate. She husbanded her attractions with judgment, and to the close of her long life retained her rank and her value. Her wealth was such that, when Alexander destroyed Thebes, she offered to rebuild the city at her own expense, provided the Thebans would commemorate the fact by an inscription. They refused. She had counted among her lovers the most famous men of the day, among whom were the orator Hyperides, whose successful defense of his mistress has already been mentioned; the painter Apelles, and the sculptor Praxiteles. It was to her that the latter gave his crowning work — his Cupid. He and Apelles were both priviliged to admire and reproduce her nude charms, a privilege rigorously denied even to the most opulent of her lovers.

Phryne was a prodigious favorite with the Athenian people. She played a conspicuous part in the festival of Neptune and Venus. At a certain point in the ceremony she appeared on the steps of the temple at the sea-side in her usual dress, and slowly disrobed herself in the presence of the crowd. She next advanced to the water-side, plunged into the waves, and offered sacrifice to Neptune. Returning like a sea-nymph, drying her hair from which the water dripped over her exquisite limbs, she paused for a moment before the crowd, which shouted in a phrensy of enthusiasm as the fair priestess vanished into a cell in the temple.

Other famous hetairae achieved political and literary

distinction. When Alexander the Great undertook his Asiatic expedition, his treasurer, Harpalus, a sort of Croesus in his way, accompanied him, surrounded by the most lovely women the court of Macedon could afford. Rewarded for his fidelity by the governorship of Babylon, and still farther enriched by the spoils of that lucrative office, Harpalus sent to Athens for the most skillful and lovely hetairae of the day. Pythionice was sent him. She was not in the bloom of youth. Some years before she had been the familiar of young Athenians of fashion; she was now the staid mistress of two brothers, sons of an opulent corn-merchant. But her talents were undeniable. She arrived at Babylon, and was installed in the palace; began to rule over the province, and governed Harpalus, it is said, with sternness and vigor. In the midst of her glory she suddenly died; poisoned, no doubt, by some one of the hundred fair ones whom she had supplanted in the governor's affections. Harpalus, inconsolable for her loss, expended a large portion of the contents of his treasury in burying her and commemorating her fame. No queen of Babylon was ever consigned to the grave with the pomp, or the show, or the ostentatious affection which did honor to the memory of the Athenian prostitute. Her tomb cost $50,000; and historians, admiring, in after ages, its splendor and its size, inquired, with mock wonder, whether the bones of a Miltiades, or a Cimon, or a Pericles lay under the pile!

Harpalus found consolation in the arms of a Greek garland-weaver named Glycera, for aught we know the poisoner of Pythionice. She, too, became Queen of Babylon, issued her decrees, held her court, submitted to be worshiped, and saw her statue of bronze, as large as life, erected in the Babylonian temples. She was a woman of a masculine mind in a feminine body. When Alexander returned from the East, breathing vengeance against faithless servants, she compelled her lover to fly with her to Attica, where she raised, by her eloquence, her money, and her address, an army of six thousand men to oppose the hero of Macedon. It is said that she purchased, at what price we know not, the silence of Demosthenes; she certainly bribed the Athenian people with large donations of corn. But she could not bribe or persuade her wretched lover to be sensible; his folly soon roused the Athenians against him, and he was exiled with his mistress. In this exile, one of his attendants cut the throat of the venerable lover, and Glycera, left a widow, returned to Athens to pursue her calling as a hetaira. She was no longer young, and needed the aid of the dealer in cosmetics; but her prestige as the ex-mistress of Babylon procured her a certain celebrity, and she soon obtained a position in the society of Athens. Out of a crowd of admirers who attached themselves to her court, she chose two to be, as the

French would say, her *amants de coeur*. One was the painter Pausias; the other the comic poet Menander. The former achieved one of his most brilliant triumphs by painting the portrait of his mistress. But, whether his temper was not congenial to hers, or his rival inspired an exclusive affection, Glycera soon discarded Pausias, and became the mistress of the poet alone. Menander, we are led to believe, was a man of a harsh, crabbed disposition; the haughty Glycera was the only one whom his *boutades* never irritated, who bore with all his ill temper. When he was successful, she heightened his joy; when his plays were ill received, and he returned from the theatre in low spirits, she consoled him, and endured the keenest affronts without murmuring. Her amiability had its reward. From being one of the most dissolute men of Athens, Menander became solidly attached and faithful to Glycera, and, so soon was her Babylonish career forgotten, she descended to posterity in the Athenian heart inseparably coupled with the dearest of their comic writers.

Another famous hetaira was Leontium, who succeeded her mistress Philenis in the affections of the philosopher Epicurus. She is said to have borne him a daughter, who was born in the shade of a grove in his garden; but, whether she put her own construction upon the Epicurean philosophy, or did not really love the gray-headed teacher she was far from practicing the fidelity which was due to so distinguished a lover. She figures in the letters of Alciphron as the tender friend of several younger fashionables; and she has been accused, with what truth it is hard to say, of attempting a compromise between the doctrines of Epicurus and those of Diogenes. However this be, Leontium was undoubtedly a woman of rare ability and remarkable taste. She composed several works; among others, one against Theophrastus, which excited the wonder and admiration of so good a judge as Cicero. She survived her old protector, and died in obscurity.

Something more might be said of Archeanassa, to whose wrinkles Plato did not disdain to compose an amorous epigram; of Theoris, a beautiful girl, who preferred the glorious old age of Sophocles to the ardent youth of Demosthenes, and whom the vindictive orator punished by having her condemned to death; of Archippa, the last mistress and sole heir of Sophocles; of Theodote, the disciple of Socrates, under whose counsels she carried on her business as a courtesan, and whose death may be ascribed, in some part, to the spite caused by Theodote's rejection of Aristophanes; and of others who figure largely in every reliable history of intellectual Greece. But we must stop.

In most of the nations to which reference must be made in the ensuing pages of this volume, prostitutes have figured as pariahs; in Greece they were an aristocracy,

JAPANESE TEA-HOUSE. MEN PROSTITUTES
Japanese woodcut

The use of philtres, or charms (of which more will be said in the ensuing chapter on Roman prostitution), was common in Greece. Retired courtesans often combined the manufacture of these supposed charms with the business of a midwife. They made potions which excited love and potions which destroyed it; charms to turn love into hate, and others to convert hate into love. That the efficacy of the latter must have been a matter of pure faith need not be demonstrated, though the belief in them was general and profound. The former are well known in the pharmacopoeia, and from the accounts given of their effects, there is no reason to doubt that they were successfully employed in Greece, as well by jealous husbands and suspicious fathers as by ardent lovers. A case is mentioned by no less an authority than Aristotle, of a woman who contrived to administer an amorous potion to her lover, who died of it. The woman was tried for murder; but, it being satisfactorily proved that her intention was not to cause death, but to revive an extinct love, she was acquitted. Other cases are mentioned in which the philtres produced madness instead of love. Similar accidents have attended the exhibition of cantharides in modern times.

HISTORY OF PROSTITUTION
W. Sanger

exercising a palpable influence over the national policy and social life, and mingling conspicuously in the great march of the Greek intellect. No less than eleven authors of repute have employed their talents as historiographers of courtesans at Athens. Their works have not reached us entire, having fallen victims to the chaste scruples of the clergy of the Middle Ages; but enough remains in the quotations of Athenaeus, Alciphron's Letters, Lucian, Diogenes Laertius, Aristophanes, Aristaenetus, and others, to enable us to form a far more accurate idea of the Athenian hetairae than we can obtain of the prostitutes of the last generation.

Into the arts practiced by the graduates of the Corinthian academies it is hardly possible to enter, at least in a modern tongue. Even the Greeks were obliged to invent verbs to designate the monstrosities practiced by the Lesbian and Phoenician women. Demosthenes, pleading successfully against the courtesan Neaera, describes her as having seven young girls in her house, whom she knew well how to train for their calling, as was proved by the repeated sales of their virginity. One may form an idea of the shocking depravity of the reigning taste from the sneers which were lavished upon Phryne and Bacchis, who steadily adhered to natural pleasures.

Scene in Montmartre, Paris: rendez-vous for tribads and transvestists. These are types of sexual deviations.

p. George Grosz

The Bath

BATHSHEBA IN THE BATH

Hans Memling (c. 1433-1494)
State Gallery, Stuttgart

[194]

The Bath

Baths and bathing have immemorially been associated with erotic diversions. In the degenerate life of Imperial Rome, public baths were in popular vogue, both sexes using them in common. It is true that the senatorial ranks and the governing body disdained such promiscuity, but the practice was prevalent among the *vulgus ignobile.* And there are historical instances that the custom was not rigidly confined to the populace. The Roman Emperor Heliogabalus himself in balneis semper cum mulieribus fuit.

The heterosexual propinquities stimulated amorous advances. As a further inducement, the attendants at these baths, that were equipped with special hot, cold, tepid and steam rooms, were regularly of the opposite sexes. Bathers and assistants were consequently exposed to sexual provocations during the entire bathing period.

In the Middle Ages, it was customary for girls to serve in similar capacities as attendants to knights and princelings during their bathing. This was the case especially in Germany, where the public baths were virtual brothels. In Japan, the custom of service at the hands of female attendants is still contemporary.

Mixed bathing — balnea mixta — is mentioned by Pliny the Elder in his Historia Naturalis. Martial the Roman epigrammatist also refers to this practice. Matrons of distinguished family, men of ancient lineage and public repute, on the other hand, were not known either to condone or to practice this habit.

For beautifying purposes, Roman women used perfumed baths. Poppaea, wife of the Emperor Nero, bathed in the milk of asses. Later ages used, for similar reasons, rose-petal baths, or baths containing crushed almonds, honey, melon juice, as in the case of Marie Antoinette.

In the major cities of Europe, in Berlin and Vienna, bathing establishments were often equipped with sleeping chambers.

H. E. W.

BATHHOUSE

Albrecht Durer (1471-1528)
Bibliotheque Nationale, Paris

BATHING WOMAN

G. Courbet (1819-1877)
Musée de Montpellier

Neo-Antiquity:
Erotic Paganism

THE PRODIGAL DAUGHTER

A contemporary symbolic fantasy of erotic prodigality.

Félix Labisse: 1943
Collection: Pierre Brasseur

Neo-Antiquity: Erotic Paganism

PIERRE FELIX LOUYS (1879-1925) was a French novelist and poet who tried to recapture the pagan amorous ecstasies and the sense of cosmic and human eroticism prevalent among the ancient Greeks. Born in Ghent, he died in Paris. He was acquainted with André Gide, Paul Valéry, Mallarmé, François Coppée, and Hérédia. He founded a poetic review called La Conque. Paul Valéry estimated the popularity of Louys' works for their 'apologies de la chair et de ses plaisirs.'

His Manuel de Civilité is a lewd guide that is reminiscent of Ovid's Ars Amatoria. His Aphrodite and Les Véritables Chansons de Bilitis made his reputation. His characteristic style is pervaded by a sensuous, poetic, erotic imagery.

H. E. W.

LES BELLES DE NUIT

Paul Delvaux: 1937
Museum, Antwerp

Exhibitionism

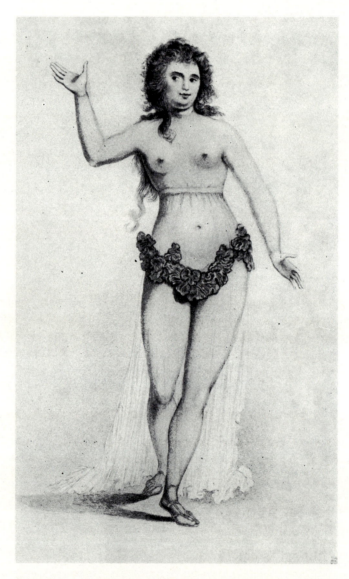

A case of exhibitionism of the 18th Century. A society woman, Miss Cudleigh, appearing at the Gran Jubilée Ball of Venice in 1749 as Iphigenia.

Exhibitionism

PAULINE BONAPARTE AS VENUS
The imperial status sees no indignity in this ecdysiastic pose.
Antonio Canova (1757-1822)

Exhibitionism is a sexual perversion not confined to males as commonly assumed. It involves public exposure of the secondary as well as primary sexual organs. Exhibitionists may be psychopathic individuals, mental defectives, or alcoholics. In most cases, the victim is driven to follow a blind impulse beyond control, with resultant relief from extreme tension.

H. E. W.

GREEK DANCING GIRL

Greek Relief: 500 B.C.
Collection of Sculpture, Berlin

VENUS

Lucas Cranach (1472-1553)
Kunstinstitut, Frankfurt

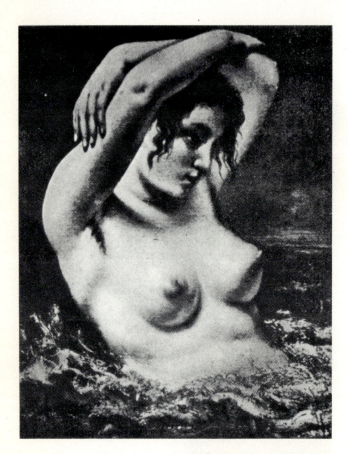

NUDE

Gustave Courbet (1819-1877)

*The actress of the Comédie Française poses as Danaë the
victim of one of Zeus' numberless amours.*

Louis Girodet (1767-1824)
Musée des Beaux Arts, Bordeaux

LEAVING THE BATH

Unknown Artist

Sadism

The Bed: An Amatory Factor

SLEEP

Vincent Van Gogh (1853-1890)

Sadism

Sadism is a sexual perversion involving erotic pleasure by means of infliction of pain or torture on others. The term is derived from the Marquis de Sade (1745-1815), a French novelist infamous for his own personal acts and for the scatological nature of his works. His novels probe into obscure sexual perversions and fantastic aberrations. Among his novels in this field are Juliette, Justine, Les 120 Journées de Sodome, and Le Petit Fils d'Hercule.

RICHARD W. NICE, in his A Handbook of Abnormal Psychology, asserts:

The sadist indulges in his sadistic actions to arouse within himself a special sexual feeling. Often the sadist is an undersexed individual who must inflict pain to experience sexual satisfaction.

Sadists are found in both sexes; although perhaps more of them are men, due to the fact that during the sexual act the man is more aggressive. However, women sadists are just as perverse and dangerous — sometimes more so. Nor is sadism confined to heterosexual activity; it is often associated with homosexual tendencies.

Influences leading to the development of sadism are often difficult to determine. Many different factors are involved. Some children learn early that violent emotions are more likely to provide greater satisfaction than moderate emotions; they tend to be aggressive in everything they do. They are interested in violent sports, football, boxing, etc., and this love of violence often extends to their sexual life. Some sadists gained the impression early in life that the sexual act is a violent attack by the man on the woman (Freud). Diseases of the nervous system may be the chief cause of sadism. Also, quite often impotence or frigidity may cause indulgence in sadistic activity in order to arouse weakened sexual feeling. Sadistic acts vary greatly and include murder, attempted murder, wounding and lesser bodily injuries, as well as sexual assault, damage to property by cutting and slashing, ink-splashing, and the like.

The most dangerous sadists are those who murder their victims. A less aggressive type of sadist may stab a girl with a pen-knife or needle as he passes her in the street, or strike at her with a stick. The dress slashers and dress defilers belong to this group. Still another type of sadism is closely related to pyromania. Such individuals derive sexual satisfaction by setting fires and watching the resulting flames.

A sadist may indulge in his abnormality only in fantasy.

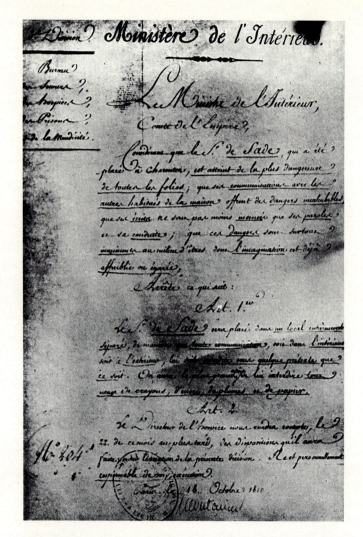

In this proclamation, published in 1810, the reference is to the Marquis de Sade, the arch novelist of sexual perversions. He was confined, in his later years, in an insane asylum at Charenton, forbidden to use pencil, ink, pen, paper.

Others cut the throats of women in photographs; still others steal shoes and other articles of clothing, which they tear, slash, burn in order to attain a sexual climax.

Another dangerous type of sadist inflicts cruelty on animals — cattle, horses, sheep, cats, dogs, etc. from which they derive great sexual excitement. This may be attributed to an early sex experience in which the child obtained sexual gratification by torturing an animal or inflicting pain on a playmate. This may have left such an impression that sadistic sexual activities are chosen rather than normal ones. Sadism may also be practiced with inanimate objects, such as clothing, books, furniture and other objects with full effect.

When associated with mental disease sadism is usually uncontrollable. The sadist may be sexually deficient; may have masochistic tendencies; may be homosexual, heterosexual, or bisexual. The degree of violence used may depend upon the delay which occurs before full sexual satisfaction is reached, that is, the greater the delay, the greater the violence. The greater the violence, the more likely is the act to be associated with mental disease.

The Bed: An Amatory Factor

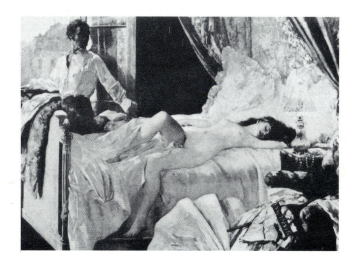

ROLLA

Henry Gervex (1852-1929)
Musée des Beaux Arts, Bordeaux

The bed or couch, basically associated with sleep and rest, became, by a natural progression, an amatory factor. It was besprinkled with balsam and myrrh, and aloes, and, from being a lectus cubiculus, it acquired the status of lectus amatorius. So the custom prevailed among the ancient Egyptians. Centuries later, Roman Juvenal speaks of gold-adorned couches. In the Middle Ages, the bed became the symbol of conjugal intimacy. In the Tristan and Isolde legend, the bed is glorified. But it also became the symbol of amorous adventure and erotic diversions: the emblem of copulatio carnalis.

In the eighteenth century, a certain Dr. James Graham described, in his public lectures, a specially constructed bed that was presumably highly conducive to amatory practices:

Suffer me, with great cordiality, and assurance of success, to recommend my celestial, or medico, magnetico, musico, electrical bed which I have constructed . . . to improve, exalt, and invigorate the bodily, and, through them, the mental faculties of the human species . . .

The sublime, the magnificent, and, I may say, the super-celestial dome of the bed, which contains the odoriferous, balmy, and ethereal spices, odors, and essences, and which is the grand magazine or reservoir of those vivifying and

[217]

(Top) *A medieval bed, made of metal and rope.*

(Bottom) *A nobleman reclining on his traveling bed.*

invigorating influences which are exhaled and dispersed by the breathing of the music, and by the attenuating, repelling, and accelerating force of the electrical fire — is very curiously inlaid or wholly covered on the under side with brilliant plates of looking-glass, so disposed as to reflect the various attractive charms of the happy recumbent couple, in the most flattering, most agreeable, and most enchanting style.

Such is a slight and inadequate sketch of the grand celestial bed, which, fully impregnated with the balmy vivifying effluvia of restorative balsamic medicines and of soft, fragrant, oriental gums, balsams, and quintessence, and pervaded at the same time with full springing tides of the invigorating influences of music and magnets both real and artificial, gives such elastic vigor to the nerves, on the one hand, of the male, and on the other, such retentive firmness to the female . . . that it is impossible, in the nature of things, but that strong, beautiful, brilliant, nay, double-distilled children, if I may use the expression, must infallibly be begotten. .

Symbolically, the bed or couch represents the supreme marriage relationship. But, by the distorted and perverse nature of man, it has also been identified with license and carnal lust. The practice of bundling, which was virtually a pre-marital experiment in the acceptability of a more

Hebe Vestina, a so-called Rosy Goddess of Health, reclining on a bed in Dr. James Graham's Temple of Health and Hymen. Dr. James Graham was the eighteenth century inventor of a Celestial Bed that was believed to induce potent erotic manifestations.

formal, stable marriage association, did not minimize possible temptation, however: for a low wooden board or a bolster divided the bed in two.

In Hungary, the bridal bed was placed on a cart heaped with the objects of the trousseau. Then the cart was drawn in procession through the village street, to the accompaniment of a nuptial paean.

In the island of Cyprus, the bridal mattress became an object of decoration and song. In the Philippine Islands, the Moros of Mindanao and the Sulu Archipelago, at a marriage ceremony, escorted the bridegroom to the bride's house. On the nuptial bed, which was decorated with the dowry of coins and paper money, the bride and her family were carried in public procession.

In Abyssinia the bridal bed was brought into Church. In Iceland, when the husband sets off on a journey, the wife leaves the bed unmade.

Hogarth depicted the bed as playing a very helpful role in the art of gallantry.

A German ballad glorifies the bed thus:

> O Bett! Du Freudensaal!
> Wo sind d'Menschen selig
> Wo ist es so süß
> Wo findt't der Mann offen
> Das Paradies
> Im Bett, im Bett, im Bett.

H. E. W.

CONTEMPLATION

Suzanne Valadon (1867-1938)
Collection of the City of Paris

Love Potions

Love Potions

The amatory urge, a primary functional characteristic of the human physiology, has, through the ages, presented a remarkable variety of permutations and deviations. In this genesiac drive, man has accumulated, in the course of the centuries, a vast corpus of devices, manipulations, and stimuli, designed to promote this erotic compulsiveness. For his basic purpose has invariably been to maintain and preserve or to refurbish and renew his vigorous faculties. This urge, however distorted it may become or channeled into furtive and untried directions, is the condition of human continuity, of racial and cosmic survival. *L'élan vital,* in the Bergsonian phrase, or the *life force,* as G. B. Shaw has termed it, is the fundamental motif that, in the male and female principles conjoined, postulates a kind of teleological cognition.

At first gropingly, therefore, with experimental hesitation and peripheral extrusions, man has sought for conclusive means of furthering his erotic tendencies. With the passing of the ages, he became more knowledgeable and consequently more assertive, more assured, more convinced of his direction. He had now amassed a store of gnomic lore, traditional hints and guidance, oral persuasions, unwritten but no less effective prescriptions, treatments, remedial designs, pillules and philtres, herbal compounds and periapts, whimsical or horrendous formulas and supplications, mystic appeals to unnamed omnipotent forces, repulsive but reputedly effectual recipes: all, either in certain hieratic combinations or cumulatively, conducive to the desired physiological consummation. The love philtre came into its own. It was palpable or visible, or it was presumed, a priori and anteriorly to its implementation, as possessed of the required, the unique efficacy. The love potion assumed an initially secretive but sequentially dominant and accepted and acceptable role in the life of the individual man and so in the social fabric itself. The philtre had acquired status. It was, if not the ultimate panacea, the final elixir, certainly the assumed conveyor of those inducements toward amatory excitations that had previously been lacking in the ministrant, the suppliant.

The term aphrodisiac, commonly used for amatory stimulants, is derived from Aphrodite, the ancient Greek goddess in her capacity as a personification of the sexual impulse. She is the generative force that pervades the entire cosmos. She is, as the Roman poet Lucretius chanted, the delight of men and gods, through whom every kind of living creature is conceived.

In a general sense, aphrodisiacs involve visual images, olfactory and tactile experience, physiological operations related to food, drink, or conceptual pictures that induce libidinous impulses. Some aphrodisiacs are, though not effective, innocuous: while others are fraught with extreme hazards. The efficacy of aphrodisiacs, in fact, is often a matter of tradition, untested for validity, but transmitted in oral sagas, in magic rituals and old wives' lore, through successive ages. Certain foods and drinks, for instance, are traditionally associated with erotic impulses. But in most of these cases no definitive pharmaceutical or medical approval warrants credence. Hence the hopeful persistence

of restorative measures. What may, however, be asserted is that an abundance of rich and appealing food, reinforced with palatable drinks, all consumed in a pleasant atmosphere in congenial company, will unquestionably induce a feeling of euphoria. This sense of physical and emotional well-being may tend toward sensual directions, and the human fallacy has been to deduce, illogically, a *post hoc* as an *ergo propter hoc*.

Aphrodite presided over every sexual manifestation. As Aphrodite Hetaira she was the patron goddess of the female

The philtre was usually a liquid concoction, compounded of various ingredients: mineral and vegetable, aromatic or stercoraceous, innocuous or disastrous in their effects. But in a wider sense there appeared in every age and throughout the continents of Asia and Africa and Europe, items that, in their own peculiar characteristics, were virtually amatory philtres or aphrodisiacs.

Artemisia absinthium, which is wormwood, was anciently dedicated to the goddess Artemis, and was known for its apotropaic virtues in warding off malefic spirits. In

REJUVENATION BATH

Martin de Vos: c. 1600

amatory companions of the Greeks. Under the name of Aphrodite Porne she was the divine protectress of prostitutes and of a variety of sexual activities. In Sparta, she was also known as Aphrodite Peribaso, Aphrodite the Streetwalker. As Aphrodite Trymalitis, she symbolized the ultimate sexual consummation.

In poetry and sculpture she was represented as endowed with such alluring charms, such sexual enticements, as to infatuate even the wise men, as Homer asserts. Throughout Greece, in temples dedicated to the goddess, her callipygian beauty was stressed as a factor in her worship.

The erotic inclination may be induced by lascivious photographs, by the reading of libidinous books, by viewing paintings and sculpture depicting erotic situations as the frescoes and wall paintings that have survived in Pompeian excavations or the Caves of Ajanta in Hyderabad.

modern times absinthe, the liqueur extracted from Artemisia absinthium, has been used as a sexual stimulant, although it involves calamitous reactions. Acorus calamus, an aromatic herb, was known as Venus' plant and was associated with aphrodisiac properties. There was affion and the agate stone. Potable gold, produced by the medieval alchemists, was designed to arouse the erotic capacities. So with almonds and ambergris, with the plant known as pellitory of Spain, with mandrake and the genitalia and viscera of animals and birds, newts and toads, fish and humans. In the same category were nuts, exotic ointments and powders.

Ingredients included the most fantastic, the rarest, the most obscene or stercoraceous items: semen virile, both human and animal: likewise the membrum virile of man and beast: the pudenda muliebria: blood and marrow:

REJUVENATION

*A pictorial presentation of the age-old search for the
resurgence of physiological capacity.*

Splendor Solis
Nuremberg: c.1600

dried skins and nails, hair and excretions. On the other hand, stimulus was on occasion provided by food and drinks that were themselves appealing: cinnamon and vanilla, wine and ginger, rhubarb and curaçao, parsley and apples, honey, black pepper, apricot brandy, elecampane, mango oil, arris root, artichoke, aubergine and asparagus. Most of these items that formed the base of aphrodisiac concoctions were innocuous in themselves, or actually wholesome and conducive to a sense of euphoria. And this sense of well-being is physiologically no mean factor as an erotic stimulation.

The Orient was highly skilled in the virtues of amatory stimuli. Hindu sexology, in particular, knew the asoka plant and the lotus, jasmine and bamboo shoots, hashish, the leaves and the seeds of hemp. All kinds of far-sought or indigenous vegetables and spices and grasses form part of the prescriptions regularly mentioned by the Hindu sexologists. Notably in such treatises as the Kama Sutra, Ananga-Ranga, and the Kama Kalpa. There is bhuya-ko-kali, whose botanical identification is solanum Jacquini. Some ingredients are difficult of procurement: some are unidentifiable in relation to Western botanical terminology:

while still others are repellent or gruesome. The bone of peacock or of hyena, the tradition runs, is an inducement to venery. Or calamint, a fragrant herb: camel bone dipped in the juice of the plant termed eclipta prostata. Or charas, smoked or eaten: cardamon, the prickly plant akin to the artichoke and known as cardoon.

Avena sativa was held to be effective. So too in the case of bananas, or basil used as a condiment. Beans were anciently endowed with powerful invigorating qualities. St. Jerome, in fact, laid down a proscription against their consumption. For their effect, he asserted, was immediate and unquestioned:

in partibus genitalibus titillationes producunt.

Beer and beefsteak and beets appear wholesome while stimulating. White beets are actually stated by the Roman encyclopedist Pliny the Elder to be promotive of amorous capacity.

In China, bird nest soup is considered a pronounced aphrodisiac. The preparation consists of the nest of the sea swallow, constructed of sea weed and highly edible. The leaves are agglutinated by fish spawn, that teems with phosphorus: and phosphorus itself constitutes a genesiac provocation.

Birthwort was a shrub favored by the Romans. Borax; brain of sheep or pig or calf, served fresh—these have reputations of high efficacy. Greek and Roman medical writers, medieval anatomists, Arab erotologists list or describe or hint at rare compounds, often unnamed, as a means of strengthening amatory practices. And the items come flowing forth in a heterogeneous plethora, all clamoring, figuratively, for their consummation, praising their idiosyncratic virtues, promising rejuvenescence and boisterous competence.

Wild cabbage belongs to this stimulating pharmacopeia, and cakes formed in genital and analogous shapes. Camel fat or camel milk mixed with honey: castor oil and, among Arabs as in ancient Greece, carrots. Celery soup was an eighteenth century dish that was popular in France, in intimate suppers, for whetting the amorous appetite. Milk of chameleon, though difficult to procure, is also equally beneficial. To the Romans, rosemary was a decided stimulant. Cherries and chestnuts too, cheese and chickpeas, cloves and cubeb pepper, rocket seed and pine kernels, nutmeg and saffron also came in for contribution. One may, in fact, postulate in a general acceptance that, for erotic impulses, one may be consuming what is normally included in simple domestic fare: dried shrimp or mushrooms, chicken liver, tripe, scallops, melons, spinach and lettuce, noodles, lobster.

Shark fin is more unique. But cider is a common commodity, and is credited with aphrodisiac property. So with cinchona, and chutney, mustard seed, mutton, musk.

Cod roe, cockles and most types of sea-food, the herb known as colewort, all belong in this designation. Colewort, in fact, was associated by the Romans with lascivious performances, and was dedicated to the phallic divinity Priapus. Cola, the native African term for which is bichy, is derived from the plant cola nitida. Cola is chewed by the native African, expectant of strengthened vigor. Cod liver oil is reputed to act as a sexual agent: also coriander and valerian, crab apples and cow wheat, cress and crayfish.

The bodies of animals and humans, the excrementitious elements in insects and reptiles were indifferently matter for amatory compounds. Even the human corpse was utilized: either in scraps of putrescent flesh, or in ashes collected after cremation. Then again, we find less gruesome but manifestly no less effective sources: the root of the cyclamen, sowbread, cuttle-fish and spiced oysters, sea hedgehogs: curry as a condiment, cumin, even cucumber, which most probably on account of its phallic formation, was associated with erotic virtue.

In Elizabethan England the philtre was a commonplace. References are numerous in the dramatists: in Dekker and Marston, in Fletcher, Ben Jonson, and Shakespeare. Falstaff calls philtres 'medicines to make me love him.' Fennel too will inspire provocative action. When mixed with ghee, liquorice, and sugar, the resultant compound, in Hindu erotology, was held to constitute a kind of sacred essence, a nectar of elixirs.

Figs, anciently associated with phallic symbolism, were reputed to have energizing qualities. The fig was also symbolic, in Hindu erotological manuals, of the yoni and the lingam. It was likewise related to the obscene digital gesture involving fingers and thumb, a gesture that was well known in the antique Roman lupanaria.

In some mythologies, the food of the gods is more than a eulogistic, figurative expression. In Scandinavian legend the reference was to the apples, that produced a rejuvenated condition in the decrepit and exhausted pantheon.

Cooked garlic may not appeal equally to all gastronomic inclinations, but it is listed, along with animal organs, by Dr. Nicolas Venette, a seventeenth century French physician, author of a *Tableau de l'Amour Conjugal.* Frogs, bones and legs, were known to the Romans for refreshing the organism. Frogs' legs were considered by Norman Douglas as a 'noble aphrodisiac.' Among milder items, the aroma given off by certain flowers creates passionate tendencies. This is especially the case with the gardenia, lilies of the valley, frangipani, henna. Among fruits, cherries and grapes are believed to be equally effectual.

The lamprey, an eel-like pseudo-fish, has a reputation for promoting seminal fluid. Lard in combination with crushed garlic is used as an ointment. Lavender causes excitation. Laurel leaves, lentils, unguents containing but-

JUAN PONCE DE LEON

Ponce de Leon (1460-1521), *the Spanish explorer, was
said to have discovered, on a fabulous island, the Fountain
of Youth, the Essence of Rejuvenation.*

Ediciones de la Universidad de Puerto Rico

ter or spurge, chives, goose fat and storax were noted by a
seventeenth century biologist as contributory factors. Lion's
fat is currently not easy to obtain, but Sinibaldus, a seventeenth century erotologist, in his *Geneanthropoeia*, published in 1642, mentions it as a popular aphrodisiac. So
with rui seed and jai leaves, with lentils and lizards and
the claw-formed plant termed lycopodium.

Rarity and repulsiveness never created a definitive
barrier to amatory manoeuvres. Men searched the far-flung
lands and oceans, or devised combinations of available
ingredients, or distilled the necessary essential properties
from herbs and animal matter, from skins and genitalia,
from pods and plants, tree bark and drugs.

In every region where communities have gathered and
settled, in Pacific Islands, in the uplands of Kurdistan,
from Kabul to the Laccadive Islands, from the Tatra
Mountains to the vast stretches of the tundras, man has

inquisitively and hopefully gone on the erotic pilgrimage
in quest of the supreme potency that would give him
genesiac immortality, that would create a timeless and
continuous vigor reminiscent of the antique gods of the
Hellenes.

Karengro is an orchid-like plant found in Transylvania.
The roots of kava piperaceae are indigenous to the South
Sea Islands. In Malaya, the bile of the King's Crow is in
use for febrile ardor. Or take the remains of a dead kite,
mixed with cowach, the prickly hairs of a tropical pod, and
honey.

Kosth and lechi, chikana and askhand, gajapimpali and
kanher root, pounded with butter, are recommended in
the Ananga-Ranga. Or lechi and asparagus racemosus,
cucumber and kuili powder and kanta-gokhru are ingredients indigenous to India and are consequently included
in the Hindu erotic treatises. Another herb, maerua

[227]

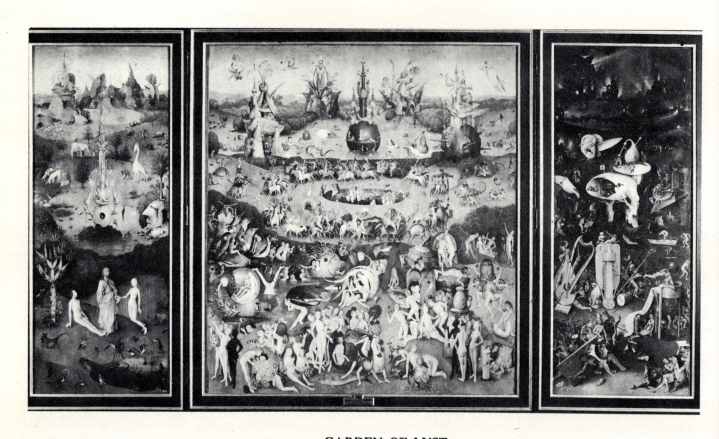

GARDEN OF LUST

*As the primary agent in the corruption of man and society, woman was
medievally depicted as the arch-exponent of carnality.*

REJUVENATION BATH

Lucas Cranach (1472-1553)
National Gallery, Berlin

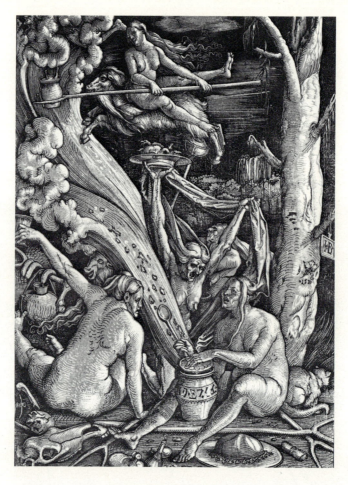

WITCH'S SABBAT

Paganism, even with the advance of Christianity, retained
furtive practices and rites until far into the Middle Ages.
The witches are here paying homage to his Satanic Majesty.

Hans Baldung (1476-1545)
Metropolitan Museum of Art

arenaria, is used in India for encouraging amorousness. Mallow may be taken innocently. But the root of mallow, in goat's milk, excites the genital urge, according to the testimony of Pliny the Elder.

Mandrake was widely used, from the earliest Biblical ages, through Hellenic times down beyond the Middle Ages. It has a long history of its own. This plant, also known as mandragore, is the atropa mandragora, mandragora officinarum, and belongs to the potato family. It has dark leaves, with purple flowers, and a tomato-like fruit, and is indigenous to the Mediterranean area, especially Palestine. It often grows in human shape, taking the form of limbs. In the preparation of love potions it was in regular use. Circe, the Homeric witch who appears in the Odyssey,

used infusions of it in her magic brews: hence mandrake was also known as 'the plant of Circe.'

The erotic nature of mandrake is illustrated in Biblical literature, especially in Genesis: also in The Song of Solomon. The Roman bucolic poet Columella calls mandrake semi-human. The Greek biographer and philosopher Plutarch called the plant 'man-likeness,' because it sometimes resembles the human form, and sometimes the testes or the membrum virile. Pliny the Elder, who compiled a corpus of strange and often unverified knowledge, declared that the plant is rarely available, but if a root resembling the male organ is found by a man, it will ensure a woman's love.

In the Middle Ages mandrake was regularly in use in

WITCH PREPARING LOVE PHILTRE

Amatory concoctions were among the usual devices familiar since antiquity, but most frequently employed in the medieval centuries.

magic rituals and in thaumaturgic experiments. A seventeenth century traveler suggested eating the root as a genesiac aid. Isaac Vossius, a seventeenth century scholar, confirms the declaration of mandrake as an amatory agent. The virtues of the plant are still credited: in Italy, in rural Greece. The legends associated with mandrake have been incorporated in a novel entitled Vampire, by Hans Heinz-Ewers.

Mango is a stimulant. Marzipan, followed by a draught of sweet hippocras, is advised by François Rabelais in a similar context. The membrum of the wolf or the hedgehog was frequently in use among the Romans. Nettles are recommended by Menghus Faventinus, an obscure medical writer. Corroboration comes from Rabelais himself, who

mentions a species of thistle called panicaut:

se frotter le cul au panicaut,
vrai moyen d'avoir au cul passion,

Aromatic mint, regularly used in flavoring food, is believed to possess restorative capacity. The moh tree, botanically termed Bassia Latifolia, produces flowers rich in sugar. In India, the liquor arrack is manufactured from these flowers. The pith of the tree, when pounded and mixed with cow's milk, is considered a sexual inducement. Even the domestic onion, in ancient Greece, had presumably aphrodisiac characteristics. It is repeatedly mentioned in literary contexts, particularly in the comic drama, as a genesiac stimulant.

To Arabs, mushroom is a significant aid. A hot mustard

bath, reputedly, increases the libido. Or an infusion of mustard seed. The brains of the mustela piscis, if obtained, were considered of marked efficacy in the case of women. Pulverized myrtle leaves, applied to the body, were once believed to arouse amatory attacks. A tonic distilled from the water in which myrtle leaves and flowers had been steeped was a putative invigorating agent. An old prescription advises an infusion of flowers and leaves of myrtle and a quart of white wine, distilled in a cold still and left for twenty-four hours. The result, it is asserted, will be a beautifying aid: and as a cordial will incline 'those that drink it to be very amorous.'

A certain Mery, a French physician, in his Traité Universel des Drogues Simples, highly recommends the partes genitales of the rooster. Peas boiled with onions are wholesome and aphrodisiac. Cake compounded of ginger, honey, pellitory, cinnamon and garlic, nutmeg, hellebore and cardamoms is prescribed by Arab erotologists.

Amatory impulses may be strengthened by perfumes. Osphresiological reactions have constantly involved erotic reactions as well. Repulsive odors of functional performances, body emanations may produce intense susceptibility. Animal effluvia, vegetable scents have been enlisted for amatory stimulation. Among the Romans, erotic urges were encouraged by the use of exotic perfumes and unguents. Perfumes were used on the body, on the head and hair, on garments. Civet and ambergris were especially popular. Aromatic spices, too, were used as an aid to sweeten the breath. Foliatum was an ointment prepared from spikenard. Nicerotiana was a scent named after Nicerotas, its originator. Cinnamon, sweet marjoram, myrrh, myrobalan were likewise used as ingredients of aromatic preparations. In recent times, Lafcadio Hearn, that synthesis of East and West, wrote a small treatise on *odor feminarum*.

In earlier times the emphasis on erotic stimulants reached the pharmacopoeia, where recipes directed to amatory capacity are described as Electuary Satyrion, Tablets of Magnanimity, and similarly by other suggestive designations.

The potion or philtre, then, in whatever form, was a staple factor in society, however remote or primitive or cultivated. In his Marriage Precepts, the biographer and philosopher Plutarch mentions them specifically. In Shakespeare's Macbeth three witches concoct a brew. Goya, the Spanish painter, has a witch in the process of preparing a philtre. Horace, the Roman poet, frequently dwells on the details and ingredients of the concoction. Propertius too, and the novelist Apuleius write of the matter as a common, accepted and acknowledged factor. The philtre, in fact, belongs in civilized society as well as in primitive communities, among the Navajo Indians no less than in Elizabethan days. In his play The Shepherd's Week, John

Gay assumes the contemporary effective usage of a love philtre. The Middle Ages, from Transylvania to the remote Scottish Highlands, abound in chronicles referring to preparations of love enchantments and brews, of rituals and formulas for love-sick knights or febrile serf, poet and princeling. Scottish witches, Irish occultists were kept constantly occupied in advising and suggesting means for acquiring the amatory power: and their recommendations brooked no hesitations. The passionate suppliant was prepared to make trial of poisonous drugs and sometimes fatal ingredients. For squire and burgher, duke and artisan were equally bent on acquiring physiological assurance, amatory arsenals.

All foods and drinks were at some time investigated for the *ad hoc* purpose of ascertaining their essential virtues. On occasion, the amatory quality was absent, but the ingredient or item itself was wholesome or innocuous as a food. Thus there came under the experimental knife, and as possible grist to the erotic mill, pineapple and pimento, pork, potatoes, pomegranates and turnips, prawns, purslane, quince, pyrethrum, the necks of snails and the Japanese root ninjin, the galanga root of India, ginseng and goose tongue and guinea fowl. Also investigated for possible amatory reactions were polignonia and nymphaea, jackal's gall and the juice of gossypion, the plant vatodbhranta and veal sweetbread, venison and truffles, mint and egg drinks, the plant emblica myrabolam. In Central Europe endive was used as a love charm. Eryngo was for centuries considered a powerful aphrodisiac. It is mentioned in this respect in Shakespeare's The Merry Wives of Windsor and in Dryden's translation of the Roman satirist Juvenal. Avicenna considered euphorbium, a gum resin derived from an African plant, as an erotic aid. Halibut and hare soup, haricot beans and the juice of hedysarum gangeticum, henna and cyclamen, herring and pizza ugurdu, fish intestines and hydromel, the water lily and juniper berries, bitter quassia and whiting, ants, woodcock and octopus: all have in their time been treated as ancillary agents in the amatory laboratory. So too with olibanum, an aromatic resin, with darnel and sperm of deer, with dill and the brains of dove, dragon's blood and drepang, the holothuria found in Oceania and the Red Sea: with yeast and the herb yarrow. Myrrh as an ingredient in powdered form had its votaries: and radishes too, pounded cloves and resins, rice oil and cod roe. Tarragon produces fragrant leaves used in flavoring: also for its putative stimulation. The testes of lamb, lion, ass and ram have been used in Tuscany and Spain, in Morocco and Provence, and have been prized for their rejuvenating action. So with certain seeds, and the Indian root uchchata, sage and the plant savory, salmon and salvia, scammony; sparrows and sturgeon, surag and gillyflower.

H. E. W.

Polygamy

Polygamy

Polygamy is the marriage of more than one woman to a man. Polygyny means a marriage in which a man has more than one wife. The first term is frequently misused for the second term. Polygyny, historically, has been widespread, especially, but not exclusively, among pre-literate peoples.

H. E. W.

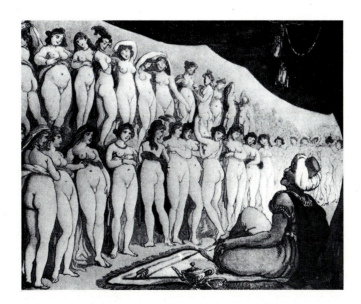

*A satirical representation of a Sultan
with his numberless wives.*

Thomas Rowlandson (1756-1827)

Erotic Academy

THE WOMAN WITH THE PARROT

Eugene Delacroix (1798-1863)
Musée de la Ville, Lyon

Erotic Academy

In 1739 there was founded in France an Académie de Ces Dames et de Ces Messieurs, that was active until 1776. Its members were young persons of the nobility and literary men interested in eroticism. Among the participants was the Countess Verrue, known as La Dame de Volupté.

H. E. W.

HARPY AT THE FOUNTAIN
In mythology, harpies were half-bird, half-woman. The water from the fountain is induced from the figure of the harpy.

Giovanni da Bologna: 16th century
Piazza del Nettuno, Bologna

[239]

VENUS AND MARS

Titian (1477-1576)
Art Gallery, Vienna

[240]

Amatory Advice:
Roman Style

VENUS AND CUPID

Francois Boucher

Amatory Advice: Roman Style

'Tis said, that Egypt for nine years was dry,
Nor Nile did floods, nor heav'n did rain supply.
A foreigner at length inform'd the king,
That slaughter'd guests would kindly moisture bring.
The king reply'd, on thee the lot shall fall,
Be thou, my guest, the sacrifice for all.
Thus Phalaris, Perillus taught to low,
And made him season first the brazen cow.
A rightful doom, the Laws of Nature cry,
'Tis, the artificers of death should die.
Thus justly women suffer by deceit;
Their practice authorizes us to cheat.
Beg her, with tears, thy warm desires to grant;
For tears will pierce a heart of adamant.
If tears will not be squeez'd, then rub your eye,
Or 'noint the lids, and seem at least to cry.
Kiss, if you can: resistance if she make,
And will not give you kisses, let her take.
Fie, fie, you naughty man, are words of course;
She struggles but to be subdu'd by force.
Kiss only soft, I charge you, and beware,
With your hard bristles not to brush the fair.
He who has gain'd kiss, and gains no more,
Deserves to lose the bliss he got before.
If once she kiss, her meaning is exprest;
There wants but little pushing for the rest.
Which if thou dost not gain, by strength or art,
The name of clown then suits with thy desert;
'Tis downright dulness, and a shameful part.
Perhaps, she calls it force; but, if she 'scape,
She will not thank you for th' omitted rape.

The sex is cunning to conceal their fires;
They would be forc'd, ev'n to their own desires.
They seem t'accuse you, with a down-cast sight,
But in their souls confess you did them right.
Who might be forc'd, and yet untouch'd depart,
Thank with their tongues, but curse you with their heart.
Fair Phoebe and her sister did prefer,
To their dull mates, the noble ravisher.
What Deidamia did, in days of yore,
The tale is told, but worth the reading o'er.
When Venus had the golden apple gain'd,
And the just judge fair Helen had obtain'd:
When she with triumph was at Troy receiv'd,
The Trojans joyful while the Grecians griev'd:
They vow'd revenge of violated laws,
And Greece was arming in the cuckold's cause:
Achilles, by his mother warn'd from war,
Disguis'd his sex, and lurk'd among the fair,
What means Eacides to spin and sow.
With spear, and sword, in field thy valor show;
And, leaving this, the nobler Pallas know.
Why dost thou in that hand the distaff wield,
Which is more worthy to sustain a shield?
Or with that other draw the wooly twine,
The same the Fates for Hector's thread assign?
Brandish thy falchion in thy pow'rful hand,
Which can alone the pond'rous lance command.
In the same room by chance the royal maid
Was lodg'd, and, by his seeming sex betray'd,
Close to her side the youthful hero laid.
I know not how his courtship he began;

[243]

But, to her lost, she found it was a man.
'Tis thought she struggled; but withal 'tis thought,
Her wish was to be conquer'd when she fought.
For when disclos'd, and hast'ning to the field,
He laid his distaff down, and took the shield,
With tears her humble suit she did prefer,
And thought to stay the grateful ravisher.
She sighs, she sobs, she begs him not to part:
And now 'tis nature, what before was art.
She strives by force her lover to detain,
And wishes to be ravish'd once again.
This is the sex; they will not first begin,
But when compell'd, are pleas'd to suffer sin.
Is there, who thinks that women first should woo;
Lay by thy self-conceit, thou foolish beaux.
Begin, and save their modesty the shame;
'Tis well for thee, if they receive thy flame.
'Tis decent for a man to speak his mind;
They but expect th' occasion to be kind.
Ask, that thou may'st enjoy; she waits for this;
And on thy first advance depends thy bliss.
Ev'n Jove himself was forc'd to sue for love;
None of the nymphs did first solicit Jove.
But if you find your pray'rs increase her pride,
Strike sail awhile, and wait another tide.
They fly when we pursue; but make delay,
And when they see you slacken, they will stay.
Sometimes it profits to conceal your end;
Name not yourself her lover, but her friend.
How many skittish girls have thus been caught?
He prov'd a lover, who a friend was thought.
Sailors by sun and wind are swarthy made;
A tann'd complexion best becomes their trade.
'Tis a disgrace to ploughmen to be fair;
Bluff cheeks they have, and weather-beaten hair.
Th' ambitious youth, who seeks an olive crown,

Is sun-burnt with his daily toil, and brown.
But if the lover hopes to be in grace,
Wan be his looks, and meager be his face.
That color, from the fair, compassion draws:
She thinks you sick, and thinks herself the cause.
Orion wander'd in the woods for love,
His paleness did the nymphs to pity move;
His ghastly visage argu'd hidden love.
Nor fail a night-cap, in full health, to wear;
Neglect thy dress, and discompose thy hair.
All things are decent, that in love avail.
Read long by night, and study to be pale:
Forsake your food, refuse your needful rest;
Be miserable, that you may be blest.
    Shall I complain, or shall I warn you most?
Faith, truth, and friendship in the world are lost;
A little and an empty name they boast.
Trust not thy friend, much less thy mistress praise:
If he believe, thou may'st a rival raise.
'Tis true, Patroclus, by no lust misled,
Sought not to stain his dear companion's bed.
Nor Pylades Hermione embrac'd;
Ev'n Phaedra to Perithous still was chaste.
But hope not thou, in this vile age, to find
Those rare examples of a faithful mind.
The sea shall sooner with sweet honey flow;
Or from the furzes pears and apples grow.
We sin with gust, we love by fraud to gain:
And find a pleasure in our fellow's pain.
From rival foes you may the fair defend;
But would you ward the blow, beware your friend.
Beware your brother, and your next of kin;
But from your bosom friend your care begin.

OVID: ARS AMATORIA
Trans. by John Dryden

The Nude in Art

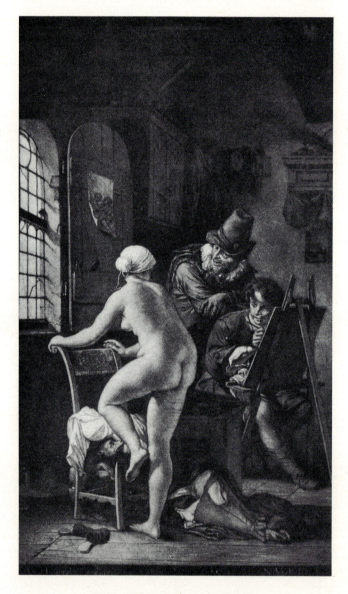

THE BEAUTIFUL MODEL

A. Houbraken: c. 1720

[246]

The Nude in Art

Pictorially and visually, the human body, male and female, has during the centuries undergone a series of evolutions. In another sense, man has looked on this same body with variant eyes; at the outset, with awed wonder at its harmony and proportion and the strange, satisfying ingenuities of its configuration.

The human figure then became idealized, and emphasis was placed by the artist or sculptor on the general recognitional effect that was produced on the spectator. The onlooker admires the sculptural skill of the craftsman, or the texture and coloring produced by the painter: and considers the nude body, in whatever pose, as a work of human talent, as a personal achievement, rather than a reproduction of his fellow man or woman.

In other directions, and chronological sequence does not here enter into the question, the human body denuded of trappings or barely draped in a minimal garment for the sake of heightened provocation, is presented in minute realistic detail, with the resultant erotic stimulations. Groupings, contrived poses, gestures, callipygian emphasis or stress on other erotogenic factors, bestialities and perversions, as in the Caves of Ajanta or the Pompeian frescoes, become the primary concern of the artist, whose motif is now the apotheosis of the sexual functions in all their diversities.

The exultant revelation of the naked form has then had its day. The esthetic mystery has vanished, and in its place appears, as it were, a pictorial, lewd voyeurism, a mixoscopic cunning, panting for participation in the priapic and aphroditic secrecies.

The great sculptors of antiquity as well as the masters of the Renaissance, the tribal cave-dwellers no less than the emotionally exhausted contemporary, have presented the human nude form either in static and normal postures, or in perverted ingenuities and associations, in paintings and frescoes, in occasional tentative studies, on gigantic canvases, in book illustration and in monumental statuary.

Basically, two motifs are apparent in the representation of the nude in art. One is an idealistic identification of the human body, as in the Venus of Milo, implying high skill and objectivity in the artist. The other type is largely realistic and arousing, emphasizing, not without skill or talent, the provocative anatomical features of the body. The Renaissance in particular stood amazed at the sensuousness or even the spirituality of the body, that could be expressed in panels and on canvas, on sculptural surfaces and statuary, but largely in the warmth and luxuriance of the painted figure. Michelangelo's sculpture of The Captive is an illustration. The nude, in fact, belongs artistically, at its apogee, to the Renaissance, when the muscular resilience in the male, the lithe sinuosity of the female, the anatomical exactitude of the human organism were rendered with the ultimate perfection. Names and figures jostle each other in endless progression: Titian's Diana and Actaeon: the sculptural Laocoon discovered in the early sixteenth century: Titian's Venus Anadyomene and his Venus of Urbino: Botticelli's The Birth of Venus and Giorgione's similar theme. The Renaissance, in short, produced the prototypes: later ages strove to imitate, although Velásquez' Rokeby Venus is wrought of startling genius.

LA FEMME

Amedeo Modigliani (1884-1920)
Gianni Mattioli, Milan

The taboo on nudity in actuality stems from the East. Genesis makes the prohibition to Adam and Eve, while Exodus issues an injunction against graven images.

Byzantine art imposed a cold rigidity on the human figure, that became alive only toward the fifteenth century.

Strangely enough, the new art that restored to the human body the form and lines that antiquity was familar with, began with the monastic illustrations to Biblical episodes. In the Middle Ages, acquaintance with the promiscuities and contiguity of the sexes in antiquity had a prohibitory result. Nudity and denudation became a matter of interdiction, and Lady Godiva became famous for the uniqueness of her daring.

By papal decree, especially that of Pope Paul IV, Michelangelo's nudes became an object of lewdness, fit for condemnation. Pius IX, Leo VIII, and John XIII equally occupied themselves with inspection of representations of nudes in churches. John XXIII in particular had the sex of angels, as displayed in the Vatican, modestly concealed. In the nineteenth century, in 1888, Emile Bayard founded in Paris a monthly review called Le Nu Esthétique. It implied that nudity, as an art motif, had arrived, that it demanded public recognition. By 1908, the nude in art had grown to a vast commercial enterprise, with the consequent intrusion of elements far removed from esthetics as such. In 1910, in France, the Salon d'Automne presented the first cubist nude. The exhibition provoked conflict and violent argumentation, public and private, individual and authoritative. In 1914 one of Van Dongen's nude paintings was torn from the wall by police authority.

A general survey of the nude form as an art subject would include monumental pictures that hang in the Museums of Europe and America, sketches, statuary, triptychs, etchings, illustrations. There is Hans Baldung's Lapsus Humani Generis, an Adam and Eve theme that belongs in the Bibliothèque Nationale in Paris. Laemlein's Le Réveil d'Adam: J. Gossart's L'Amour: Memling's Bathsheba's Bath all belong in this category. So with Hieronymus Bosch's The Garden of Delight: Crispin de Paffe's Lucretia Borgia: Giovanni Pedrin's Cleopatra: Parmigianino with his Diana Surprised: Antoine Wiertz' woman looking into a mirror and seeing her Satanic self: Janssen van Nuyssen's Lascivia: Joseph Heinz with his Lot and his Daughters: and the same subject treated by Adrian van der Werff. Subjects for nude depiction came from history and mythology, from Biblical literature, from the sacred and the profane. Goya has La Maja Desnuda: Guérard, The Harem: Modigliani, Femme Nue Endormie: Albrecht Dürer, Le Nu et l'Artiste: Cranach, Earthly Paradise: Johann Matsys, Suzanna at the Bath.

The moderns and contemporary are possibly less spacious in concept, but more prolific in execution. Auguste Rodin's The Kiss is sui generis. Among recent and contemporary artists are Félicien Rops and Hans Bellmer, Marcel Gromaire and Franz Hirmann, René Magritte and Maillol.

H. E. W.

Narcissism

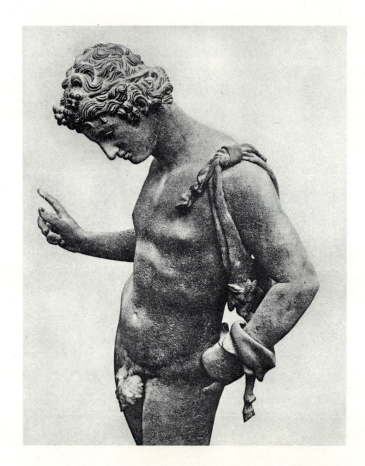

Narcissus, shunning all feminine love, saw his reflection in a pool. Falling in love with his own image, he pined away. The name of the sexual perversion Narcissism is derived from this mythological tale.

National Museum, Naples

Narcissism

A form of auto-eroticism that displays itself, in its extreme forms, by highly neurotic and morbid manifestations. One of the simpler directions that narcissism takes is in auto-reflection in a mirror, a procedure that dates back at least to the Roman poet Ovid.

Mythologically, Narcissus was a handsome youth who fell in love with his own image reflected in water.

H. E. W.

QUEEN ELIZABETH

In this Judgment of Paris, Queen Elizabeth, as Paris, awards the apple to herself, thus confirming herself as the goddess of beauty. In mythology, the three contestants for the prize of beauty, the golden apple inscribed 'To the Fairest', were Aphrodite, goddess of beauty, Minerva, goddess of wisdom, Hera or Juno, wife of the supreme god Zeus or Jupiter. The judge was Trojan Paris.

Hans Eworth
Hampton Court, England

THE COMPARISON

A. F. Lejeune: c. 1885

Masochism: Sexual Slavery

A SLAVE MERCHANT

Victor Giraud
Museum of the Luxembourg

Masochism: Sexual Slavery

SQUIRES EXCHANGE SERFS FOR DOGS
In Czarist Russia the human value was equated to a canine.
Taras Shevtshenko (1814-1861)
Old print

Masochism is a sexual perversion involving erotic pleasure derived from the infliction on oneself of pain or cruelty. The term is derived from Leopold von Sacher-Masoch (1835-1895). He was an Austrian writer whose novels depict this abnormality. He is, in fact, the arch-exponent of masochism. Among his works are Venus in Furs and Les Batteuses d'Hommes.

The concept of masochism is a complete physiological and erotic submission to the female partner, a reduction to an amorous and voluntary slave condition.

The Austrian novelist, Leopold von Sacher-Masoch, is associated with the term masochism. He produced a number of popular, sophisticated plays and tales. He himself appears to have experienced erotic reactions from violence inflicted upon his person. This circumstance became the theme of a number of stories, collected under the title of Cain's Heritage. His major work in this field is Venus in Furs. The protagonists are Severin, the willing victim, and Wanda, the woman who is responsible for producing the reactions. When the author died, in 1895, Venus in Furs had become the literary symbol of masochism throughout Europe.

H. E. W.

[255]

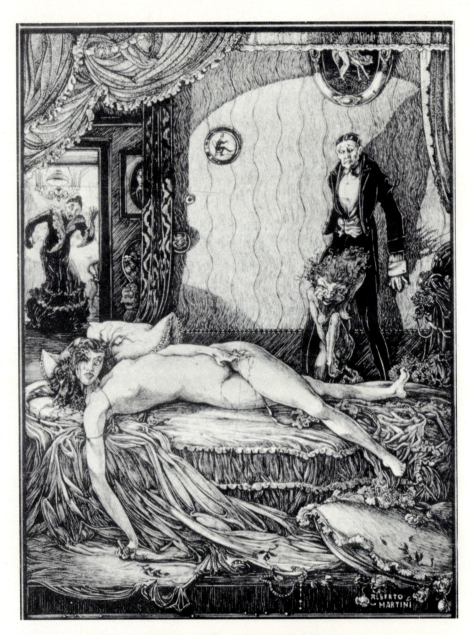

THE ASSAULTED VIRGIN

Alberto Martini
Dictionnaire de Sexologie,
Jean-Jacques Pauvert
Editeur, Paris

PSYCHODYNAMICS OF MASOCHISM

Of the two forms of masochism, the sexual and the moral, the latter is by far the more important. It represents a definite and frequent character structure, participates in the symptomatology of all neurotic conditions, and plays a fundamental part in Western culture. Indeed, moral masochism is so universal in human life that it was not recognized as an entity until the description of the sexual masochistic perversion sixty years ago threw a sharp spotlight upon it and gave it its name. The concept of moral masochism had, historically, a bad start. The analogy with the sexual perversion is the general and basic form that furnished the ground upon which, in a minority of persons and under certain circumstances in psychosexual development, the perversion may evolve.

Freud assumed masochism to be the manifestation of a death instinct. Prior to this theory Freud had stated that masochism is the sadism of the individual turned back upon himself. Most of those who are not inclined to accept the theory of the death instinct resort to this earlier definition. Freud said little about how and why this reversal occurs. The explanation given in his great paper, A Child is Being Beaten, namely, that it is motivated by a sense of guilt from the oedipus complex, fits some cases and does not fit a great many others. However, this theory has led to the widespread misconception that masochism is in any case the reflection of a person's own hatefulness and destructiveness and has to be interpreted as such. This is not only incorrect, but does injustice to the patient and harm to our therapy.

In a previous presentation, I suggested the theory that it is not the sadism of the masochist himself that is turned upon his ego, but the sadism of another person, a love object. The subject accepts the sadism of the love object for libidinal reasons and turns it upon himself by way of introjection, identification and superego formation. In this concept masochism is neither an instinctual phenomenon (death instinct) nor the expression of a component sexual drive of which moral masochism would be a so-called desexualized form. It is a disturbance of interpersonal relations, a pathological way of loving, which only in a minority of cases affects sexuality proper. In all cases the disturbance of interpersonal relations leads to and is maintained by a particular character formation. Masochism is a character neurosis. Thus it is taken out of the scope of the id and considered a function of the ego, namely a defense mechanism of the ego against an instinctual conflict.

Masochism means loving a person who gives hate and ill-treatment. In sexual masochism this person may be a voluptuous woman with a whip who needs sadistic stimulation for her sexual gratification, or a fantasy of this kind; or it may be a prostitute hired to act this part, thus materializing the fantasies of the lover and procuring sexual gratification while degrading him to the status of a naughty boy or a slave. This performance usually depicts a punishment. Moral masochism is devoid of overt sexuality. In Freud's definition, the suffering itself is sought without regard to the person administering it: 'It may even be caused by impersonal forces or circumstances, but the true masochist always holds out his cheek whenever he sees a chance of receiving a blow.' The motivation of this self-maiming attitude was deemed by Freud to be an unconscious sense of guilt or need for punishment. However, in analyzing this form of masochism, we find that it means as well loving a person who ill-treats and hates one. The subject re-lives and re-enacts in interpersonal relations a submissive devotion to and a need for the love of a hating or rejecting love object, who was originally a parent or some other unfriendly person of his childhood, and who lives on in his superego. It is the superego that keeps the original situation alive through transference to any suitable person or set of circumstances in later life.

In the history of every masochistic patient we find an unhappy childhood, often to such an extreme that we are led to wonder if the development of a masochistic character was not a protection against a schizophrenic or depressive psychosis. In these cases the function of masochism as a defense soon becomes evident. The basic emotional disposition is founded on the need for being loved at the level of oral and skin eroticism. The infant is not only absolutely dependent on its environment, but also biologically attached to it by its libidinal needs, i.e. love, which is like a psychic umbilical cord. If the early love objects treat it with hate or the hostile component of ambivalence, the infant is unable at first to perceive it, but later its instinct for self-preservation and an imperative need for love may motivate it to repress the perception (denial). The normal adult, experiencing an absence of love, hates in return and gives up the love object. The dependent child, in order not to lose the vitally needed love object, submits and accepts the suffering which the object imposes as if it were love, and is not conscious of the difference.

The child introjects the pain-giving object because of an oral need for its love. Simultaneously it represses any hostile reaction against the loved object because that also would cause its loss. The child does not love suffering or ill-treatment — nobody does — but because it loves the person who gives it, the ill-treatment is libidinized. Masochism is the hate or the sadism of the object reflected in the libido of the subject. Love and sadism are instincts, masochism is not; it is the defense of the ego against, and the neurotic solution of, conflict between manifestations of those two instincts: the need for being loved and the experiencing of hostility instead. Primarily it has nothing to do with the masochist's own sadism.

A simple form of masochism is illustrated by the fairy tale of Cinderella, who responded to hateful treatment with humble devotion, who knew that she was good and loving, and had the undying hope in her heart that one day she would be rewarded. Innumerable variations of this fantasy occur in patients, who derive a compensation for suffering from the feeling of their own goodness and lovability. Suffering enhances the individual's sense of his value as a love object, and he may therefore feel good. Here the defense is a retreat into a narcissistic position. The consciousness of the value in terms of love in suffering is a protection against being crushed by the hate of the loved objects. Likewise feeling sorry for oneself feels good because suffering has come to mean being worthy of love.

In real life however this narcissistic defense usually fails. Under its compensatory surface there remains the detrimental disposition to act out continually the old trauma. In a previous paper I described a girl who spent her childhood in great poverty, was completely unwanted and mistreated by her mother, and became depressed to the point of a suicidal tendency which she expressed: 'My greatest guilt is that I did not do away with myself to please my mother.' In spite of this misery she grew up to be a young woman of great physical beauty, which may well have been a psychosomatic effect of her compensatory narcissism. A Prince Charming came in the person of a wealthy and kindly man who fell in love with her, married her, and provided her with a life of luxury. She 'could not take it.' She was frigid, lived in constant anxiety and depression, and counteracted her happiness in every possible way. She forced her husband into the role of her hating and punishing mother, and went on acting out the part of the hated and unwanted child.

This is an example of a great multitude of similar cases. The person acts out the old situation without knowing what he is repeating, taking the situation thus re-enacted erroneously for actuality and reality. The deeper underlying motivation of this unhappiness is the wish to please a hating parent, to placate or to ingratiate himself with the parent by being unhappy, by failing or, in other cases, by being helpless or stupid. It is the wish to be loved by a parent who hates or depreciates.

Freud understood moral masochism as the expression of an unconscious sense of guilt and need for punishment. The feeling of guilt is present in all masochists, but it can not be considered an ultimate explanation. The disposition to guilt is certainly a phylogenetic inheritance; however, to regard it as the sole explanation of masochism leads therapeutically into the same blind alley as the theory of the death instinct. Analyzing the content of the guilt in the individual we find in the masochist, in contradistinction to the obsessional neurotic, that it is not the reaction to anal-sadistic impulses, but has a more asthenic character; it stems from the oral love for a person who hates and engenders guilt. This love sees the other person right and the self wrong. And is these a need for punishment? Yes, if the ill-treatment which was lovingly introjected took the form of punishment or discipline which is often but a rationalization of hate for the child, which then makes itself the whipping boy for the benefit of a sadistic parent. In adult proportion, any external reality or fate may take the place of this parent.

A patient said: 'As a boy I took my spanking when I deserved it and then went for more. My parents paid no attention to me when I was good; they did so only when I was bad.' For him being spanked had come to mean being given attention, being loved. He ingratiated himself in this way with the punishing parent so that, to some extent, he could enjoy punishment as a substitute for love. He derived no sexual stimulation from being spanked. Whenever this occurs, through erogenous irritation of the skin, it does not seem to be a primary factor but merely an intensification of the loving attachment to the pain-giving object of love.

Punishment is also sought because it helps curb one's own aggressiveness which may cause the loss of the love object: thus, with denial and libidinization, it is an additional means of defense. The masochist invites punishment by demonstrativeness, accusations, naughtiness, aggressiveness, as if he would say: 'Punish me and help me to be good so that I will be loved by you.' Or he punishes

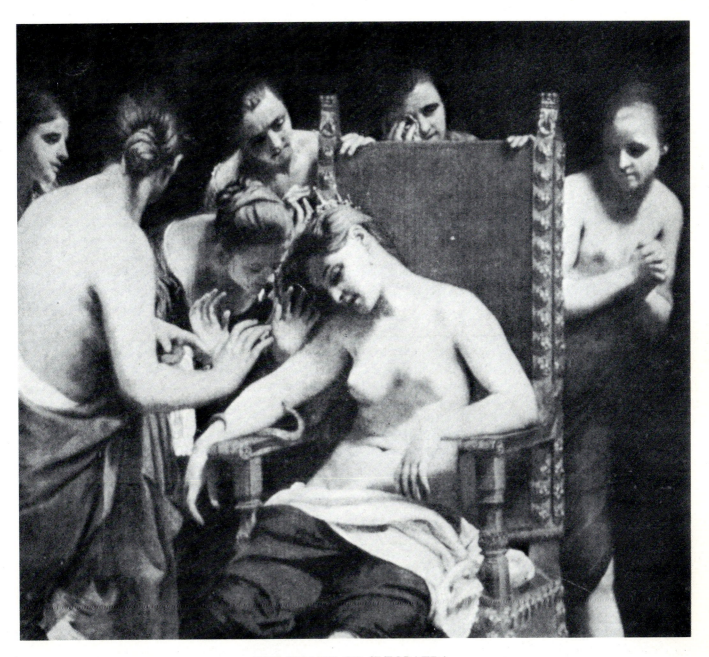

THE DEATH OF CLEOPATRA

G. Cagnacci
Kunsthistorisches Museum, Vienna

himself with the idea: 'Look, I took care of my punishment myself; you need not punish me any more; you can love me again, and love me all the more because I am so good in my suffering.' Need for punishment or self-punishment is thus a bid for affection; it is the need for the love of a person who punishes. Without this reference to an individual, a need for punishment as the moral form of an instinctual 'lust for pain,' does not seem to exist.

The objection may be raised against this concept that it neglects the importance of the fear of castration and feelings of guilt connected with it. Castration fear of course occurs, but it is experienced against the background of the repressed preoedipal suffering; the specific masochistic defense (libidinization of suffering motivated by oral need for love) applies to it too. In other words, fear of castration is not specific for masochism. It conditions the masochistic sexual perversion; not however moral masochism.

The provocative behavior of moral masochists gives again and again the impression that they need, and often almost passionately ask for, punishment. However, if we base our analytic interpretation upon this observation we encounter the strongest resistances, often in the form of negative therapeutic reactions. Severe cases of this kind are those mentioned by Freud, '... which we have not yet succeeded in understanding completely.' This difficulty led me to adopt a different point of view whose results, observed over many years, give me confidence that it is correct.

Masochistic aggressiveness appears in two ways. First it is an intensified bid for affection. The search for love through suffering is not superseded by aggression; it remains the basis of operation for the latter. When the masochist markets his suffering with demonstrativeness or the exhibition of martyrdom he feels it gives him a claim for being loved, and also for prestige and domination. He welcomes being hurt, not because it hurts, but because it makes him right above others. He would rather be right than happy. He gains not only love-worthiness but also strength of ego from suffering. Inflicting himself upon the love object is a magic gesture devised to induce the object to change its mind and to give more love. The idea that the object may dislike this provocation is repressed. He behaves as if presenting an old unpaid bill for love, and he puts pressure on the love object, refusing to believe that his bill may not be paid. The attitude to which Edmund Bergler refers, in his description of the 'mechanism

of orality,' of maneuvering oneself into being wronged, often with no more than some contributory negligence or a subtle setting of the stage, is in my opinion not so much a springboard for aggression, as Bergler sees it, but an attempt to provoke others to come out with tokens of love. Thus the love of a partner may be put to tests which are impossible to fulfill: the old frustration i sre-enacted. I agree with Bergler that masochistic aggression (or pseudo aggression, as Bergler calls it) is a cloak for the deeper, repressed masochistic wish.

Secondly, masochistic aggressiveness is a more intense form of the magic gesture characterized by the idea: 'You will be sorry.' It is revenge which, however, is veiled from consciousness by its libidinization. It is the love object toward which vindictiveness is directed but which also cannot be given up. Making someone sorry, by self-sabotage, is intended both to hurt the love object and make it concerned for the subject. The violent claim for love gives the masochist the feeling that he has a right to punish his love object. This drive to punish the love object impresses me as much more important than the 'need for punishment.' If we understand the drive to punish only as a projective defense against a sense of guilt we fail to see its specific masochistic structure.

These two forces and their ambivalent interplay are responsible for the great perseverance of the masochistic character: the need for the affection of a frustrating love object and the drive to punish the object. The beloved partner, or his proxy who is to be punished, has to be provoked and put in the wrong and simultaneously the illusion of being loved by him has to be maintained. It is this magic thinking, obstructing any testing of reality, that makes the condition so persistent.

Seen against the deeper background of the oral need for love this aggressiveness of the masochist appears clearly not as the primary driving force but as a secondary defense against masochism. The primary defense against suffering at the hands of a love object, its denial and libidinization, is unsuccessful because, like neurotic repression, it does not remove its objective from existence but preserves it in the unconscious, making it a permanent pattern of behavior. Against this painful condition the secondary defense of aggression is directed; it is a conversion of passivity into activity which not only fails to remove the suffering but preserves it. I feel inclined to compare this defense with the counterphobic attitude described by Fenichel, and to call it a 'countermasochistic' attitude.

THE THREE WITCHES

Antoine Watteau

The basic pattern of the drive to punish is of course the traditional attitude of parents toward their children, fusing and often confusing love with punishment, rationalized with the deep-rooted philosophy that the child must not be spoiled, or that it is born wicked and has to be made good by chastisement. Some parents thus prejudiced or possessive in their own claims for affection — this being of course a matter of degree and usually entirely unconscious — would rather see a child guilty than love it, and they rationalize, if not the very existence of the child, then its early biological and later social naughtiness, as justification for their sadism. The sense of guilt thus planted in the child is sometimes a defensive camouflage of its unconscious drive to punish the parent, a kind of projection of the act of making guilty, as if saying, 'I do not see you being guilty. You (the parent) shall see me to be guilty.' The child's feeling of guilt, then, takes the place of what may be called its unconscious sense of the guilt of the parent. It is the defense against realizing the guilt of the parent for fear of losing him as a love object.

The drive to punish is associated with a feeling of righteousness. However it is not the feeling that punishing the rejecting parent would be a just revenge. That would not be masochistic at all. It a feeling of righteousness that arises from the superego. Analysis regularly reveals that the person feels he is doing the right thing according to the sadistic object whose love he craves; and that he will gain the love and approval of the object when he expresses aggressive trends which copy those of the object. These aggressive trends, originally experienced in the love object appear in two ways: they are directed against the ego, causing self-inflicted suffering or what appears to be self-punishment; or they are directed against the external world in the way the original love object has treated or would treat external objects.

The permanent wish to please the once rejecting, introjected object causes the person to lose his identity. To accommodate a hating parent he may make himself as unlovable as he feels the parent wants him to be. He may deny his good qualities or his intelligence, often to the degree of pseudodebility; he fails to exploit his opportunities or to seek legitimate enjoyment, confusing an irrational asceticism with virtue that earns love; he 'lives down' to the views of those who resent him, in order to be accepted by them. He feels that he has to make efforts and sacrifices to reconcile the world with his existence, and he does so by suffering as well as by being hostile or mischievous, which lowers his value as a love object and releases the hater from having to love him. He is stigmatized with unwantedness and displays his stigma as his bid for affection.

On the other hand, with submission to parental power, the masochist borrows the authority for the drive to punish. That feels good, and indemnifies him for his suffering passive submission. The aggressiveness of the masochist is not the manifestation of his primary sadism; the latter only furnishes part of the energy with which the identification with the hater is set into action. It is this imitation, out of his search for love, which makes the masochist feel that by being aggressive he is the way he is supposed to be. This accounts for the fact that these persons are often so astonishingly unaware of their provocative behavior. The superego shields the ego and furnishes the motives for aggression.

A simple and frequent example is the mother who has the habit of nagging her husband and drilling her children into an overconformist attitude. She is identified with her mother whose educational principles, exaggerated sometimes by spiteful submission, she imposes on her husband and children, so that they will be approved of by her mother. She has no intent of being unloving, feels only that she is right according to her mother's standards.

The need for punishment which Freud considered the central motive of moral masochism is the acceptance, in form and content, of the drive to punish which operates in the love object, resulting in punishing oneself and in punishing others, thus developing one's own drive to punish and passing it on to the next generation. The identification with the parental drive to punish seems to be the strongest foundation of our moral standards, but it makes freaks of them. It accounts for the universality of moral masochism in our culture. No death instinct needs to be postulated to explain masochism.

Finally, a word about differential diagnosis. Moral masochism is often confused with compulsion neurosis. The prevailing definition, that masochism is a way in which a person deals with his feelings of guilt about his own sadistic impulses, applies actually to compulsion neurosis, not to masochism. This definition is not even consistent with Freud's statement that in obsessional neurosis there is the turning of sadism upon the subject's self, but without the attitude of passivity towards another person. 'Self-torment and self-punishment,' Freud says, 'have arisen from the desire to torture, but not masochism.' Very often,

LOVE AND DEATH

Johann Heinrich Fussli
Zurich Museum

however, we find masochistic and obsessional phenomena co-existing in the same individual because all neurotic conditions overlap, and symptoms are mixed. Superficially masochism and compulsion neurosis may look very much alike, as far as the self-harming attitudes are concerned. The differential points, however, are the following.

Masochism develops from oral erotism and is the libidinal reaction to another person's sadism. Compulsion neurosis stems from anal erotism and from the subject's own sadism and the fear of its consequences, although masochistic motivations often assist in this development.

The masochist has a weak ego, is dependent, love-seeking, and forms a strong transference in therapy. The compulsive neurotic has a strong ego supported by anal aggressiveness, is stubborn, often negativistic, having little need for love. This need may be repressed, or warded off by isolation which never occurs in the masochist. The compulsive neurotic has difficulty in forming a transference.

The basic unconscious idea in the compulsive neurotic is: 'What have I done?' The aim is to avoid anxiety. The basic unconscious idea in the masochist is: 'What has been done to me?' The aim is to gain love. The compulsive neurotic is paying imaginary debts, not knowing what the real debt was: the masochist is presenting an old unpaid bill for affection.

BERNARD BERLINER, Ph.D,. M.D.
Encyclopedia of Aberrations

Flagellation

Flagellation

Flagellation is a perversion involving whipping and flogging for the purpose of arousing erotic reactions. In antiquity, flagellation as a means of sexual excitation is rare. It occurs, however, in one of the Dialogues of the Courtesans by the Greek satirist Lucian (c. 120-180 A.D.), in which two courtesans, Ampelis and Chrysis, discuss the practice.

The Marquis de Sade's novels contain many frenzied descriptions of fustigation. So too with Leopold von Sacher-Masoch's works, particularly Les Batteuses d'Hommes.

In the Orient too flagellation has been prevalent in an erotic direction.

Seneca, the Roman Stoic philosopher, considered flagellation as a remedy for the quartan ague. A later writer, Jerome Mercurialis, describes flagellation as an aid in increasing the weight of lean persons. Galen, the famous Greek authority whose reputation lasted well into the Middle Ages, adds that it was used by slave merchants as a method of making the slaves plump and more appealing for sale.

Richter, in his Opuscula Medica, refers to the treatment as a sexual stimulus:

ex stimulantium fonte, cardiaca, aphrodisiaca, diaphoretica, diuretica, aliaque non infimi ordinis medicamenta peti.

In the seventeenth century Meibomius extensively advocated this remedy. He wrote a monograph on the subject, entitled De Flagrorum Usu in Re Venerea.

A couplet, introducing the book, runs as follows in the English rendering:

Lo! Cruel stripes the sweets of love insure,
And painful pleasures pleasing pains procure.

Millingen, in his Curiosities of Medical Experience, similarly declares that the effect of flagellation may be readily referred to the powerful sympathy which exists between the nerves of the lower part of the spinal marrow and other organs. Artificial excitement appears in some degree natural; it is observed in several animals, especially in the feline race. Even snails plunge into each other a bony prickly spur, that arises from their throats, and which, like the sting of the wasp, breaks off, and is left in the wound.

The Abbé Boileau, in his Histoire des Flagellants, has this to say:

Necesse est cum musculi lumbares virgis aut flagellis diverberantur, spiritus vitales revelli, adeoque salaces motus ob viciniam partium genitalium et testium excitari, qui venereis illecebris cerebrum mentemque fascinant ac virtutem castitatis ad extremas angustias redigunt.

On the testimony of Pliny the Elder, Cornelius Gallus, friend of the Roman poet Vergil, had to resort to the scourge in order to achieve amatory consummation.

Another instance refers to a notorious Italian libertine, who used a whip steeped in vinegar:

FLAGELLATION

The Flagellants were medieval religious enthusiasts who administered self-floggings in penance for sin.

Miniature in 15th century manuscript

Plus on le fouettait, plus il y trouvait des délices, la douleur et la volupté marchant dans cet homme d'un pas égal.

A French epitaph alludes to a similar circumstance:

Je suis mort de l'amour entrepris
Entre les jambes d'une dame,
Bien heureux d'avoir rendu l'âme,
Au même lieu où je l'ai pris.

It has also been conjectured that Abelard employed this means. In writing to Héloïse, he declares:

Verbera quandoque debet amor non furor, gratia non ira, quae omnium unguentorum suavitatem transcenderent — Stripes which, whenever inflicted by love, not by fury but affection, transcended, in their sweetness, every unguent.

Again, he rebukes himself:

[268]

KNEELING WOMAN

Toulouse-Lautrec (1864-1901)

Thou knowest to what shameful excesses my unbridled lust had delivered up our bodies, so that no sense of decency, no reverence for God, could, even in the season of our Lord's passion, or during any other holy festival, drag me forth from out that cesspool of filthy mire; but that even with threats and scourges I often compelled thee who wast, by nature, a weaker vessel, to comply, notwithstanding thy unwillingness and remonstrances.

The same practices are recorded in the case of Tamerlane, the Asiatic conqueror, who was also a monorchis.

A certain Abbé Chuppe d'Auteroche, who died late in the eighteenth century, asserted that in Russia, in the vapor baths, stripes were administered to the frequenters as a stimulus to the venereal appetite.

Jean Jacques Rousseau was likewise susceptible to flagellation:

> J'avais trouvé dans la douleur, dans la honte même, un mélange de sensualité qui m'avait laissé plus de désir que de crainte de l'éprouver derechef.

H. E. W.

Deviations and Aberrations

THE MAN OUT OF PLACE
Illustration for La Fontaine's Le Rossignol.
Hyacinthe Rigaud (1659-1743)
New York Public Library

Deviations and Aberrations

Variations and aberrations from normally and socially acceptable standards of behavior have always included, among other divergencies, those of a sexual nature. In some instances these divergencies were inspired by religious or spiritual motives: in others, by physiological and emotional conditions.

TRIBADISM

TRIBADISM: Tribadism is an etymologically variant designation for Lesbianism. It is the female counterpart of homosexuality. This type of association was anciently linked with the island of Lesbos, the birthplace of the Greek poetess Sappho. Sappho is the literary spokesman for this practice. Sparta, too, or Lacadaemon, was known for the same abnormality. The Greek satirist Lucian, in his Dialogues of Courtesans, treats the subject at great length, making a certain Megilla the mouthpiece as it were of her fellow practitioners.

The names of actual tribads known in antiquity have come down to us. A certain Philaenis of Leucadia wrote and illustrated a treatise on tribadic activities. The most famous of them all is of course Sappho, who was born c. 612 B.C. Her poetry is pervaded by the feminine passion. Among her friends were Euneica, Gongyla, Megara, Anagora, Atthis. Sappho displayed, in her febrile poems, such intense amorous feelings, especially in the case of this Atthis, that the Roman poet Horace calls her masculine — mascula.

In the course of time the tribad, the Lesbian, acquired in public a condemnatory stigma. A Lesbian, in fact, became equated with a harlot. Another Lesbian, known by name, was Nossis, of Locris in Italy. She belonged in the fourth century B.C. and was also a poetess. Centuries later, in France, there was a club of tribads known as Les Chevaliers du Clair de Lune.

NECROPHILIA: The practice of erotic association with a corpse was known to the ancients. A certain Dimoetes, on finding the corpse of a beautiful woman washed up on shore, consummated his lust on the body: when disintegration of the body set in, he committed suicide. An Egyptian embalmer likewise abused the corpse of a woman, as the historian Herodotus recounts. Again Periander, ruler of Corinth, similarly maltreated the body of his dead wife Melissa.

In the obscure legends and folklore of Central Europe

THE GOAT FIEND

A witch is sacrificing a human being
to the goat-formed Archfiend.

Goya (1746-1828)
Metropolitan Museum of Art, N.Y.

necrophilia was frequently associated, in the popular mind, with vampirism. The subject is treated by Lombroso and Krafft-Ebing.

BESTIALITY: Physiological and erotic relationship between human beings and animals were often represented on the antique stage. Among the subjects treated in pantomime, in Roman Imperial times, was the story of Pasiphae's passion for the bull: also the tale of a matron of Thessalonika and her amorous adventures with Lucius, the hero of the tale, who had been changed into an ass.

The perversion of bestiality or sodomy, as it is variantly termed, is frequently mentioned in the Greek writers. Europa and Zeus in bovine form were a stock theme.

The crocodiles of Egypt, too, mentioned by Plutarch, and the snakes that were so well treated in Rome, according to Suetonius the Roman historian, were also associated with this practice.

Many deities and zoo-anthropomorphic semi-deities were the products of sexual unions between mortals and the animal-formed protean divinities of the ancient pantheon. Jupiter, for instance, often assumes the form of a familiar animal: a pig, or eagle, a bull, a cuckoo.

In a literary sense, bestiality has inspired many novels, especially in France: e.g. La Belle et La Bête, by Mme. Leprince de Beaumont: L'Histoire de Wardân le boucher avec la fille du vizir. Honoré de Balzac's tale Une Passion dans le Désert relates the amorous adventures of a soldier and a panther. John Collier's Le Mari de la Guenon and Monique Watteau's L'Ange à Fourrure belong in the same category.

E. A. Poe's Murder in the Rue Morgue is of the same genre.

The cinema has borrowed the theme to produce horror episodes. Mighty Joe Young, Congorilla, and Konga are extensions, however crude, of essential bestiality.

In the Middle Ages and during the Renaissance bestiality was practiced in rural and isolated areas. Confirmatory testimony appears in Ludovico Hernandez' Les Procès de Bestialité au XVIe et XVIIe Siècles. A certain Jean Vigeon, for instance, was burned at the stake for his associations with his hen-house.

In the Orient, in North Africa, in Saigon and other Eastern cities, establishments were set up that presented to visitors unions between farmyard creatures, donkeys, goats, sheep, mares, hens, dogs, and humans.

Pictorially, Les Deux Femmes au Tigre, by Zita, and Entre la Bestialité et la Mythologie, and Une Circé Moderne are contemporary instances of the practice.

Bestiality, as Plutarch realized, is the renunciation of the human status: 'No man has ever been invited to coition by any animal, though you constrain beasts forcibly to the act as well as to other shameful pleasures.'

A young and an old witch are on their way to a Sabbat,
by means of levitation.

Goya (1746-1828)
Metropolitan Museum of Art, N.Y.

[275]

HERCULES AND OMPHALE

Hercules, to expiate the murder of his son Iphitus, was sent by the Delphic oracle to work for three years at the court of Omphale, queen of Lydia. Hercules was turned into an effeminate creature, spinning wool, dressed in woman's clothes, while Omphale carried his club. Later, Hercules became Omphale's lover. The tale contains elements of transvestism.

Louvre, Paris

The vice is known to the Bible:

Neither shalt thou lie with any beast to defile thyself therewith; neither shall any woman stand before a beast to lie down thereto.

Leviticus 18. 23.

And again:

And if a man lie with a beast, he shall surely be put to death: and ye shall slay the beast.
And if a woman approach unto any beast, and lie down thereto, thou shalt kill the woman, and the beast; they shall surely be put to death; their blood shall be upon them.

Leviticus 20. 15-16.

Sodomy was the result of Egyptian and Asiatic luxury, evolving from the religious cults. The Egyptians, in fact, had Mendes, the sacred goat, worshipped through Sodomitic practices by female votaries.

In the temple of Aesculapius tame snakes were believed to have been employed for the purpose of sodomy.

MESSALINA

Messalina, wife of the Emperor Claudius, was, even in Imperial Rome, noted for her profligacy and licentiousness. The satirist Juvenal thunders against her monstrous lewdness and her disregard of all public and private moral standards.

Antique Sculpture
Uffizi Gallery, Florence

Among the Roman women the ass, notorious for salaciousness, was similarly used. In this regard mention is made by Juvenal, the Roman satirist, in the sixth satire.

Among practitioners of sodomy was Giorgio Basta, an Italian general of Greek descent. In the Duke of Parma's campaigns in the Low Countries, in Germany, Hungary, and Transylvania, Basta was credited with being regularly accompanied by a goat that he abused as a mistress.

Another sinister figure with like tendencies was Louis de Gonzaga, who married Henrietta of Clèves in 1565.

VOYEURISM: Also called, by Greek etymological associations, mixoscopy. This is a sexually perverted condition reputed to stimulate the erotic sensibilities. There are many descriptions of voyeurism in the novels of the Marquis de Sade. In Les 120 Journeés de Sodome a typical episode occurs:

Il vint un homme chez moi me faire une singulière proposition. Il s'agissait de trouver des libertins qui s'amusassent avec sa femme et sa fille, aux seules conditions de le cacher dans un coin pour voir tout ce qu'on leur ferait.

ZEUS AND LEDA
LEDA WAS THE MOTHER OF HELEN OF TROY
National Museum, Athens.

These secret observations were not unknown to the ancients. In Homer's Odyssey, Hephaestus, husband of Aphrodite, wishes all the gods to observe the lascivious spectacle of his wife in sexual embrace with Ares, the war god. In this instance, observation did not involve secrecy.

Herodotus, the Greek historian, describes a case of mixoscopy in the story of King Candaules. The king, proud of his wife's beauty, induced his friend Gyges to conceal himself in the nuptial chamber and witness the unrobing of the queen. Aware of the situation, the queen was shamed, and made this offer to Gyges: "Either slay Candaules my lord and gain the kingdom of Lydia, or be content to die at once yourself where you are." Gyges slew Candaules, married the queen, and became king of Lydia.

IRRUMATION: A sexual perversion that is described as membrum in os adrigere.

FELLATIO

A sexual perversion that employs the lingua or the

[278]

OEDIPUS AND THE SPHINX
*The Sphinx, half human, half bestial, sometimes called
'the wise virgin', propounded a riddle that brought death to
the unsuccessful contestants. Oedipus, answering the riddle
correctly, assumed the throne of Thebes and later married
unwittingly his own mother.*

Terracotta Vase, Berlin

labra. Both these vices are mentioned by the Greeks and
the Romans: by the lexicographer Hesychius, by Lucian,
and Cicero.

The Church Fathers fulminate specifically against them.
Martial the Roman epigrammatist makes reference to
the abnormality:

That you gladly pass the night with the over-
flowing wine-cup, may be excused: that is Cato's
vice, Gaurus, that you have. That you compose

poems without the aid of the Muses and Apollo,
deserves praise. You have Cicero's fault. That
you vomit: that was Antony's way. That you are
an epicure: so was Apicius. That you are a fel-
lator, whose vice is that, tell me.

HERMAPHRODITISM: The androgynous concept, both biologically and in a cosmic sense in general, was familiar to
the Greeks. On the island of Cyprus an androgynous deity
was worshipped at Amathus. The cult involved a form of
couvade: a young man annually lying in childbed and

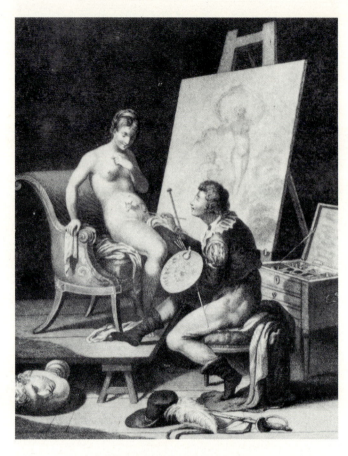

LE BAT: LA FONTAINE
This painting illustrates La Fontaine's Le Bât: the reproduction of the donkey is a witness to the woman's fidelity.

imitating labor pains.

There was a hermaphroditic divinity called Aphroditos, who wore a beard but had a female form and feminine dress. Public buildings, baths, private houses displayed statues or pictorial representations of Hermaphroditos. The deity is also sculpturally depicted as being embraced by the Satyrs or Pan himself.

Another deity of the same type was Leucippus, whose festival, called The Festival of Undressing, Apodysia, was celebrated in Crete.

The Greek and Roman comedy writers depict hermaphroditic scenes.

Biologically, the androgynous form is not unknown in medical history.

EUNUCHISM: Etymologically, as a Greek derivative, the term means a bed-watcher. In antiquity, the priests of Cybele, the Galli, castrated themselves in a religious frenzy. Catullus, the Roman lyric poet, describes the rite in one of his poems entitled Atys.

Eunuchism involves castration, although there are cases of biological eunuchs. In the Orient the eunuch was attached, innocuously, to the guardianship of the harem. Voluntary eunuchism was not unknown among religious

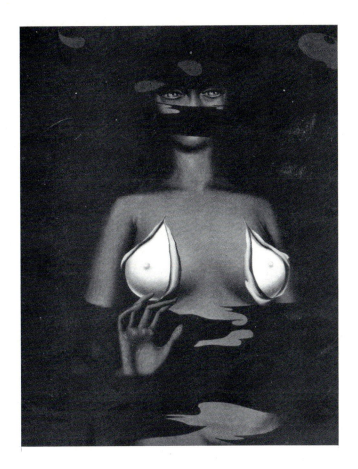

THE FUTURE VEILED

Felix Labisse

ascetics, especially in the Middle Ages. It was a means of eliminating lust and carnal desire. Abelard is a case of enforced eunuchism.

The eunuch, in ancient Rome and in the Orient in all ages, played his part. Ovid, the Roman erotic poet, elaborates on the offices performed by the eunuch:

Ay me, an eunuch keeps my mistress chaste,
That cannot Venus' mutual pleasure taste.
Who first deprived young boys of their best part,
With selfsame wounds he gave, he ought to smart.
To kind requests thou would'st more gentle prove,
If ever wench had made lukewarm thy love:

Thou were not born to ride, or arms to bear,
Thy hands agree not with the warlike spear.
Men handle those; all manly hopes resign,
Thy mistress' ensigns must be likewise thine.
Please her — her hate makes others thee abhor;
If she discards thee, what use serv'st thou for?
Good form there is, years apt to play together;
Unmeet is beauty without use to wither.
She may deceive thee, though thou her protect;
What two determine never wants effect.

H. E. W.

[281]

THE KISS
Edvard Munch (1863-1944)
National Gallery of Art, Rosanwald Collection

SEXUAL PERVERSION

The generalized psychiatric acceptance of the term perversion has broadened to that which includes any deviation of the normal heterosexual act of coitus which tends to be fixed and exclusive in its nature. Freud has attempted a somewhat more specific designation by dividing perverted acts into those which take place as an anatomical transgression from parts of the body designated by nature for sexual union or a deviation from a normal sexual aim. Thus, perversions of the first class would be fellatio, cunnilingus, anilingus, whereas those perverted sexual acts which use a substitutive object from the normal one would include fetishism, necrophagism, coprophilia, and kleptomania. It will be noted, therefore, that one of the essential elements of the definition of perversion implies the existence of a love object. The love object may be phantasied or be inanimate as in necrophagia or be a substitutive object as in fetishism. Masturbation without phantasy, therefore, is not a perversion, whereas with exhibitionism, it becomes such an act. This distinction is of importance inasmuch as failure to consummate the sexual act is a frustration of the race propagation of the community, whereas otherwise it becomes merely an offense against the individual himself.

Much confusion exists among sexologists as to the delimitations of the various perversions. There is a constant tendency to broaden the scope of each designation. The Law itself is quite vague in this matter and in many states penalties are laid down for a wide number of

THE KISS

Georges Grosz

perverted acts coming under a common designation. Thus, Sodomy has been designated by law in several states to include unnatural acts between human beings, whereas its original designation limited the act to one between an animal and a human being. In the forepleasure of normal coitus, modified forms of sexual perversions may occur. If these do not pervert the participants from the consummation of the normal act and if these abnormalities in themselves do not become fixed and do not become the prime object of satisfaction, then they are not to be considered perversions. A great many forms of perverted sexual acts are known but those of chief interest from the point of view of culpability in the eyes of the law are as follows:

Anilingus, the commission of a perverted sexual act by the use of the mouth on the anus. Individuals so indulging have regressed to the anal erotic level of development. It is essentially an infantile act.

Cunnilingus, the commission of a perverted sexual act by the use of the mouth upon the external genitalia of the female. This frequently occurs between homosexuals of the female type. Not infrequently it is one of the perverted acts found in the forepleasure of normal intercourse. Individuals indulging in this perversion have regressed to the infantile oral erotic level. Emotionally, they are sexually fixated on the primary oral erotic zone.

Exhibitionism, or indecent exposure. The exposure of the genitalia to one of the opposite sex constitutes, in general parlance, the perversion of exhibitionism. Usually this offense is committed by the male in the presence of one or more females. Socially accepted sublimated acts of exhibitionism, however, occur among females in Terpsichorography, in burlesque shows, and in choruses, as well as in diving, swimming and bathing, while among males well-recognized forms are oratory, acting, boxing and wrestling. Psychogenically, the perversion of exhibitionism seems to have its origin in a failure to resolve thoroughly the elements of the Oedipus situation. The victim through attachment to one of his parents identifies the love object with his own body (Narcissism). Tensional states are built up frequently by masturbation. The compulsion arises to exhibit the genitalia to the opposite sex but in so doing the individual hopes that the woman, in turn, will likewise expose herself.

Even the phantasy of being approached sexually for the purpose of intercourse is indulged by the male but unconsciously he revolts against this idea, does not desire it and in some instances would even flee if such an attempt were made upon him. Castration fear is deep in these cases. As a boy he has been unconsciously in love with his mother and fears revenge from the father whom he fears might deprive him of sexual competition through his castration. Through exhibitionism he attempts to eliminate this fear by reactivating the unconscious phantasy he had as a child of being a woman with a penis. Thus, self-identification of the exhibitionist with his love object becomes affirmed. The compulsive nature of tensional releases through exhibitionism is well known and has caused many investigators, notably Freud himself, to believe that there is a constitutional component compelling the individual toward a repetition of this act. Other investigators, such as Fenichel, deny the constitutional element of the act. There is no doubt that the act itself is a substitutive one and is a compromise of the individual with himself for the consummation of the normal heterosexual act of which he is usually incapable. The personality of these individuals is characteristic. There is little evidence of aggressive tendencies and the men tend to be shy and timid. They frequently come from puritanical homes where sex discussion is avoided and a very proper attitude toward sex problems is maintained. Such an individual may have the highest type of ideality and pursue many idealistic avocations. The Law, however, treats the offense with considerable severity. There is an increasing tendency on the part of the judiciary to refer these cases to psychopathic clinics for observation and report back to the court This perversion is frequently allied closely to that of pornography, obscenity, voyeurism, toucherism.

Fellatio, carnal knowledge of an individual by or with the mouth. Freud explains the origin of this perversion by stating that it arises from a fixation of the psychosexual development of the individual at the so-called oral erotic level. During the normal development of an individual certain areas of the body, known as erogenous zones, become stimulated. These are primarily the mouth, the urethra and the anus. The zone about the mouth is stimulated by suckling of the mother's breast. The anal zone becomes stimulated through the process of defecation. The third zone is that of the urethra, which is stimulated through urination. All these processes have intense interest for the developing infant and, therefore, these three zones become highly emotionalized. As the development of the child proceeds, a large part of this emotionalized interest becomes diverted into other channels. Some individuals, however, are so conditioned to this emotional response that the zones become highly erotic and it is then a frequent and simple matter for the individual in his adult life to regress to the level in which these zones seek stimulation. The courts affix judgments of this act as an act of sodomy.

Fetishism, a compulsive perversion of the substitutive type in which an object possessed by the loved person replaces the love for that person herself. Thus, the fetishist employs the art of magic in investing an intimate object with the attractive evaluation of the individual himself. The object which serves as a fetish is a symbol. It embodies mysterious qualities which are considered by the victim to emanate from the loved one. By over-evaluating an object, such as a shoe or a stocking, the hair or any other portion of the loved one's body, the fetishist relinquishes the aim of accomplishing the normal heterosexual act and accepts a mystical substitute which to him offers even more miraculous qualities. A perverted sense of smell frequently accompanies the perversion of fetishism. The odor is often that of a portion of the body of the love object.

Psychogenically, an individual suffering from this perversion has a fear of being rejected by the love object and thereby being humiliated by the opposite sex. Through a symbolical possession of a portion of the love object, he magically assumes control of the whole individual without fear of rejection. Often there is a strong tendency toward self-degradation in this process. These individuals are usually quite masochistic. Anthropological literature is replete with instances whereby an object assumes all the magical powers of its possessor. Primitive extensive use of totem and taboo arise from the magical use of symbolical objects which are considered to be surcharged with power, authority, ability to exact revenge and above all, the most desired qualities of the original owner. The

EVE

Hans Baldung Grien

CLEOPATRA

Rembrandt van Rijn

fetishist is enabled through the use of a symbolized over-evaluated object to carry on all of his love-making with the exception of the actual heterosexual experience itself. He no longer desires this since he can accomplish everything else without fear of rejection.

In those cases in which the object sought by the fetishist has a symbolic equation with the female genitalia, such as velvet, fur, and underclothing, the basic perversion of the fetishist becomes most apparent. He fundamentally has an aversion to real female genitals on the basis that there is no evidence of a phallus, thereby symbolizing a fear of castration and so he turns to substitute objects for the genitalia. This permits him both a denial and assertion of the fact of castration and the avoidance of rejection if heterosexual advances were to be made to the female.

Fetishists often annoy the police through their breaking into houses and the stealing of unusual objects therefrom. The objects removed often seem to be of no value and the conduct seen is bizarre and inexplainable to the police. The same residence may be burglarized frequently and usually the same type of article is removed or despoiled. These may be shoes, lingerie, stockings or other female wearing apparel. Sometimes lingerie put out on the clothesline in the backyard for drying is thus despoiled during the night. Seminal emissions are frequently noted on such wearing apparel. The law considers the fetishist as a misdemeanant and is inclined to refer the case to a psychiatric clinic for further observation.

Kleptomania (Cleptomania). The uncontrollable compulsion to steal. This perverted act has a close resemblance to that of fetishism. The object stolen has symbolic meaning to the offender. It is the act, however, rather than the object which invests the offense with a value to the offender. In fetishism the object becomes magically invested with all kinds of authority and promise to the lover. In kleptomania the objective is revenge instead of adoration. The Freudian concept is that the stealing is associated with penis envy. The stealing from someone in authority or more powerful than the offender himself deprives that superior one of an object of power and authority. The object therefore symbolizes the penis and, the stealing is an act of castration of the father. This offense is nearly always a female offense. The woman in stealing, therefore, castrates her father and limits his power and authority over the mother.

Punishment of these individuals is singularly ineffective inasmuch as the punishment emotionalizes the act and, therefore, makes it all the more exciting to the doer. It is well known that pathological stealing occurs very frequently in cases of wealthy women who could afford to buy the object stolen ten times over. It is the act of stealing itself which invests the situation with exciting satisfaction rather than the object taken. Franz Alexander and Karl Abraham believe that the roots of kleptomania reach back to the first source of pleasure to the infant; namely, the mother's breast. The withdrawal of the nipple from the child has brought about a sense of frustration which has never been entirely overcome. The act is an obsessive one and, therefore, the individual is a psychopath. Lorand believes that, in addition to the penis envy and the loss of the mother's breast another factor in this perversion is defective critical appreciation of the factors of reality. He found in all of his studies of such cases that there was an instinctual drive which crowded the function of the critical faculty. While these cases are of great interest to the student of abnormal pathology, they are relatively rare and from the point of view of the police do not constitute a great source of annoyance. For every case of true kleptomania there are perhaps fifty cases of outright shoplifting where the motive is pure greed and gain.

Masturbation. Genital excitation caused either psychologically or by mechanical manipulation which leads to ejaculation. The act without phantasy may be purely automatic and, therefore, does not constitute a perversion. Habitual masturbation is not a disease of the mind in itself but is a sympton of an underlying conflict of the personality or an actual neurosis. A well-known fact is that masturbation may be a bridge in the psychosexual development of the individual between narcissism and the divergence of the libido into more socialized channels. The period in question occurs about the age of puberty and such act should not be classified as a perversion.

The practice is very common in groups of men who are removed from association with the opposite sex for long periods of time. It is doubtful that such a method of sex expression should be classified as a perversion. Mutual masturbation in which the act is performed by two individuals, usually of the same sex, simultaneously upon each other is a perverted act inasmuch as the possibilities of normal heterosexual relationships are transgressed to a deviated abnormal method of expression. Here again the offense is against society more than against the individual himself. The practice of masturbation is so universal at some time in the course of the life of the individual, both male and female, that many theories and legends have grown up regarding self-abuse. The most prevalent of these is that the act engenders insanity. This belief has largely been discredited, but the fact is well recognized that excessive masturbation leads to moodiness, periods of depression and a chain of symptoms closely resembling neurasthenia. The mental reaction of the individual himself to the act and his feeling of guilt with respect to his committing something which he recognizes as being condemned by society and the extensiveness of the phantasy accompanying the act, are the most potent sources of injury to the individual. There is a certain compulsion to the act, but it does not have the elements of incurability that many of the obsessive, compulsive perversions exhibit. Psychic masturbation which results in ejaculation without mechanical excitation of the genitalia is often associated with other perverted tendencies, especially that of fetishism and toucherism.

The initial phase of the masturbatory act is one of phantasy. The phantasy-life in connection with this act is of more psychological importance than the act itself. A certain amount of dissociation of the personality occurs during phantasy and this in itself may become the basis of schizoid tendencies of some duration. Many schizophrenics are known to have a prolonged and continuous history of masturbation, although this must be construed as a symptom rather than a cause of schizophrenia itself. The fixation of the libido at a narcissistic level obviously is an obstacle in the psychosexual development of the individual toward the ultimate goal of heterosexuality. The length to which this goal is deferred becomes an increasing detriment to the individual. He tends to become more withdrawn in his personality, more inclined to avoid social contacts, and has a deeper feeling of guilt as time goes on. Such individuals may continue their practices throughout life and are generally known to be inadequate in their personality, vacillating with respect to decisions, and lacking in firmness of character necessary for leadership. The individuals recognize these deficiencies thoroughly with a consequent deepening of the feeling of inferiority so that a vicious circle is thus established. Castration threats frequently made by parents upon children addicted to masturbation may be carried into adult life as the roots of an anxiety neurosis and the castration fear.

Sometimes the child resorts to a substitutive act, namely enuresis, particularly of the nocturnal sort. Masturbation in itself is considered by adults to be a childish manifestation. The police are usually concerned with this in connection with exhibitionism. Conviction is usually for a misdemeanor, and in many instances the case is referred to a psychiatric clinic for observation.

Necrophilia, copulation with a corpse. This revolting act probably is more frequent than the paucity of scientific literature on the subject would indicate. Courts and juries are usually so horrified with these revelations that much of the confidential material dealing with acts of this kind does not become public or even available to the reporters themselves. History plainly indicates that the perversion was well known to antiquity and there are many allusions to the practice in the literature of ancient Greeks. Certain perverted acts of mutilation upon dead bodies as exhibited by the Axis Powers during the recent World War II in-

dicate that the perversion is by no means a rarity. The sadistic feature of the act is clearly realized.

A certain parallelism is to be noted between necrophilia and bestiality. In each instance the love object is defenseless, and incapable of resisting maltreatment. A peculiarly revolting feature is the nature of the love object itself with associated odors. Coprophilia which is a perversion of the sense of smell is closely associated with necrophilia. In some instances where corpses are not available the necrophiliac requests prostitutes to dress up and act as corpses. Associated with this also is the perverted act of permitting the body to be saturated with excretory material or in the case of some types, particularly those who are psychotic, the ingestion of feces. The peculiarly revolting nature of these perverted acts has led many investigators to conclude that the offenders are degenerates. Certainly the incidence of psychosis is much higher in this group than in almost any other type of perverted offender.

Almost all investigators are inclined to the belief that a constitutional factor is involved, in addition to certain psychogenic elements. These cases manifest unusually perverse desires at an early age. Many seem to be totally devoid of superego development, so that the question of guilt and the feeling of having transgressed the tenets of the community are almost non-existent. Almost all the cases show a marked generalized development of erotic sensitization over the entire skin area instead of localized erogenic zones as in the normal individual. Many of the cases seem to be lacking entirely the sense of smell or they may have a perverted sense of smell in which the stench of decomposition or the odor of the products of defecation becomes pleasant rather than repulsive. The judiciary is inclined to consider such individuals essentially psychotic, and reference to a State hospital for prolonged observation is commonly the disposition.

Pederasty. Coitus per anum. The individual who indulges in this act is considered to be psychosexually fixed at the anal erotic level. The anus is a primary erogenous zone as explained in the topic under the heading of Fellatio. The law deals with this act as one of sodomy and imposes penalties accordingly.

Pedicacio, sexual excitation incurred only through the love of children. The sexual act usually engaged in is that of pederasty and fellatio. Individuals of this type are usually sexually impotent and cannot derive any sexual satisfaction except with young children. Individuals indulging in these practices are usually psychopaths and show many mental abnormalities in addition to their sexual perversions. *Carnal abuse of a female child* brings severe reprisals on the part of the law. Any adult who abuses the body of a female child under the age of ten years is adjudged to have committed a felony. If the child is be-

SEATED NUDE

Eugene Delacroix
Musée du Louvre

BACCHANAL

Pierre Dernarteau

tween the ages of ten and sixteen, according to the New York State law, the offender is guilty of a misdemeanor for the first conviction, and for a felony for the second conviction. Carnal abuse includes not only attempted intercourse but the indulging in any indecent or immoral practice with the sex parts or organs of a female child. A sentence not to exceed ten years may be imposed by the court for the commission of such a felony.

Pornography, the expression of lewdness and obscenity through written language, pictures, or other forms of images. The distribution or possession of obscene books, pictures, literature or other objects frequently approaches the status of a cult among many individuals of high cul-

ture, good intelligence, and often high social status. The practice may be quite esoteric. Thus, a small, highly-gifted and cultivated group of individuals may collect and exchange pornographic literature and objects with the same keenness shown by a collector of vases of the Ming dynasty, for example. On a lower social scale the interchange of crude and exceedingly lewd pictures of the so-called "French photographs" may occur. Of greatest interest perhaps is the wide distribution of pornographic literature in thinly disguised forms, such as nudist magazines, so-called art studies, salacious literature and highly ambiguous paintings.

Distributors of these pornographic articles are highly

AMOR AND PSYCHE

J. Renaud

organized to secure a wide market and are frequently subjected to legal prosecution. The difficulty with which they are brought to judgment indicates the cleverness with which the pornographic nature of the articles is thinly but effectually disguised legally. Furthermore, the existence of a large quantity of this material is indicative of the great number of consumers ready to receive it. The true pornographic pervert is likely to be either a frigid woman or an impotent man. A history of disastrous attempts at the heterosexual level is often revealed. The turning to the lewd article thus becomes, in effect, a securing of sex satisfaction through a symbolic object. The motivation thus becomes somewhat like that of fetishism without, however, having quite as strong an obsessive component. Psychosexually these individuals seem to be fixated at the early erogenous zone stages of development. Many of the lewd scenes depicted have elements of cruelty traits, revenge, horror, and other primitive emotional attitudes. There is very little subtlety of erotic expression. Closely allied to the perversion of pornography is that of obscenity making itself known through the repetition of lewd stories or the exhibitions of a lewd nature which are commercialized, and are presented to limited audiences. Finally there is the so-called "poisoned pen" writer who exhibits sadistic impulses through hurting others by means of letters written anonymously.

The law is inclined to group pornography with the perversion of exhibitionism. Each is classified as a misdemeanor and is so punished, but the courts usually refer the exhibitionist to a psychiatric clinic for observation, study, and report, whereas the individual addicted to pornography is dealt with more directly by the law as an offender. Undoubtedly, the crime of blackmail has its roots in the same level of psychosexual development with frustration of the kind found in the case of pornography.

Sado-masochism. Because of the close linkage between these ambivalent tendencies, sadism and masochism should always be considered coincidentally. Sadism is the sexual excitement engendered by inflicting cruelty and punishment on another individual. Masochism is the pleasure derived from suffering pain, ill-treatment, and humiliation either at the hands of a sadist or through other sources.

In many instances the two states are intermingled or there is a quick and sudden swing from one state to the other. It is doubtful that either state exists in its true form in complete absence of the other. The term sadism, as is well known, was derived from the name of Marquis de Sade, a French writer who gave voluminous and detailed descriptions of the infliction of cruelty upon others. It is obviously a source of intense sexual satisfaction to all concerned. Sadism during the course of love-making may take almost any kind of violent action toward the love object. The most frequent perhaps are biting and scourging with whips. Religious cults, known as the Flagellants, exhibit a mass form of sadism. The greatest exhibition of mass sadism is encountered, of course, during war. The violent forms of sadism are highly perverted sexual deviations but mild forms occur regularly in almost any kind of human relationship whether on an erotic or other level. One of the most devastating, although little known, forms is that of mental cruelty often exhibited toward the love-object itself.

Without exception these cases are obsessive neurotics. They possess the anal sadistic character. In the second or third year of the life of these individuals intense curiosity is manifested in the excretory processes. According to Freud, children of this type will resort to retention of excrement for the purpose of deriving greater pleasure at the moment of defecation. Also, the act of defecation is utilized as an expression of pleasure toward the person whose admiration was sought. The whole act of defecation thus becomes emotionalized. Also, the child by means of controlling the process of defecation through his own will is able to frustrate the desires of his parents who are attempting to establish normal toilet training habits in him. In a certain sense, then, the child through these processes gains mastery over those who are in authority above him.

Through the process of reaction formations in later life the ego is reinforced and the earlier anal sadistic traits are developed into more socially acceptable expressions, such as that of self-sacrifice, desire for justice, social improvement, meticulous attention to details, a passion for orderliness and precision and other manifestations leading to an opinionated, rigid type of character. In many instances excessive thrift and parsimony is shown. The anal character of these obsessive neurotics shows decisive, aggressive trends against those individuals who are at variance with the inflexibility of the anal sadistic neurotic. He regards the genital impulse for coitus as being an excrementitious function and, therefore, a subject to be avoided as a dirty or filthy procedure. Such type of reaction from the earlier infantile high regard for excrement is, of course, a reaction formation. Regression to the early anal sadistic level, therefore, becomes frequent in these individuals. After regression takes place, the individual acts in a cruel manner toward the love object with the especial objective of debasing that love object, dominating, soiling, and physically abusing her. Fixation of the psychosexual development, however, occurs in the oedipal situation. The sadist constantly shows a tendency in a choice of sexual objects which have a symbolic significance or are unconscious representations of the mother. During this stage of his development the individual probably has lived in a relationship of infantile submission which is only lip service, so to speak, inasmuch as intense hatred toward the parents is unconsciously felt. Regression to the anal sadistic level reinforces this passive feminine relationship toward the paternal images. It conflicts with the aggressive tendencies of the individual toward active rivalry and with his passive submission. Thus, the sadist and the masochist are in the position of showing an ambivalence; namely, in quick swings toward one or the other manifestation. They may be aggressively violent toward the love object or suddenly yield to a feminine type of submission.

In the former instance the pervert adopts a virile, active attitude, often showing intense cruelty traits. In the latter instance there is considerable phantasy formation and the submissive act becomes symbolic of castration. Nevertheless, the masochistic attitude of entire submission may in itself be a very potent weapon of revenge for the phantasy castration because there is no real giving in to the lover and he never succeeds in actually obtaining possession of her. Thus, again masochism may be utilized and frequently is so utilized as a weapon of cruelty. Here again the inflexibility of the obsessive neurotic is clearly shown. Moreover, the fluctuating character exhibited by the obsessive neurotic in the manifestations of sadism or masochism leads to a vacillating, indecisive nature often incapable of strongly-drawn decisions.

The ego in its struggle against unconscious tendencies

ALINE THE MULATTO

Eugene Delacroix
Musée de Montpellier

of the anal erotic stage finds that its best weapon of nullification is that of repression. These repressed instincts, of course, merely accentuate the genital conflicts which are the basis of the obsession neurosis. Another method is displacement toward insignificant acts which lead eventually into highly ritualistic procedures. Thus, the obsessive neurotic sets up routines of procedures or avoidances in which he lives psychically in an animistic world. A procedure of this nature is closely allied to the use of magic found in fetishism and other perverted acts. Through such ritualistic behavior the ego is enabled to neutralize some of the strong guilt feelings of the superego. The obsessive neurotic has a full understanding of his tendency toward vacillation, conflicts and doubts and learns through processes of isolation, nullification, denial of existence, and repression to avoid painful affects growing out of feelings of guilt. Thus, the desire to seek expiation may become so intense that the individual readily yields to physical abuse. Counterposed to this submissive attitude toward the superego is the intense ego striving to free itself of the repressive influence. This, of course, may break forth as an explosion of aggressive nature leading to highly sadistic acts. The aggression commonly takes as its purpose either the destruction of the object or its complete control. Thus, it will be noted that these tendencies revert directly back to the Oedipus situation itself.

With respect to the application of the perversion of sadism toward the criminal, in all probability many sex crimes showing atrocious violence toward the love object often to the point of murder, have their source directly in this perversion. The body may be greatly mutilated. In many instances, the mutilation is self-inflicted, often in the form of attempted castration. It is a matter of common knowledge that many hold-ups are accompanied by intense sadism and that a great deal of unnecessary violence is perpetrated upon the victim. So prevalent is the sado-mesochistic attitude that is pervades the very court itself. The attitude of the public in general and of some of the judiciary in particular is a direct expression of sadism toward the criminal. The history of the handling of criminals is replete with instances of the utmost cruelty at the hands of their captors. It is this element of sadism so prevalent in the community toward the criminal that is the most effectual check against intelligent and progressive advancement of penology. The science of penology has lagged perhaps more than any other type of human endeavor, particularly among the social sciences, due directly to the sadistic attitude of the community as a whole.

Sodomy (Bestiality). The psychiatric acceptance of this term limits the field to the performance of sexual relations between human beings and animals. The law, however, takes a broader view of the matter and is inclined to consider that any person who has intercourse with another individual by means of the anus or mouth or submits to such deviated acts or has carnal knowledge with a dead body is guilty of sodomy. Thus, the legal definition includes the psychiatric conceptions of bestiality, fellatio, pederasty, and necrophilia. Bestiality is not uncommon among farm laborers in remote rural sections. Many of these individuals are feeble-minded. The factors of low moral standards, lack of opportunity for indulgence in normal intercourse, narrow economic margins under which the individual lives, lack of opportunity for mingling with others in a community are probably more potent factors in inducing this type of perversion than are constitutional factors themselves.

The act of sodomy is viewed with considerable horror by the community. Some allowances are made legally by the court in the matter of sentencing individuals convicted of bestiality. The law as applied, however, to abnormal relationships between human beings as indicated by the law is treated most severely. A large number of states impose a penalty up to twenty years of servitude for the commission of such an act.

Toucherism. An irresistible impulse to touch the body of another person. Toucheurs are frequently encountered in large crowds. They obtain considerable sexual excitement by touching the breasts of women inadvertently or pinching of the buttocks or merely by casual contacts. If they rub against the other individual, they are known to be *frotteurs*. The condition is closely allied to that of fetishism and has strong, compulsive, obsessive trends. These individuals are psychopaths and may in many instances be suffering directly with a full-fledged neurosis. The law views them as misdemeanants, of an annoying character since the depredations are childish, but they are irritating to the victim herself.

Transvestism, the wearing of clothing of the opposite sex with the erotic desire of simulating attributes thereof. The practice is not uncommon among homosexuals and is seen in its full-fledged state in male individuals who make themselves up as females and parade the streets in open solicitation. In less public form homosexual parties may be devised, a portion of the members of which may dress themselves in female costumes and behave as females to other members of the party. Certain modified forms of this are seen on the stage as female impersonations. The law makes provision for the punishment of the wearing of clothing of the opposite sex but the law is not rigidly enforced. Male transvestists are well known to the police and are able to ply their trade upon the streets in a surreptitious manner only. They are not usually brought to judgment except in connection with other offenses.

Transvestism among females is very common and seems

CAMP FOLLOWER

Urs Graf

CYTHERIA, THE ISLAND OF LOVE

Hans Baldung

to be socially acceptable, the concept of the community being that it has no particular sexual significance from a perverted point of view and is more or less of a gay prank. Certainly the use of male attire by females does not possess the perverted interest that is shown by the male in such action. In this respect there is a parallelism in the perversion of exhibitionism. Transvestism among females is often encountered among women who have an unusually large male component in their makeup. Such women dress mannishly, particularly in business pursuits and are usually frigid and unattracted by the opposite sex. Homosexuality in this group is proportionately less than might be assumed, but these personalities are rigid and without richness in emotion. The Law does not consider transvestism in the mannish woman as being punishable.

Uranism, the perversion of Homosexuality. The term was widely used a number of years ago but is rather infrequently encountered in present times.

Voyeurism (Peeping Tom) (Scoptophilia). The derivation of sexual excitement and satisfaction through viewing the genitalia or the nude body of an individual. The perversion is closely linked with that of exhibitionism. The exhibitionist exposes himself to view to another individual, whereas the voyeur seeks gratification in looking at others. Usually, he prefers to remain unseen and gets especial delight in viewing the disrobing of women. The perverted interest shown by such individuals is really a fixation of an infantile curiosity instinct. The young child learns his relationship to other people sexually and socially through observation. He endeavors to learn the functions of his own body by observing those of other individuals. A certain amount of peeping is required for this. If such process becomes unduly emotionalized and remains of emotional interest to the individual in his adult years, he may find himself in the position of deriving his chief satisfaction through this infantile practice. The practice is frequently associated with masturbation.

Accommodations for scoptophiliacs are maintained in some special establishments in metropolitan areas, particularly on the Continent, for the unseen viewing of acts of defecation, masturbation and other procedures both normal and abnormal.

V. C. BRANHAM, M.D.
formerly, *Chief,* Outpatient Section
Neuropsychiatric Division
Veterans Administration
Washington, D.C.

The Sexual Dilemma

THE SAME EVIDENCE
Labisse
Athol Publications Limited

The Sexual Dilemma

Homosexuality exists in men as an overt sexual practice and also in an unconscious (latent) form. The latter plays a more or less important part in men who might not even be aware of the fact that they are possessed by a substantial homosexual component.

Overt homosexuality is frequent; we cannot tell how frequent because we lack reliable statistics on it. Some speak of four per cent in the civilized nations of the West; this figure is probably understated. In the Orient and among primitive people, homosexuality is so frequent that we may call it endemic.

There is, however, a difference between primitive and the majority of civilized homosexuals. The Anatolian peasant, Arabs and other half-primitive people practice homosexuality according to stimulus and response, i.e., they accept a man as their sex object when a woman is unavailable. In this same sense the primitive shepherd has intercourse with his animals because being too poor or for other reasons he cannot have a better object. There is, however, no doubt in him that a specimen of the other sex would be preferable to any and all surrogates; he acts like a homosexual but is not necessarily so. It seems that we must regard homosexuality in ancient Greece in the same light, particularly before Plato. Pre-Platonic Greek literature hardly mentions homosexuality.

Homosexuality as a modern phenomenon among civilized people is different from its primitive appearance because as a rule it implies a rigid fixation on objects of the same sex. In their great majority our overt homosexuals have no use for objects of the other sex. They are either indifferent to them or — particularly when forced to practice intercourse with them — they feel fear of and repugnance toward them.

Homosexuality always has been a scientific enigma. Nature is full of the most complicated arrangements for safeguarding propagation. There is no end to propagative devices in the animal and vegetable kingdoms from the lowest to the highest species. Homosexuality runs counter to the aims of propagation involving for individual pleasure a stimulus which nowhere else in nature has any other aim than propagation. In this sense homosexuality is puzzling to biology.

Anatomy is a little closer to a solution of our problem, showing that rudiments of the other sex exist in all men: the male has nipples and other bisexual anatomical formations. Many males display feminine sex characteristics, such as feminine distribution of fat and females masculine traits like hairy legs and moustaches. One might suspect that homosexuality of men is attributed to a more feminine anatomy. This, however, is not always so, not even in the great majority of homosexuals. We see males looking "womanish" and females looking "mannish" who are not at all homosexual. On the other hand, we see homosexual men who look athletic and women very attractive to normal men because of their feminine beauty, although they themselves have no use for men.

To the physician also homosexuality is a puzzle, because it looks like a disease — which it frequently is — but often the homosexual himself does not feel ill or ailing by any means but on the contrary, satisfied with his perversion without suffering except for his social inferiority and even that not in all cases. Let us add that the concept of ailing involves diminished efficiency. We know, however, that unusually efficient men — in the higher strata artists, writers, scholars among them — often are homosexuals. Hence it is difficult to call homosexuality a disease.

Quite unimpressed by the puzzle is the legislator when in his penal codes he brands the homosexual a criminal and punishes him accordingly. The laws of most civilized countries establish a difference between male and female homosexuals. Female homosexuals have a psychology different from the male's anyway. Woman because of her position as a potential mother is prepared to love both sexes, boys and girls. The primitive form of homosexuality as described above seems to be more frequent among Lesbians than among homosexual men. They are rather bisexual than homosexual and more frequently than men do they find their way back to accepting the other sex as mates.

For about fifty years attempts have been made to explain homosexuality by assuming a general bisexuality. It is presumed that components of both sexes exist in all men, in the psychological as well as the anatomical sense. The homosexual component comes to the fore under unfavorable circumstances intensified by undesirable training in the formative years, morbid interrelations in the family and — there is no denying it — by inherited characteristics. This hypothesis was strongly supported by discoveries of biochemistry. Feminine and masculine products of the sex organs (Estrogen and Androgen) could be found in the urine of men and animals of both sexes. However, the bisexuality theory does not quite harmonize with the statistics on homosexuality either. We come to the conclusion that homosexuality with the exception of a few extreme cases is a psychogenic phenomenon. Psychoanalysis has contributed considerably to the understanding of its origin. We must, however, refrain here from giving an account of these doctrines.

By far more interesting than overt homosexuality and more important for sociology is its latent aspect. Some of it has to be expected in all men, if we think the theory of bisexuality to its logical end. Actually, psychoanalysis could prove a homosexual component of which they are not conscious in all men. The differences in various individuals are not so much inherent in the mere existence of this ubiquitous component but in the varying degrees of fear of it and in the defense mechanisms in which men take refuge. Fear of unconscious homosexuality can reach enormous heights and then release a kind of panic which was discovered in soldiers during the first world war. Living together in close quarters and prolonged separation from the other sex are responsible for an advance of the homosexual component generating anxiety over some unknown danger. Men in this condition behave in such a way that in bygone days they were convicted because of cowardly conduct in battle. Nobody realized then that a phenomenon existed which about thirty years ago was given the name of "homosexual panic." This tremendous anxiety connected with latent homosexuality was never completely explained. A forcible switch from heterosexuality to homosexuality is actually a social danger. However, anxiety as expressed in homosexual panic by far surpasses the rational importance of this danger and probably is rooted in some fear of disintegration of the entire personality which actually occurs at the onset of certain psychoses. These psychoses are very often connected with an advance of homosexuality. Psychoanalysis sees a connection with the phenomenon of neurotic castration fear. It is perhaps not superfluous to emphasize here that the overt homosexual is free of homosexual panic; he has accepted his perversion as such, and therefore is not afraid of it any more. All other men are more or less exposed to the danger of homosexual panic. Overt homosexuals are usually harmless and friendly. However, when hunting sexual mates they often happen upon latent homosexuals who are attractive to them while the unconscious homosexuals, not knowing of their perverted instincts, are afraid of the tempter and seducer. Relations of this kind frequently end with homicide and atrocities which are reported in our newspapers without the foregoing psychological interpretation.

The anxiety of latent homosexuals has produced a great number of defense mechanisms which play an important though not yet adequately appreciated part in our culture. We refrain here from speaking of complicated neuroses and psychoses arising from the conflict between unconscious homosexuality and defenses against it. One of the most important defenses is *cruelty* and *compulsive destructiveness*. Aggressiveness and lust for destroying seem to be rooted in the animalistic understructure of man, but are often enormously increased by fear of an inner feminine drive. Some men wish to give evidence that they are not feminine by any means because of their being capable of committing atrocities. Even little boys know of no more terrible disgrace than to be called a "sissy." A boy has to fight and to be "tough." This is inculcated in them from early childhood by their teachers and by other children of their own age who often feel like crying rather than fighting; but fight they must, in order not to be called feminine.

From here the road leads to the theory of the *superman,* of whom we do not have to say much because it has been sufficiently discussed in recent years. *Megalomania* and *persecution mania* belong to one another. A demi-god or whatever term he chooses as an expression of his megalomania, does not have to be afraid of his feminine component any more. But then one has to be afraid that actually he might not be a demi-god: a cause for persecution mania. Only a few people are quite free of persecution ideas. A mechanism is here at work which modern psychiatry since Freud has been calling a projection of an inner voice to the outside. Actually these people feel persecuted by their own feminine component (in women it is the masculine component) without being aware of it. By projecting the danger outside they build up an illusion that other people — individuals or groups of men — persecute them and by so doing they feel somewhat removed from their vexing internal problems. They could not possibly act against an unconscious voice within, but if they can denounce other people they secure for themselves a right to hit back, to persecute their persecutors.

Another defense mechanism is *erotomania*, known in the figures of Don Juan and his feminine counterpart Messalina. Don Juan proves by his apparently insatiable sex-life — and mind you: exclusively with women — that he is not feminine. It is, however, easy to expose his feminine trends, just as the aggressive "oversexed" woman betrays her identification with men. A real man or woman, feeling within the completeness and certainty of his own sex, does not have to play a mad erotomaniac. In contrast to normal men, Don Juan cannot keep the conquered woman. On the contrary he has to run away from her as if haunted by furies. The real Don Juan is comparatively rare. Much more frequently do we see his rudimentary edition traveling all over the land, so to speak, burning and ravaging without ever reaching his goal. This variety of Don Juanism has been called the "kissing menace."

There is a form of *jealousy* to be booked in the catalogue of our defense mechanisms. Jealousy is a normal phenomenon which so definitely belongs to love that we have a right to doubt the presence of genuine love if jealousy is completely absent. However, there are pathological forms of jealousy based on the fact that one man is in love with another man. The layman cannot easily grasp the idea that a man can be in love without knowing it; yet it is one of the most common occurrences — and he experiences his own latent homosexuality in such a way that he is jealous of his wife or his sweetheart as though she and not he were in love with that man: another form of projection. In this way strange triangles arise of one woman and two men, not at all in the sense popular with novelists and playwrights. In the triangles which we have in mind, the most important line is the one between the two men and the line leading from the men to the woman is unimportant.

In addition to individual defenses we have to consider collective measures offered the individual by the various civilizations in which they live. Here we have to mention all kinds of *organizations* (covenants) *of men*. Religious associations like monasteries, religious knights and soldiers of Christ and well-disciplined and, particularly, fanaticized armies belong here, as well as certain fraternities and also involuntary groups as in prisons, or explorers on trips of long duration. In such associations the homosexual com-

ponent is intensified, but as a rule checked by the regulations and practices of the group.

There are two ways leading out of the hardships of latent homosexuality.

Either man withdraws from the sex struggle for a love object, dodging the difficulty by changing into a *Narcissus,* in love only with himself like the youth of the ancient saga. Then he is not interested in anyone, either of his own or the other sex, only in himself. We cannot call him an ordinary egotist because he avoids association with his fellow-men even if they offer him personal advantage. He lives a lonesome life and by renouncing social life gets away from a fight of which he is afraid. In this camp we meet eccentrics of all kinds, misers, collectors, book-worms, also exaggerating lovers and protectors of animals who prefer pets to men, because animals are no danger to them. Being a gregarious animal, man cannot be happy as a narcissus and often deplores his lonesome life, but is not able to change it. As the alternative to homosexual panic he chooses narcissism because it promises him peace.

The other escape from fear of the homosexual component is called *sublimation*. If we can sublimate a drive we do not have to suppress it any longer. On the contrary its permanent practice and enjoyment are made possible in such a way that society and hence also the individual who sublimates are satisfied. An example of this is genuine friendship which — as we know — is not far removed from erotic warmth. Another example is charity of any kind which always has been felt to be identical with love. Generally speaking, devotion to any social cause which is not quite egotistic satisfies a piece of libido which if suppressed and pent up might become a danger for the individual. Different nations and different times have produced different collective possibilities and the individual can become a gentleman by sublimation of his instincts according to the taste of the people in whose midst he lives.

It is not always easy to differentiate between sublimation and repression. Not only does hypocrisy play an important role, but even with an actual benefactor, it sometimes is doubtful whether he has sublimated his cruel drives into charity or has remained cruel underneath and occasionally shows it. As an example of this kind we mention the philanthropist who builds orphanages for children whose fathers would have survived were it not for the cruel business methods of the philanthropist. Consider the Grand Inquisitor who by burning heretics alive, pronounces himself a philanthropist because by tormenting them here he saves the souls of his victims from eternal flames in hell.

Extremely momentous is the flight of latent homosexuals into liquor. Drug addicts (morphine, opium, cocaine, etc.) present more sinister a problem than the alcohol addict, but the social importance of alcoholism is infinitely greater because of the tremendous number of alcoholics in many countries of which unfortunately America is one. Many a man is driven to drinking habits because of his fear of unconscious homosexual tendencies. When intoxicated people drop their inhibitions, often enough the latent tendency comes to the fore and shows its existence even to the untrained eye of the observer. The defense is double barreled by encouraging what it was supposed to overcome. In view of this danger the alcoholic continues to drink until he eventually passes out or incapacitates himself in some other way. He then exchanges his dreaded homosexual component for narcissistic loneliness.

To summarize, we have described four categories of defense mechanisms against latent homosexuality:

Morbid defenses such as cruelty, megalomania (the superman), persecution mania, erotomania, pathological (paranoic) jealousy, and collective defenses.

Regression to narcissism which terminates the struggle in its particular way.

Sublimation into desirable social activities.

Borderline cases between sublimation and morbid reaction formations.

* * *

Almost all men who are afraid of their own feminine component have one characteristic in common: they hate and despise women. They rationalize their feelings about the female sex in various ways. Women who suffer under this persecution can avoid these men's hatred only by renouncing their prerogative as sex creatures and identifying themselves with men as much as possible. In this way a race of masculine women is fostered who deal with men, their jailers, as they deserve, i.e. they torture them and make them unhappy. Sometimes it looks as though education and national training — in past history as well as in present times — have produced men who cannot love their women. Accordingly, an unhappy generation may ensue living in permanent restlessness who will not permit other nations either to pursue their natural and peaceful happiness. We reach the conclusion that there are not only economic but also psychological causes for good luck and aggressivity of peoples and those who undertake the job of educating and re-educating nations should consult psychologists.

FRITZ WITTELS, M. D.
Psychiatrist
New York City

The Sexual Offender

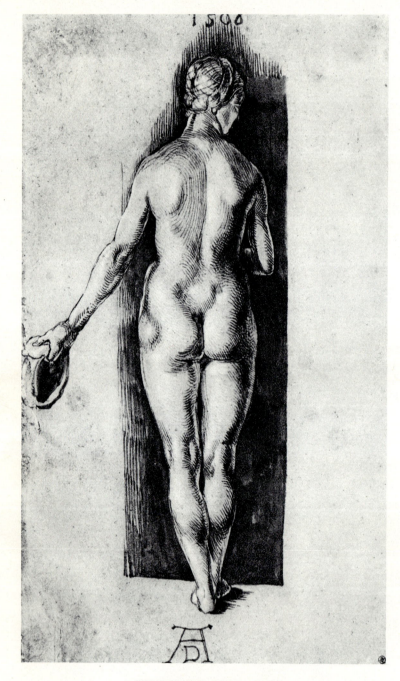

STUDY OF THE NUDE

Albrecht Durer

The Sexual Offender

The mind of the sexual criminal is a complex one. His crime is a type of sexual behavior characterized by socially prohibited aggressiveness, and lack of regard for the unwilling participant. It is compulsive and irresistible in nature. It is committed under the influence of a strong and overwhelming urge.

The sexual criminal is a pervert, whose offense may be legal when no other person is involved against his will (homosexuality, sado-masochism, etc.), or illegal when socially prohibited (incest, pedophilia, etc.). Sociologically, sexual offenses go beyond the barriers of race, class, culture, or social position.

There is no direct relationship between sexual criminal activity and nonsexual criminal activity. An individual sexual offender is not often involved in other types of criminal activity; the nonsexual criminal is not very likely to be involved in sexual offenses. There are, however, instances, where both types do occur.

The sexual offender is very rarely sorry for his victim. His regrets, if any, pertain to himself, to what may happen to him if he is apprehended. However, these regrets are not sufficiently strong to act as a deterrent to repetitions of his sexual crime. The sexual offense is not a substitute for normal sexual intercourse, for many sexual criminals have sexual relations at regular intervals.

Dr. Bernard C. Glueck arrives at the following conclusions: Sexual offenders are of average intelligence. Many have definite physical deformities. Quite a few show marked social awkwardness, stemming from their withdrawn, isolated patterns.

Many sexual offenders have the ability to hide ideas and experiences which they have learned are not acceptable to their families or friends. Distortions in their perceptions of reality may be very subtle. It is the initial perceptive distortions, magnified and further altered by disturbances of mood and affect, that may, in some instances, lead to the antisocial sexual act. Their capacity for object relationships is disturbed, largely as the result of incapacitating inhibitions and fears over establishing emotional contact with others. These disturbances result in an infantile type of behavior toward libidinal objects.

Frequently, the sexual offender is not a sexual fiend, motivated by an uncontrollable need for gratification. He is satisfying some other need while performing the aberrant sexual act such as retaliating for the trauma experienced with a hostile, rejecting, or castrating mother or wife. His lack of integration, extending to chaotic confusion, is based primarily on the intense sexual years generated by traumatic childhood sexual experiences.

In a study of sexual offenders, conducted under the direction of the Commissioner of Mental Hygiene of New York State, the following facts were elicited.

1. *Mental Disorder*: Of the 102 men studied, every one suffered from some type of mental or emotional disorder.

These varied in type and intensity from phychosis to neurosis. The disturbances and symptoms were often of a mixed nature. While sexual crime is often a manifestation of a mental or emotional disorder, there is no known mental disorder that predisposes the commission of sexual crimes.

2. *Deprivation in Childhood*: Almost all the men had histories of unusually unfavorable childhoods with severe emotional deprivation.

3. *Hostility*: There was an overwhelming amount of hostility in all the sexual offenders, which often expressed itself as extreme brutality (sadism) in their criminal acts. This hostility appeared to be directly related to the hostility or neglect to which they had been subjected as children.

4. *Resentment Against Authority*: Most of the sexual offenders displayed, to a potentially or actually dangerous degree, a hatred and resentment against authority. This could be explained as a carry-over from earlier unexpressed resentment and hostility against parental authority.

5. *Alcoholism*: The excessive alcoholic consumption so often found among sexual offenders is a means of release from intense anxiety and a vicarious gratification of other deeper needs.

Abnormal brain function certainly plays a considerable role in the etiology of the criminal sexual psychopath. However, other factors are also of great importance, Endocrinology, psychology, heredity, and environment are also involved.

In the main, psychopathology of sexual perversions consists of faulty psycho-sexual development — "fixation" at an infantile or childhood level, or persistence in infantile attitudes, resulting in an inability to attain mature sexual attitudes later in life.

The sexual impulse is one of the two primary drives of the human being. Had it been less compelling, the human race could not have survived the rigors to which it has been subjected during the course of its development. But today, under conditions far different, the impulse needs to be controlled in the interest of social welfare. In modern man, it has been estimated, the sexual impulse is four times as strong as it need be to perpetuate the race. Such control is much more difficult in a society of clashing cultures, disintegrating codes, and uncertain sanctions.

R. W. NICE, in *A Handbook of Abnormal Psychology*

GABRIELLE D'ESTRÉES AND HER SISTER
School of Fontainebleau, Louvre

The Art of Taking a Wife

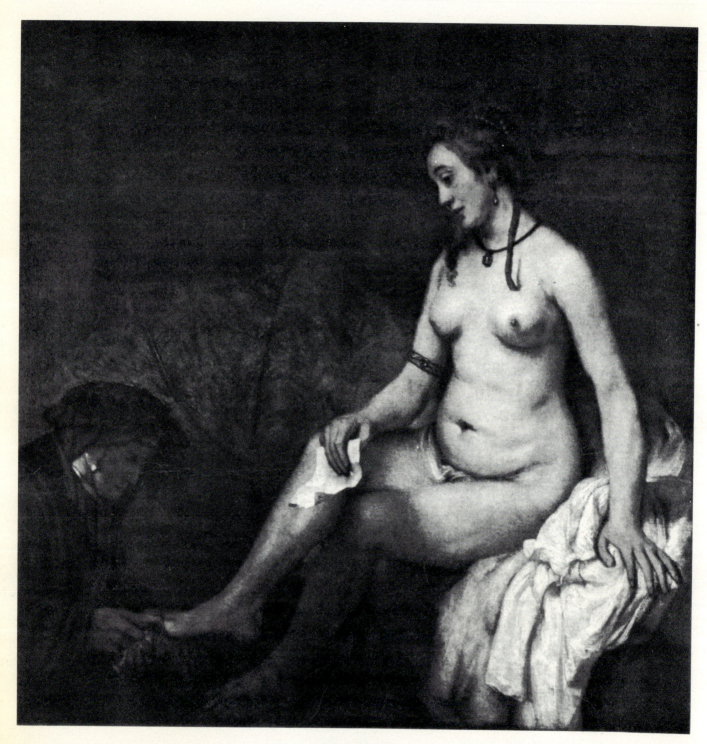

BATHSHEBA

Rembrandt

The Art of Taking a Wife

There are two principal ways by which we may arrive at the fatal *yes,* that terrible monosyllable which must decide our happiness or misfortune; that *yes* which may make for us a paradise on earth, or a hell of twenty-four hours for every day in the 365.

Either love first and marriage after, or marriage first and love after. Which of these two ways is the better, and the most certain to lead us to the paradise of two?

Theoretically, the answer cannot be doubted; one ought to love first and marry after.

In practice, however, it is not always so. Many marriages inspired by love end badly, while others, planned by reason more than the heart, turn out well.

And why? If the theory is true, it ought to accord with the practice, and if it contradicts the practice the theory must be mistaken.

The apparent contradiction can be explained at once if we reflect that love is every day spoken of as the desire for the possession of the woman, and this alone is certainly not sufficient to make two people happy. Give love and lust their real names and every difficulty immediately disappears, and we then see the happy dogma, *Love first and marriage after,* shine out in all its splendour. If by legal means alone a man can possess the woman he loves and if the passion be violent, the greatest libertine, and even the enemy of matrimony, bow their heads under the *Furcae Caudinae* of female virtue and the civil code, and marry. It is a stony road and full of pitfalls, but one which, nevertheless, may sometimes lead to the happiness of the two. Gradually there becomes associated with the desire of the senses, that more valuable sense of the affinity of hearts, and when the desire is satisfied there remains still the enjoyment of the more delicate dainties

of the understanding and affection. To transform lust into love is a difficult work, but worthy of woman's holy virtue, and the woman can succeed in doing so, even when possession has cooled desire and age dimmed her beauty; but she must be a sublime being and possess lasting gifts of sentiment and thought; if her companion be also an elect soul, who knows how to value this lasting and solid virtue, and who understands ideality of spirit as well as grace of form, so much the better.

Sublime beings and elect souls are always exceptional, and if, in the innumerable crowd of husbands and wives, they have reached the *yes* by the way of desire of the flesh, they soon find that the game was not worth the candle, and that the muddy swamp of weariness and animal familiarity of sex follows upon the first outburst of voluptuousness. The woman sometimes succeeds in fanning and reviving it with inexhaustible coquetry, but one gets scorched, and the distaste may become even more obstinate the more ingenious are the remedies used to oppose it. A marriage inspired only by the desires of the flesh, maintained only by the bread of lust, is a very poor and abject thing, that can very rarely give peace to the mind, and much less happiness. Even in the most vulgar and sensual natures, there is something that rebels against the permanent animal, and raises its voice in demand for a more human form of food. Man, like the swine, wallows in the mud, but with this difference: he likes to wash himself, and to look up to the heavens from the trough. It must be added that in marriage the dignities of father and mother only increase the responsibility of the two consorts to animate and enlarge the human nut at the expense of the animal pulp. The spirituality of the family impresses itself upon the coarsest nature and the most obtuse nerves, by warming the atmosphere and revealing a streak of blue in the heaven above.

Woe to the man who, in solitary and sad contemplation of his wife, says to himself: *My companion is only a female!*

Much worse is it, and woe to that woman who, in the night watches, looking at her husband as he snores, says in a low, fretful voice: *My husband is only a male!*

* * *

There is hardly a man who would confess to his friends, or even to himself, that he married a woman to possess her. Even if it were true, modesty and pride fight against the confession, and with one of those clever self-deceptions with which we know how to embellish and deceive our own consciences, we exclaim in a decided and convinced tone, *I love her!*

If it be so difficult a thing to distinguish between gold and its alloy, true and false diamonds, eastern and Roman pearls, imagine whether it is easy to distinguish between the desire of the flesh and true love. Yet this is just one of those most dangerous and hidden pitfalls which bring death to happiness in the battle waged in our minds between the to be or not to be, when we have to decide whether or no we ought to give the holy name of wife to the woman we desire. In other books of mine I have ventured to give some advice to those aspiring to matrimony to enable them to distinguish between true love and carnal excitement, which only affects one organ.

As I believe, however, that we have here before our eyes one of the gravest and most vital questions in the art of taking a wife, I may be allowed to enter more minutely into particulars.

Always doubt a sudden impression so called a *coup de fondre*, if it has seized you after long abstinence from woman's society.

* * *

For love also, and perhaps more for love than for the brain, it is prudent to remember the fasting Philip.

* * *

If you fear being enamoured of a young girl and are not disposed toward marriage, go and see all the married and young ladies most famed for beauty, grace, and elegance, and make your comparisons. If they be unfavourable to her, doubt directly the seriousness and depth of your passion.

This has to do only with what we call physical love, but I speak of it at some length as it is the first door opened when a man and woman see each other for the first time. But I do not mean that it is the only one which leads you to the fatal *yes.* It ought only to give you an entrance into the ante-chamber where you must wait patiently until heart and mind open the doors of the inner rooms, where you will have to live all your life.

If there has been no *coup de fondre*, but the sympathy came gradually, developed and grew until it became a real passion, then all my counsels of examination and experiment will be perfectly useless. At each visit you unconsciously, and without thinking of it at all, correct or confirm the first impression — now trimming, now increasing the warmth of the original sympathy. How many wooings, how many marriages have miscarried in our fancy without our knowing a word of it, or even having spoken an affectionate word to the person who awakened so sudden and strong an impression in us! A being suddenly appeared on the horizon, perhaps in an hour in which we felt the weight of solitude, the tortures of abstinence, and we said to ourselves directly: What a charming and sweet creature! Why do I not take her for mine . . . and forever?

The apparition passed from our gaze, but we carried it home with us carved, or rather written, on our minds in fire. We saw her between the lines of the book we read, in our dreams, everywhere.

A few days later we see her in the street, or in society, and we vainly endeavor to reconcile the reality with the figure we saw in our imagination. The discord is complete. The woman is not the same, and smiling to ourselves over the love which we had dreamt of in the silence of our minds, we exclaim, "How could I ever have admired this vulgar, ugly, faded creature and wished to have her for my own!"

It is well, indeed, when the sketch can be corrected so soon; unfortunately it sometimes occurs after several visits, when we may have compromised our heart and perhaps our word.

Prudence, then, *adelante Pedro con juicio!*

* * *

Science teaches that no force in the world is lost, no energy consumed, but that force and energy transform themselves one into the other without loss at all. Then I ask myself — but all the desires that men and women breathe out in the streets, in society, in theatres, or wherever they meet, where do they end? All those glances of the eyes which carry fire enough in their rays to burn and consume the whole planetary system; all those heart beatings which make the face burn and attract two beings, two organisms, two lives to each other; when (as in most cases) they pass like meteors without fructifying the earth, where do they go? Those terrible energies, the fruit of the most intricate and sublime mechanism of our brains and nerves; into what do they transport themselves when they produce neither words, tears, lust, crime, matrimony, nor sin?

And yet these desires are many; they meet day and night in the crowded streets, in the whirl of railway car-

DIANE OF POITIERS AT HER TOILETTE

riages, in the dense crowd, in the solitary mountain paths; they plough through space, and if we were able to see them we should see the air lighted up by them as by the convulsive lightning of a tropical tempest.

But where do they go? Where is so much light consumed? Who warms himself with all this mighty heat? And where are the ashes of such a fire?

I know not; perhaps biologists and physicists of the future will tell us.

* * *

Another elementary, but most important aid toward the wise choice of a wife, is to see a large number of women before choosing her to whom you wish to give name, heart, and life.

If you have chosen your companion in the narrow circle of a village without leaving it, you may be proud to have gained the prettiest girl among a dozen companions. But woe to you, should you suddenly go to other villages, or still worse to some large city; you may find the comparison odious, most odious, and yet irremediable.

This is why men who have seen and travelled a great deal generally make the best husbands; for making their choice on a larger basis, there is great probability of their choosing well, and perhaps also for another reason, women more easily pardon some former gallantry in their fiancés than a too ingenuous virtue. Don Giovanni has always seemed more pleasing to them than the chaste Joseph.

A woman who knows that she is preferred and chosen as a companion, by one who has seen and known a hundred or a thousand other women, is proud of it, and with reason.

I do not know if all women will share my opinion, but those who know most of the science of love will most certainly think with me. Were I a woman, my ideal of a husband would be a man who had travelled in all the six parts of the world, and had seen and admired all the women there.

And continuing my Utopia, but bringing it down to the level of earth; were I a woman and had I doubts about the sincerity of the passion awakened in my fiancé, I should wish him to make a journey through all Europe which should last a year, and if on his return he still found me worthy of him, I would give him my hand with the certainty of having a loving and faithful husband.

Time is a valuable element to add weight to our choice; it is one of the best gauges of comparison by which to distinguish true love from carnal excitement. It is an old axiom, confirmed by universal experience, that time cools and extinguishes the small attacks of love, but strengthens and invigorates the more serious ones. The fatal brevity of our lives, the natural impatience of all those in love, conspire together to hasten marriage, but as far as I know and am able, I recommend men and women to acquire the sainted virtue of patience. I pray women again and again in their love affairs (in which as people say they are more *men* than we are), to follow the tactics of Fabius the temporizer: wait, wait, and still wait. Love is centered in a most serious moment, one most pregnant with consequences to our whole lives, and a month or two more will only increase the dignity of the choice, and be a guarantee for the future. The honeymoon will shine all the longer above our horizon, the more we wait for it, with the poetry of desire and the ideality of hope.

PAOLO MANTEGAZZA.
The Art of Taking a Wife: 1896
Trans. Anon.